ATLANTIC CIRCLE

ATLANTIC
CIRCLE

Kathryn Lasky Knight

PHOTOGRAPHS BY
Christopher Knight

W·W·NORTON & COMPANY
New York   .   London

The text of this book is composed in Bembo, with
display type set in Centaur. Composition by Com Com.
Manufacturing by Haddon Craftsmen.
Book design by Jacques Chazaud.

Portions of the chapters on Europe appeared originally in different form in *Sail*
magazine.

First Edition

Library of Congress Cataloging in Publication Data
Knight, Kathryn Lasky
   Atlantic circle.

   1. Leucothea (Yacht) 2. Voyages and travels—
1951– . 3. North Atlantic Ocean. I. Knight,
Christopher G. II. Title.
G470.L34 1985   910'.091631   84–4888
ISBN 0-393-03295-7

W. W. Norton & Company, Inc., 500 Fifth Avenue, New York, N. Y. 10110
W. W. Norton & Company Ltd., 37 Great Russell Street, London WC1B 3NU

1 2 3 4 5 6 7 8 9 0

To Max and Meribah
With Love

ATLANTIC CIRCLE

Foreword

Atlantic Circle may well be the wittiest, most incisive book on sailing in many a season. Mercifully free of nautical jargon, it combines delightful bits of travelogue from Norwegian fjord to Vineyard sound, enticing morsels of haute cuisine, and a running account of connubial bliss between a gifted pair of young Americans. But LOOK OUT, you guys, you male chauvinist, yo-ho-ho skipper types, it's one heck of a lot more explosive than that. It will, no doubt, prick inflated he-man pretense as lethally as a shark's tooth piercing a rubber life raft.

While you were sacked out in your bunk there with a Hornblower paperback, enjoying your off-watch, this Kathryn Lasky Knight, for all her endearing young charms, has been fashioning a subversive harpoon of a book. With devastating accuracy, she describes the misery endured aboard a small yacht by the womenfolk whose mates can't see the need for a warm, fresh-water shower more than once a week. She has struck a blow for equal rights at sea. Her story could become the *Uncle Tom's Cabin* of the women's movement afloat.

"There are moments in sailing," she writes, "that others find inspiring. Even during a cruise these often come in the form of self-testing, when we measure our limits in terms of our patience, resources, and adaptability. We either fail or succeed, and we talk about these moments later, especially if we succeed.

"There were two such moments on our own honeymoon. Although I passed them quite admirably, I really did not like it and found that they did not increase my own sense of self-worth in the slightest. So what if I had explored a few frontiers previously unknown to me. It didn't make me a better person. As a matter of fact there are certain kinds of self-improvement that I am absolutely loath to pursue." What male would dare say that?

In both moments, Kathy showed her mettle. Nine days bathless, and blocked everywhere in Eastport, Maine, from even a shower, she persuaded Chris to cross over to Canada. When a new halyard had to be rigged, she, "a notorious acrophobic," chose to have Chris winch her up the mast rather than risk him to her dubious cranking power. No doubt she inherits the direct approach from her mother, a belle from Indianapolis who married the son of Russian Jewish émigrés. When he took to racing his Thistle, a high-performance dinghy, he recruited her as crew. Preparing for the spinnaker run one afternoon on the lake, she became entangled in the sheets. When told to get on with it, she replied with dignity from the bilge, "Marven, you know what you can do with your goddamn spinnaker?"

Despite the fact that Kathy found that "this world of string and wood, spar and canvas, wind and water . . . didn't do much for me," she persevered. She screwed up her courage for a North Atlantic crossing aboard *Leucothea*, the thirty-foot Cheoy Lee ketch that was a wedding present from her parents, then mostly enjoyed three summers' cruising in the Baltic and across Europe from Denmark to the Mediterranean by canal before enduring the long voyage back across to Grenada.

It represented miles enough to allow her to hobnob with the saltiest in the yacht club bar, but that's not Kathy's style. Harken to this:

"It is a difficult task to name a boat, especially from a woman's point of view. Boats for the most part are named after women. To my way of thinking, there is going to be the suggestion either of something shared or something adversary between the boat's name and the woman who sails that boat, a reflection, whether positive or negative. Even if this is not precisely so, people unconsciously project such a relationship. It begs for comparison. So there is always this peculiar tension that exists between a boat's name and the woman on that boat."

She searched the *Odyssey,* rejected "Calypso" as too common. "Circe was out from the start. I am not into women with that brand of heavy magic. Turning men into swine is inappropriate on every level from poetic metaphor to politics. They do not need our help." Then out popped the story of Leucothea, whose veil saved the drowning hero.

Pick up *Atlantic Circle* anywhere and you're soon intrigued by a fresh insight. Take this appraisal of "boatie" life: "They don't sail; they drift. They don't have adventures; they maintain the boats that keep them adrift. They can perceive little beyond the boundaries of their fiberglass or wood capsules. They are en-hulled, so to speak, physically and mentally. They are not voyagers of the world's oceans; they are self-selected inmates of boats, and they might just as well be in a supermarket pushing a cart from produce to frozen foods as on a boat sailing from Fiji to Tonga, because that is largely what boaties talk about: the price of things in one port as opposed to another."

But not the Knights. Chris, a filmmaker of distinction whose *American Challenge* documentary of the 1980 solo transatlantic yacht race won rave reviews, shares his bride's love of gourmet food and off-beat sightseeing. She may roll her eyes over his puns, but devotion and admiration flow between them even when cabin conditions deteriorate in storm or fog.

How well she writes. It flows on like silk, shimmering with good metaphors, brightened with saucy retorts and discoveries. How come? She's worked at it. First as a fashion copywriter for *Town & Country,* eventually as the author of twelve children's books, fiction and nonfiction, surely the most demanding school of all. It has given her prose an elegant confidence. She will be discovered now by adults as a talent. Even if, to their loss, book editors mistake this to be a book "for yachties only," there'll be a next and a next and the alert will spot her irrepressible energy today.

I like this description of groping for a landfall in a Maine fog: "in visibility like the inside of a full milk bottle we saw a feeble pulsing glow off to port," the Minturn Harbor lighthouse. Every down-east sailor knows the relief of it.

And take the chapter on "climbing up and down mountain ranges" in France aboard *Leucothea,* with her masts lying on deck so she can pass under bridges. "Far in the distance across one of these fields loomed the flamboyant Gothic twin towers of the grand basilique of St. Nicholas. I was becoming quite attached to this business of sighting Gothic towers in the morning mist rather than whistle buoys in a Bay of Fundy fog." It's a journey through paradise filled with merry encounter and good food. Hard work, too. Getting caught in a lock with the prop wash of a big barge buffeting their boat was "like square dancing with elephants."

With the birth of Max, and then Meribah Grace, voyaging, perforce, gives way to gentler coastal cruising for the Knights. But they've worked out nets and tricks to keep the kids from falling overboard. No doubt there'll be sequels of adventures *en famille* to beguile us, volumes that, like Kathy's sole quenelles, "as the supreme Jewish accolade goes, 'You could die from!' "

Philip S. Weld

PART I

Leucothea *under sail on Penobscot Bay.*

CHAPTER *1*

On a calm clear day, you can see the roots digging into the sea floor. It's possible to imagine that they grew upwards over millions of years until finally the rocky crowns broke through the surface of some nameless bay to become islands. There is a mythic quality in their thrust out of the sea. From three thousand feet above the water's surface, one can almost picture what a poet once called the beginning mists of time.

Some people can imagine those mists. Not me, however. Not when I am three thousand feet above Casco Bay being piloted in a single-engine flying machine that I consider strikingly similar to the models I found in the cereal boxes of my childhood. When my eyes aren't fixated on the gas gauges that are registering three-quarters full, I am scanning the water below for the clods of dirt and rock that might provide an adequate strip of earth for an emergency landing. We are in no actual danger. The flight has been smooth. The engine, whose thrumming vibrations I monitor like a cardiac patient, is performing excellently. All is, in the parlance of the aerospace program, A–OK, except for me. My fuel gauges are measuring E, and my vibrations are lousy. Hovering over these seemingly mythic islands, I am consumed with thoughts of mortality—my own. And rather than the beginning mists of time, it is a fiery final perdition I contemplate.

Chris, my husband, is waxing ecstatic over the grandeur of the coastline. "Where else can you see this sort of stuff. I mean look at these islands—a string of emeralds!" He rotates the wheel and steps on the rudder peddle as he banks the plane steeply so we can skim closer. He performs an adorable little wing waggle over a sailboat. I close my eyes and lean back in my seat. Is it a figment of my imagination, or do I actually hear Chris humming "America the Beautiful"? He is not a superpatriotic sort, but he is obviously finding this scenery so spectacular and uniquely American that he feels compelled to sing. Meanwhile, William Blake's "Jerusalem" is running through my mind, somewhat feebly, and I am thinking about our little chariot of fire making a neat plummet into the deep with the sea closing over it in a final sizzle.

"There's the *Blue Dolphin.* Let's say Hi."

Tied up to a dock in Boothbay Harbor is a sister ship to the legendary schooner *Bluenose.* Chris feels a personal connection with the *Blue Dolphin* because of a lengthy college courtship with Mary Nutt, whose family owned this 110-foot piece of nautical tradition. We circle several times around the schooner so Chris can examine her. We do this every time we fly to Maine so Chris can scrutinize her condition. "Looks like they've stripped her decks . . . yeah. Yeah, definitely. Look, they've taken part of the deckhouse top off. Wonder what they're doing that for. Maybe they're really getting ready to sail her again. I think they've taken all the hardware off the forward mast!"

"Hardware! For God sakes, Chris, we've flown too close!" Chris pulls back gently on the wheel and we float off.

"She's old but elegant."

"Mary Nutt?"

"No, *Blue Dolphin.* Mary's about your age."

"You should have married her."

This comment does not shock Chris. I have said it several times during our marriage, particularly on those occasions of physical duress and imminent danger.

"Now, now, Kathy." He pats my knee reassuringly. "Still not getting used to the flying, huh?"

"No," I say quietly and think how I never will. Mary Nutt would probably be wing walking right now rather than sitting here scared stiff watching the fuel gauges.

The Nutt family lives up to its name admirably. And lest anyone think that because they are the owners of a classic schooner they somehow fall into the Merriweather-Post-Rockefeller-Vanderbilt category, such notions should be dispelled immediately. Beany Nutt, the father, a Dartmouth professor of oceanography, had done extensive Arctic research after World War II using *Blue Dolphin* as his research vessel. He and his wife, Babs, became Arctic addicts and together with their six little Nutts cruised Labrador and Newfoundland for many summers. The children all grew up brainy and tough, becoming world-class kayakists, sailors, marine biologists, etc. Mary Nutt, Chris's friend, got married and took her honeymoon on a Hobie Cat in the Caribbean. That should suffice to explain her. The parents, Babs and Beany, gave up sailing when their children were all grown and took up flying. Babs, pushing sixty, became a glider-pilot instructor. They later bought a dear little airport in Post Mills, Vermont, and have been spending their retirement years in the air either in their amphibious plane or in separate aircraft, as Beany tows Babs's glider up and drops her at four thousand feet.

It has always seemed to me that the Nutts would have been the perfect family for Chris to have married into. An appropriate match in every sense of the word. Whereas . . . I do not finish the thought. The question hangs in the air as ominously as *Three Four Juliet,* the Piper Cherokee we are flying. For diversion I pick up a small paperback that Chris carries aboard, *How To Survive in the Wilderness.* I begin reading. I am familiar with the shelter and first-aid stuff. It is the solutions to starvation that I find unsettling, in particular the one that suggests the nutritional value of drinking rabbit's blood. I never get past page 15 of the book. Any further contemplation of that beverage and I am thoroughly convinced that I would choose death and find a place in heaven next to Beatrix Potter. Such are my survival instincts. We are now somewhere between Port Clyde and Vinalhaven, and I am shifting my thoughts from Beatrix Potter to Tom Watson, the IBM chief, who summers on the island. This is a non sequitur indeed considering that I don't even know the man. But I needed a distraction from the rabbit's blood, so my nimble mind virtually flies from consideration of lapine sangria and Beatrix Potter to computers and Watson. It is at this rather insignificant juncture in my hiccuping consciousness (for me it rarely seems to be a stream) that Chris turns and says, "I have a modest proposal." I actually hiccup at his phrasing, my thoughts having so recently been on rabbit's blood.

"What?" I ask.

"I'll give up flying if you'll sail across the Atlantic with me."

I look down. I think of our thirty-foot ketch *Leucothea,* sturdy and sea-kindly, sails full and driving us toward a distant shore. How sensible it all seems. The beautiful simplicity of ropes, wind, dacron, three thousand pounds of lead in the keel, as opposed to this antigravitational device that looks like a cereal-box toy.

"It's a deal!" I respond. I sink back into the seat and hope that *Three Four Juliet* will just get us to Deer Isle, where Chris's family is waiting for our arrival at their summer home.

CHAPTER 2

This was the summer of 1972. It would be two more years before we would actually begin to fulfill the bargain in the sky. I have already hinted amply that there were some rather fundamental differences between Chris's and my own backgrounds and rearing that made him eminently suitable for such a venture and me eminently unsuitable. Whether it was to be a challenge of the "spacious skies" or the "sea to shining sea," I was strictly an "amber-waves of-grain" sort.

Deer Isle, Maine, the destination of most flights on what Chris called

Chris and Kathy on the rocks in front of the Deer Isle house. Their official engagement picture.

Fly-By-Knight Airways, was the ancestral home of the paternal side of the Knight family. A few forebears were scattered about in the Martha's Vineyard-Nantucket-Rhode Island area, but it was Deer Isle that people tended to think of as the familial turf. Chris's grandfather Dr. Charles Knight had been born there, and though he eventually went off to Harvard Medical School, he returned to the island in the summer to lobster in a dory for his tuition.

On their honeymoon in 1905 he and his bride, Sadie Ellis, rowed from Deer Isle to Marshall's Island, some twenty miles away, for some privacy. Although I consider this slightly less harebrained than honeymooning on a Hobie Cat, it was apparently just about as wet when a heavy rain began to fall. The bride, who wore a brand-new purple hunting outfit, discovered much to her horror that she had been dyed bright purple when they pitched their tent that night.

Although they settled in Boston, Charles Knight kept the old family farm on the Reach, a lovely stretch of protected water between Deer Isle and the mainland. Sadie was never too keen about the house, but summers were spent there with their two sons, Peter (Chris's father) and Jack.

Going farther back in the Knight family tree, one sees the professions of cooper, shipwright, mariner, and increasingly in the late 1800s that of master mariner listed. Many served on Grand Banks schooners and some in the China trade. A certain William Torrey was lost at sea rounding Cape Horn, and more than a few were lost on the Grand Banks. One was a captain of the *Charles W. Morgan*. He and his wife had a daughter born aboard in Hawaii. On the Ellis side there was a Quaker who was shot three times during the Civil War, which goes to show what ambivalence in the face of a bullet can do.

For real exotica in the family tree, there was a certain Meribah Wardell, who was half-Indian. Her mother, also named Meribah, was married to Jonathan Eaton of Rhode Island. During a period of unrest between the settlers and the Indians, she was captured by the Indians and (as it is so delicately reported in a family history) "compelled to become the chief's wife." Hence little Meribah. The account goes on to say that upon the return of peace between the whites and the tribe Meribah was "delivered up" to her husband with her new child.

Among the duller ancestors were a sprinkling of *Mayflower* types in the direct and indirect line. It is always hard for me to believe that so many people in this country can claim kinship with the *Mayflower* crowd. If it were really true, I think the boat would have sunk. So I have settled on incest as the explanation for all these claims. Names like Thankful and Theophilus, Ebenezer and Mercy, Uriah and Josiah abound. They all looked toward the sea for their living. They were all hardworking, stalwart types, until November 28, 1847, when along came Levi Knight and the work ethic went out the window. Notorious for his laziness, Levi did it all under the guise of godliness. In fact Levi was probably a folk hero before such types were appreciated. He is certainly my favorite dead Knight relative, if one can claim to have such favorites.

Levi was named for an uncle who was captain of the schooner *Elizabeth,* which was lost off Bay Chaleurs, Canada. He became a fisherman out of Deer Isle, but Levi soon decided that it was ungodly to catch the good Lord's fish, so he took up farming at the Reach on Deer Isle. Pretty soon he decided that plowing God's earth and slaughtering innocent animals was not any more godly than fishing, so he gave up farming and opened a small tobacco shop. Long before anybody had ever heard of the surgeon general, that Surgeon in the Sky spoke to Levi, and soon he gave up selling tobacco. He then proceeded to spend the rest of his life sitting in his wife, Francena's, kitchen. Francena worked tirelessly raising the five children, including Dr. Charles Knight, Chris's grandfather. Nobody knows for sure exactly how they supported themselves, but the inclination toward hard work was resumed immediately by Levi's offspring, and that might be a partial explanation. Levi died in 1931, and most people who knew him remember him as a grouch and a bore, but I remain firmly convinced that if Levi really was grouchy it was only because he was born too soon. Had he lived today he most certainly would have been a guru. So I prefer to think of Levi wrapped with saffron robes, cheerfully boring people in his down-east accent in some Himalayan mountain retreat or at least an ashram in Cambridge.

Chris's father, Pete Knight, was Levi's grandson. He graduated from Harvard's School of Design with a landscape architecture degree in the late

Rusty at the Maine house.
Chris, three and a half years old,
is at lower left.

thirties, when work was hard to find. A good job offer brought him to Cleveland, Ohio, with his bride, Lillian (Rusty) Balboni, and he enjoyed the less-rigid social atmosphere there. But there were still trips to the East. Doctor Knight had died relatively young, but his widow, Sadie, lived on Joy Street on Beacon Hill, and around the corner at 78 Mount Vernon was Doctor Balboni, Lillian's father. Gerardo Balboni had arrived here from Cento, Italy, at the age of thirteen speaking no English. He went to work in a pharmacy whose proprietors found him to be a bright, hardworking sort and encouraged him to go to college and then on to medical school at Harvard. He became a beloved physician in the North End of Boston and at the Massachusetts General Hospital.

For the Knights in Cleveland, Boston became a stop on their way to or from "the Maine house." The old farm on the Reach was now a summer house for Rusty and Pete and their four children: Peter, Chris, and the twins, Judy and Jonathan. The house had no running water and no electricity. But it did have a sailing canoe, a millpond where you could make model boats out of shingles, and endless adventures. Pete Knight received only two weeks' vacation a year, but Rusty would spend whole summers there in the primitive house with her four kids and a college girl to help out. Water had to be hauled, cooking had to be done on a woodburning stove, children had to be kept from drowning, but there was plenty of time to whittle model boats, make miniature diving boards for the frog population near the millpond, and chew the fat with cousin Francis while his delivery of ice in the back of his truck melted in the hot July sun.

CHAPTER *3*

Island life requires versatility for survival, and Chris's cousin Francis was no exception. He had on various occasions cut lumber, worked for the roads department, or whatever they call it on an island, certainly not highways. He had fished, and he had cut ice from ponds in the winter and delivered it in the summer for the old-fashioned iceboxes, which still provided refrigeration. What was unusual about Francis was his mechanical ingenuity. He was the Yankee Tinkerer par excellence. What Robert Goddard was to rockets, Francis Williams was to sunken boats and cars stuck in the mud flats. He had assembled an incredible array of junk into a line of Rube Goldberg-type machines that could accomplish any task. Need a mooring dropped or pulled? Francis would come chugging into your harbor with his floating crane, which consisted of some gear salvaged from a wrecked trawler affixed atop a platform that was floated on a small population of oil drums with an outboard attached. "One of them tourist folks" from New York pulls off the side of the road to admire the sunset at low tide and finds himself stuck in the clam flats with the tide starting to turn. Along comes Francis in his truck. Or is it a truck? It looks more like the offspring of an unfortunate union between a pickup truck and a piece of heavy wrecking equipment.

What Francis's machines lacked in refinement, they more than compen-

Francis Williams in his boatyard at Burnt Cove, Deer Isle, Maine.

sated for in character, and what they might have lacked in horsepower could always be provided by Francis. He was a massive man, and his hands were the strongest I have ever seen. I will always remember Francis's huge hand wrapped around a champagne glass at our wedding as he recounted a joke he had heard about a man who inquired of his hostess whether a lemon had wings. "Why, no," replied the woman. "Well, Ma'am, I think I just squeezed your canary into my drink."

It was inevitable that Francis, with his assortment of equipment, would one day get into the boatyard business. "The boys had boats to haul, and I had a place to put them, so . . ." So from November to April Francis's front yard in Burnt Cove became crammed with lobster boats and more than a few sailboats, dinghies, and sundry pleasure craft. The boats, as his wife, May, put it, "just kind of crept up" out of the water and across the lawn. Pretty soon they were up to the drive. Then before you knew it they were right there in with the petunias. With the boats came the usual concomitant load of junk that seems to breed in boatyards—old wire spools, cradles, trailers, rusted-out engines, etc. All strewn about in total disarray. None of this really bothered May that much. She was used to confusion. One entered May's house and was in immediate danger of becoming lost or crushed while threading through stacks of old *National Geographic*s and *Modern Photography*s (May was a photo buff), sewing projects in progress, pattern books, and grandchildren's toys. Musical scores were scattered everywhere as May was the choir director and the church organist. There were textbooks as May had decided to start college in her fifties to get her B.A. in music. She commuted regularly to the university in Bangor even during the worst of winter. There were always term papers to write and choir practices to get ready for, plus her weekly column in the *Island Advantages* newspaper to write, so dishes were washed just a couple of times a week and seldom put away because "after all you have to get them right back out again." There were always scores of newborn kitties that tumbled about the place like dandelion fluffs, and there was an enormous Newfoundland called Tuffy Bear that lumbered about like a canine version of Francis.

In spite of her own disdain for order within her house, some of Francis's machines plus the ever-encroaching tide of boats must have given May a few trying moments. Francis's priorities were different from many people's, and it took May the longest time to finally get him to install a bathroom in the house. It always seemed as if there were another boat to haul or mooring to drop before he could get to it. May, however, is a unique and strong woman. Despite the chaos in her house, she has a keen aesthetic sense and a talent for accomplishing things. She takes the music education of the island seriously and devotes countless hours to teaching children and exposing them to good music. She has formed music groups for the elderly. I doubt that Francis gave a hoot about music, but it was her love of it and her genuine appreciation for beauty in life as well as art that made many a harsh and ugly island winter survivable for May. Maine islands between December and March are not easy places to be. Men often drink because they cannot fish, and women get fat and dream of other places and other men and other lives. But May was different.

I remember when May called to tell us that Francis had died of a massive heart attack. He had been unconscious for a day. The family was keeping a vigil by his bedside in the Blue Hill Hospital when suddenly he opened his eyes and sat up. In a perfectly clear voice he asked what day it was and the time. The family was dumbfounded.

"Francis," May said. "You sure are tough!"

"Tough as a boiled owl," he replied and promptly died.

CHAPTER *4*

Chris's fascination with Francis began in those summers of his early youth on Deer Isle. The highlight of every week was the ice delivery and the chance for making snowballs in July from the ice chips as Francis sawed the blocks. When he brought the horses for haying the fields, Chris would beg to ride on King or Queeny. Sitting by the woodshed, Francis carved scraps of shingles into tiny square-rigged ships that Chris found irresistible. He taught Chris to make his own, and soon fleets of them were voyaging across the millpond, pushed by the summer sea breezes. Perhaps I should blame Francis for dreams of ocean crossing planted in Chris's head at the impressionable age of four or five.

Of course the best rides of all were the ones in the sailing canoe when Pete Knight arrived for two weeks at the end of the summer. A sailing canoe requires more in terms of skillful handling than any sailboat a person is likely to encounter. Steering with a paddle, shifting leeboards on each tack, trying to keep the narrow unballasted hull upright, in the canoe the Knight children first learned to sail.

In the last week of summer there was usually a cruise on a smart little schooner or ketch with a name like *Rogue's Moon* or *Black Bird*. Of the four Knight children Chris seemed to inherit the strongest love of the sea. It seemed to come fairly directly from his father, who taught him with skill and patience about weather and navigation and wind and boats, but perhaps more than that Pete and Rusty Knight taught their children about risks—risks well taken and the trade-offs between living well and living securely.

A young Chris at the helm of Black Bird,
on a summer charter with his parents.

When Chris was a freshman in high school, landlocked and bored in Cleveland, he remembered his father's old scrapbooks hidden behind the first row of books in the living room bookcase. Put together by Sadie Ellis Knight, they recorded a phenomenal adventure undertaken by his dad and a friend, Harold Putnam. The two young Dartmouth students set out in the summer of 1933 in a kayak and began a circumnavigation of New England that started on Lake Champlain. From Champlain they went out the Richlieu River to the Saint Lawrence, then into the Gulf of Saint Lawrence, round the Gaspé Peninsula, down the Nova Scotian coast, through Maine's maze of islands, and finally on to Boston and New York.

Chris was fascinated as he poured over the journal entries, photos of campsites and seal hunts, yellowed news clippings of adventures with whales and gales. The coast that young Knight and Putnam had traveled was riddled with bays and channels and islands to explore. The idea of a grand adventure started to grow. In his senior year in high school, while studying in the library, Chris came across a fairly detailed map of Alaska. He noticed that the southeastern coastline of Alaska was as convoluted and thick with islands as anyone might imagine. The map indicated spectacularly high mountains that plummeted into the sea. This inside passage from Skagway to Seattle looked ideal for kayaking. Laced with channels and fjords that were protected from the open sea and braced by mountains, it was a kayakist's dream.

After two full years of planning, Chris, now a nineteen-year-old sophomore at Dartmouth, and his brother Peter, a senior, set off for Alaska with

Chris and his brother Peter a few miles out of Skagway at
the start of the great Alaska kayak adventure.

Chris, in the bow, and Peter, in the stern, sidle up to
an iceberg in Tracy Arm, Alaska.

a kayak called *Wasso III*. Specially designed and built to their specifications in Västervik, Sweden, *Wasso III* was a sleek mahogany needle weighing only fifty pounds but capable of carrying two hundred pounds of camping equipment and the two boys.

The southeast coast of Alaska, although protected for the most part, was a rugged one. There were small gaps with direct exposure to the Pacific and the sucking Japanese current. There were killer whales, and mostly there was wilderness. The boys would have to hunt for food to supplement what they could carry. The equipment stowed in the boat had to be as reliable as possible, because replacements would be unavailable along the way. In case of medical emergency they would have to use their ingenuity. There were few towns on the charts, and many of these had become ghost towns when the mines or salmon canneries had closed down.

The risks in short were formidable. They would travel for days without seeing another human being. Death was a distinct possibility, but Peter and Chris's focus was not just surviving but also enjoying the wilderness. For two years with the guidance of their father and support of both parents they had tested various kayaks and modified their ideal one. They had studied every chart and current table of that coast. The equipment had been tried on a number of practice trips that refined their boat-handling skills as well.

Everyone except Chris's parents had been opposed to this trip. From the Knights' friends in Cleveland to Alaskans who heard about their idea, most thought that the trip was impossible. People at their kindest were skeptical and at their worst condemnatory. Rusty Knight once told me that everyone in Cleveland "thought Pete and I were either nuts or negligent as parents."

CHAPTER 5

Back in Cleveland, Pete Knight, Senior, followed his sons' progress on a duplicate set of charts. Although he had never seen the Alaskan coast, every current and tidal change was printed in his mind and every hazard and wind variation was imagined and plotted. Because a kayak has no chart table for on-the-spot course work, Pete had precharted several options for the boys based on prevailing wind patterns and tidal currents. There were two places that had direct exposure to the Pacific: Dixon's Entrance near Prince Rupert and Queen Charlotte Sound. The passage across Queen Charlotte Sound was about thirty to forty miles long. Pete, Sr., had plotted a course several months before, taking into account the thicket of rocks close to shore and the big Pacific waves that had built uninterrupted from Japan for some four thousand miles. It was a pounding, monstrous surge. The run was long, not one that could be done in a single stretch, but landing on the coast without being splintered was impossible. Thus, the first leg was set for Egg Island, which was in the middle of the sound and had a semiprotected backside. Beyond Egg Island was Cape Caution or, as the boys came to call it, C-c-c-c-ape C-c-c-c-aution. They were then to proceed on a compass course Pete, Sr., had set for a rock some twelve miles off. Wrecks and killer whales were prevalent in the area, but the real danger was being caught by bad weather with no place to hide.

Throughout the stifling summer nights in Cleveland, Pete Knight worried about this passage as letters from his sons and his own calculations warned of their approach to the sound. He imagined the rumble of the immense surge like artillery fire in the distance. He imagined the sun that would set and rise with each swell and the straight lee shore with nowhere to land if the weather blew up. He imagined all this—the wet silver spray flying like wings off the bow, the long Pacific swells occasionally humping up into thundering breakers on deeply buried ledges, the mahogany needle splitting through it all, powered by his two sons.

They made it across the sound and continued their trip. Sixty-one days after setting out from Skagway, the great adventure was completed. The perverse southeast wind that was rarely supposed to blow had indeed blown like a demon all summer and twenty miles from Seattle had at last turned around into a tail wind.

Two years later Chris and a group of Dartmouth friends from the Ledyard Canoe Club paddled the entire Danube river from its source in Ulm, Germany, to the Black Sea. Photographed by Chris and fellow classmate Dick Durrance II, the story appeared in *National Geographic*. In 1966 Chris was back in *Wasso* photographing another story for *National Geographic*. A group of ten Dartmouth friends and English students paddled in kayaks through the inland sea of Japan from Shimonoseki to Tokyo.

Summer work stints with the *Geographic* supported Chris's graduate studies in architecture at Harvard and kept his taste for adventure alive. It was during this time that I met Chris.

CHAPTER 6

It seems that ever since the Knights had left Deer Isle as a permanent home in the early 1900s, they had been trying almost desperately to "go down to the sea again." The only island of ancestral import in the Lasky family, however, was Ellis, which hardly evokes nostalgia among any of our kin.

The Laskys, shortly before leaving Russia— left to right, Ida, Kathy's grandmother; her son, Louis; Kathy's great-grandmother, holding granddaughter, Cecile. The child standing is Kathy's aunt, Ann Lasky Smith.

Nor had we been yearning to return to our home places, Odessa and Nikolayev in Russia and a small town in Poland the name of which I can never remember, but it sounds something like the name of one of those smoky sausages.

There is no family tree for the Laskys as far as anybody can ascertain. "Shrub" would better describe the known genealogical shape of things. However, poking into the shrubbery reveals some interesting if not dazzling types on both my father's and mother's sides. To take a slight leap back in time, around the turn of the century (this one) the Russian policy toward Jews was even worse than it is today. Jews were required to serve in Tsar Nicholas II's army, and ironically they were just as likely to be victims in pogroms by the tsar's forces. In short, they were catching it from both ends.

Once a man had served he could still be called up again. In fact the only sure way not to be called again was death. A great-great-grandfather of mine and his wife were murdered in their beds because the tsar's troops wanted their two silver wine cups, and thus they did avoid recall. But service or death were two unacceptable choices for my own grandfather Joseph Lasky, a machinist in a factory outside Nikolayev. In 1904 he packed up his wife, three kids, father, and sister and left. Somehow they got hold of a wagon (any conveyance was an almost unheard-of luxury for Jews then), and they traveled a number of days to a border where the guard was bribed. We are not sure which border. The next thing my Aunt Ann remembers (she was four at the time) was boarding a boat in Le Havre for Liverpool.

In Liverpool they took a ship, the *Halifax*, traveling steerage and sleeping on the floor. They had to bring their own food, which consisted of dark bread, salamis, tea, and hard candy. When they arrived in the States, it was thought that my great-grandfather, Joe's father, had contracted trachoma and would be detained indefinitely. The family was very nearly hysterical over this, but miraculously Great-grandfather Sol's eyes cleared, and the family continued to Duluth, Minnesota, where two uncles had settled three years before. Duluth, although hardly exotic, can be thought of as somewhat unusual in terms of Jewish migration patterns. It was here that Joe and his wife, Ida, settled and had three more children including my father, Marven. Joe found work as a machinist.

Trying to imagine life in that household in the early 1900s is odd. Here was an intensely Jewish family transported to the relative wilderness of a northern almost pioneer town. Grandfather Sol drank his glasses of sweet tea, stayed warm in the kitchen, and alternated between growling at the kids and giving them rough but affectionate pats. He walked doubled over with a cane never raising his eyes from the ground, and once when my dad asked him why, he barked in reply, "to find money!" The older people in the household did learn English but often spoke Yiddish, especially if they did not want the children to understand.

My Aunt Ann was very musical and wrote a few songs that were eventually published. My father was apparently spoiled rotten by his sisters, but this did not interfere with his love of adventure. I get the distinct impression that he itched to escape the thickly feminine world that seemed to dominate the home front. He worked in a logging camp one winter during a school vacation when he was ten or eleven. His job was to wake up the loggers in the morning, which must have been something like tapping a shark on the shoulder at breakfast time. He loved the outdoors, and his father made him a pair of skis from barrel staves on which he blithely went all over Duluth and into the northern woods. He also became an excellent swimmer and in 1924, at the age of seventeen, traveled to Indianapolis for the Olympic swimming trials. He did not make the team, but he did meet his future wife, Hortense Falender. One could hardly call their courtship whirlwind. They went out together for eleven years before finally deciding to get married. "People thought about things in those days." This is a favorite remark of my mother's. I have often wondered what else they did besides think during those eleven years.

Although my mother is Jewish, my father could not have found a family more different from his than hers. Prosperous and very urbane by comparison, the Falenders lived in a Mediterranean style house (they would have been loath to call it a villa) designed by my grandmother Belle on the loveliest street in Indianapolis. They had six children—one boy and five lively girls who were considered quite striking in appearance. One in fact was offered a movie contract. They were all college-educated, a remarkable feat for those times. It must have been a sparkling household during the twenties, with musicals, endless pranks, and a constant flow of young men courting the girls.

Kathy's parents,
Marven and Hortense Lasky,
pose on the beach
during their courtship.

They had a six-and-one-half-foot black gentleman, War Leader Bell, who functioned as a combination butler-nursemaid-handyman-chauffeur. A powder blue Model-T took them on summer trips to Lake Wawasee in northern Indiana and sometimes even as far as Atlantic City. The object of these trips was to display the fabulous Beatrice, eldest of the sisters and recipient of the movie-contract offer. One of the most fun summers ever was when Bea was taken to Cuba and the other girls were left at home to fend for themselves, which they did rather nicely. My grandmother was quite laissez-faire about certain things.

Everyone in my mother's family including her parents adored my father, which really speaks well of them because it would have been easy to try to tag a penniless Olympic-team reject courting a lovely well-off girl as a fortune hunter. But he was not, and they saw him for what he was—bright, ingenious, hardworking, and kind. He was working then as a lifeguard and attending night law school. We never could figure out how one went to law school without having attended college. He never did finish law school and went on to a series of jobs—more lifeguarding, one with Johnny Weissmuller in Florida, another also in Florida of tending alligators in a Seminole Indian village where the Indians wrestled the reptiles. He became at one time a ladies' hat salesman and then after prohibition a liquor salesman.

Over an eleven-year period from his late teens to his late twenties, he would turn up at the Falenders', always welcomed and sometimes pressed into service to escort a younger sister of my mother's to a prom after a sudden breakup with a beau. My mother, an eminently sensible sort, refused to marry him until he had found a steady job. She in the meantime had finished college and was working as a social worker. Trips to Russia, Norway, and Europe with her sister Mildi and a good friend, another Hortense (Hortense Davis), were frequent during the prewar years. My father bore all this fairly patiently, even other intermittent boyfriends. There was, however, a fistfight at a country club dance between him and another one of my mother's suitors. My grandparents were at the dance too and evidently when my mother went crying to her mother over this shameful display, Belle merely waved her hand and said, "It's your problem, Hortense."

Finally, however, they did get married. My father had found a niche for himself in the liquor business and eventually started his own company, with no help from my mother's family because by this time they had lost all their money in the depression. My father had a bottling and distribution company in Indianapolis. In what will always seem the oddest reversal of things, wine in tank cars was driven from California to Indiana and put in bottles at his plant. His label, Melody Hill, though hardly a grand *cru,* really did take off. The anthropomorphized grapes emblazoned on the sides of trucks also sang on radio and television, "I'm sherry, I'm port, try me, muscatel and zinfandel!" As cute as Shirley Temple, these little animated grapes tap-danced their way into the hearts, minds, and bloodstreams of the unsophisticated wine-drinking public in the Midwest.

But it was strictly grapes of wrath as far as my older sister Martha and I were concerned when my father would arrive in the blue van with the little dancing grapes painted on the sides and the horn that honked the first four notes of the commercial's song. We were victims of a common adolescent disease—terminal embarrassment caused by parents. This van was the bane of our existence. God forbid a peer should actually see us being driven in it by our dad, who could have been the sixth grape with his bald head and smiling countenance. Several years later my father sold out Melody Hill to Gallo. Ernest Gallo was the first famous person I ever met. He came to our house for dinner with his wife, Amalia, whose name I thought was the most beautiful sound I had ever heard.

CHAPTER 7

When we were growing up in Indianapolis, there was a reservoir outside the city, and when they started a sailing club my father bought a small sailboat, a Thistle. Unfortunately, neither Martha, my mother, nor I could bear to subject ourselves to the rigors of being his crew. He was fiercely competitive to the point of tyranny on board, and we were apparently untrainable in the fine art of spinnaker management and the myriad of other skills necessary for small-boat racing. I have one vivid image of my mother having fallen down in the boat after a bout with the spinnaker, one leg straight up in the air, scratched, bleeding, and entwined in the spinnaker lines, and my father at the tiller yelling at her that so-and-so had just gotten a full boat length on us and to get the thing up. My mother, still bleeding, her leg still straight up in the air, turned to him and in a dangerously sweet voice said, "Marven, you know what you can do with your goddamn spinnaker?"

In general, Indianapolis had little to offer in the way of sports and entertainment, aside from minature golf. As an alternative, Martha and I were sent to fancy summer camps—some where you spoke nothing but French. Although I was a good swimmer, I avoided the waterfront like the plague. Boating bored me. It seemed to be all knot tying and standing with oars in a line on a pier while a gravel-voiced counselor, who doubtlessly had gone to Buvee Boston College, shouted commands like "Oars up!" at which point we were all supposed to salute or something. All I ever wanted to do was say "Up yours!" and crack her on the head with my paddle. As a matter of fact my real forte in those days was track rather than the waterfront. On one parents' weekend I came within four inches of winning the broad jump. My jump had remained unmatched through seven attempts to smash it in one meet. Then along came Sylvia Sakowsky—stubby-legged Sylvia with God knows what kind of lungs and a will of steel. "Kiss good-bye to those four inches, Lasky!" Just before she flew off the mark, I remember her taking a huge breath of air, as if she were inhaling the whole camp. She absolutely jetted across the sand pit. There was a loud expulsion from her lungs midair and when she landed a throaty, ecstatic *"Oy vey!"* It was at this point that my mother turned to my dad and said, "One thousand dollars a summer and they still say *oy!"* Not that my mother minded the *oy.* It was the non—*oy* part of the camp that got her. She found it pretentious and snobbish. This was long before anyone had ever heard of that now-overused expression "Jewish American princess," but this camp certainly was a hothouse for their cultivation. Martha's French camp was nice, but she was terribly homesick and, although an excellent French student, found it absolutely torturous to have to speak French, canoe, and miss home all at the same time.

Were we Jewish princesses, Martha and I? I'm really not sure. I have always found it an exceedingly offensive term that was really no more descriptive of an individual's nature than debutante, Southern belle, WASP, or any number of supposedly clever nomenclatures that are intended to say it all about a group. They are ultimately racist tags that make it easier for nonthinking people to categorize other human beings. But still I won't beg off on the question. If Jewish American princess means to have money and privilege, then we fit the term. We were indulged, but we were not spoiled. There is a difference, I think. By indulged, I mean that we were allowed special pleasures and experiences of a material kind because money could buy them. But we always realized that this was a privilege and not a right, and we were never excused in terms of conduct because of privilege. Always there were standards, expectations, and values. We learned that privilege was a limited thing that money could buy, but standards and values had no price.

Part of what this money could buy was the privilege of escaping Indianapolis during the winter every year. When I was quite young, two years old at the most, I was a runny-nosed, skinny, allergic kid, and my parents felt that extended doses of sunshine might be the answer. So we all migrated to Florida for the winter, a practice we kept up long after the nose had dried up. We would stay in the Hollywood—Miami Beach area. This was back in the heyday of the grand hotels like the Rony Plaza and, somewhat later, the glitzy but gorgeous Fontainebleau. My parents felt that such lodgings were too rich for our blood and too cushy for young girls. So we settled into a lovely apartment. In boat terms it was somewhere between a kayak and a gold plater. We would swim madly all day long. Esther Williams was a heroine for Martha and me. We each had an elaborate bathing cap festooned with flowers. I remember that I had one with sprin-klings of violets on it. The little petals flapped when you swam. My sister had one that was covered with roses. Together we would choreograph elaborate water ballets, our rather uninspiring forms moving through back dolphins, tucks, and watery arabesques. For the better part of a day, all that was visible of either of us were our rear ends turning somersaults or our flower-bedecked heads.

All of this paid off lavishly when I went on to college and took water ballet in order to fulfill the gym requirement. Eventually I became the lead dolphin in a group called The Wet Dreams. However, in Florida Martha and I for the most part did not attend schools but brought schoolwork from home and were taught by our mother. We seemed to survive this casual academic training fine. My parents always had the bedrock belief that family vacations were just as valuable as school, and they went to great extremes to protect what they felt was an inalienable right in terms of our education. I do know that the reading I did during those vacations, although little of it was in textbooks, was far more extensive and richer than what I would have been doing during school, and both my parents encouraged my inclination toward writing far more than any teacher ever had or would.

The Florida trips stopped being extended ones when my sister neared high school and I was about a fourth-grader. We had switched from public to private school in Indianapolis at about this time. The school was a peculiarly anachronistic institution, even for those days, being very long on tradition and short on psychology. It was headed by a starchy Scotswoman

Kathy at thirteen, having last-minute adjustments made in her grade-school graduation dress by her mother, who made the dress.

who was about as charming as a kipper and knew as much about kids as Mae West knew about Sanskrit. She ran the place with appalling efficiency. There was indeed plenty of individual academic attention, and she had an impressive track record for getting her girls into good colleges, especially Eastern ones. I doubt if it would disturb her eternal sleep much to hear me say that I don't think I learned a damn thing except for the Lord's Prayer while I was there. She never did think I was much of a student, at least nothing compared to my sister. But I did make a lot of good friends there, which is the most valuable contribution any school can make to one's life.

Despite its shortcomings, the school was in many ways a lively and unique experience. Where else would a Jew get a chance to say the Lord's Prayer and sing the Doxology once a week? It was quite an exotic experience, almost heady. A dangerous foray in uncharted waters. In those first few years of Monday morning chapel, it was like playing Russian roulette with God to sing those last few words, "Praise Father, Son, and Holy Ghost." If I were feeling chicken I would cross my fingers while singing. But crossed fingers or not, at the end I would always roll my eyes heavenward, not in praise but in apprehension to see if any bolts of lightning would come cracking down and strike me dead right there in the study hall where we had chapel. I felt as though I were on the razor's edge theologically. It was an incredibly exhilarating experience within an extremely stuffy and rigid environment.

I was glad when I got out of high school. I went to the University of

Michigan, and after my graduation, like all young dreamers, I did not simply "go," I "set out" for New York with fantasies of becoming a writer. My dream was to work for the *New Yorker* and hang out at the Algonquin. I thought that I could begin modestly, a researcher, perhaps, who finds those funny little malaprops that have appeared in newspapers and are reprinted at the bottom of the *New Yorker* pages. Then I thought I could advance to writing small stylish pieces for the "Talk of The Town." Then finally one day they would come to me and say, "Gee, Kathy, so-and-so just suffered a coronary, so could you finish the profile for him on Adlai Stevenson and maybe start thinking about one for the September issue on Ella Fitzgerald?"

There were not any openings at the *New Yorker.* Instead I wound up working for *Town & Country.* Talk about anachronisms; I was a walking one during my tenure at the magazine. A child of the sixties, just a few years behind Tom Hayden at the University of Michigan, and it had all culminated in my working for a glossy fashion publication. People were protesting Vietnam, working on voter registration in the South, and I was writing fashion copy for *Town & Country* magazine, or "Cappy and Piggy," as one of my friends called it. But I just had to work. I had to know that somebody thought my writing was good enough to pay for it, even if it was only sixty-four dollars a week after taxes. I was ashamed to admit my minuscule salary to anyone, and my tenure at *Town & Country* was hardly a happy one. There were no Dorothy Parkers, Genets, or E. B. Whites treading the corridors. Instead there were a lot of junior-college girls with names like Muffy and Bambi and Lacy who had different Pucci dresses for each day of the week. These girls were in fact the fashion editors of the magazine. I must explain that these were not editors of the ilk of a Diana Vreeland or China Machado. Taste was required, but not style. Indeed, the ones who worked there when I did had barely discernible brain waves, but they were superior clothes horses, and all they had to do was pick out a variety of stuff gathered from the small coterie of American designers and match it up with the debutantes of the year and the names that continually cropped up in the *New York Times* society columns.

Town & Country never used professional models, and these editors would call up the rich and the pretty and ask them to pose in this Bill Blass or that de La Renta. One of my first assignments was to write a small article on the fashion philosophy of the ten best-dressed women in New York City as selected by *Town & Country.* I had to call them up on the phone and interview them briefly on the subject. Granted the whole idea is rather insipid, but all of these women, except one, were so unbelievably inarticulate and stupid, at least over the phone, that I decided it was best just to forget it and make up a philosophy for each person. It would be to their benefit.

Most of my work at the magazine consisted of staring at designer dresses on pretty ladies and trying to write something about the clothes that was "fresh" and "exciting" and would make people want to spend ridiculous sums of money. I actually became quite good at it. I knew that I had arrived at the rather unlofty pinnacle of success in this field when a very good but small advertising firm began doing hilarious parodies of what I was writing for a fashion account of theirs. When these ads began appearing in fashion magazines, there was a tempest in the *Town & Country* teapot. The editor in chief met with the Hearst publications' lawyers. There apparently had been no copyright violations, and there was not a darn thing they could do about it. In the end they decided it would probably do them more good than harm. I was actually complimented for my stylish copy.

I immediately decided that may be that ad agency would be more the ticket for me. So I went over there and announced myself as the one whose copy they had been parodying. I had a nice interview with the president. She said they were not taking anybody on then, but perhaps they might be using some freelance people. At the moment they were working on a campaign that used real superstars, almost legendary types, to promote mink coats. They needed one dynamite line. I tossed off a couple and, when I got a half block away, thought of two more, one of which I wrote on a scrap of paper and ran back and left with the receptionist. My entries were "What makes a legend great?" and "What becomes legends most?" I never got a job or a credit line or a cent, but for many years I have seen the line "What becomes a legend most?" under pictures of Marlene Dietrich, Liza Minnelli, Barbra Streisand, etc.

I continued at *Town & Country* for a few months more. While Chris was paddling the Inland Sea of Japan I was writing such memorable lines of fashion copy as "takes a dazzling plunge at the neckline and comes up ruffling."

Our paths finally crossed in Cambridge, Massachusets. Chris was a graduate student at the Harvard Design School. I had decided that my tenure at *Town & Country* was beginning to have ever-diminishing returns and that self-esteem and immortality were not going to be found on the fashion pages of any magazine. I went to Cambridge and signed on as a part-time student at the Harvard Divinity School. Some might take this as an extreme reaction to Cappy and Piggy. It was not really a reaction at all. It was more of a holding action while I sorted out what I wanted to do. I had a lot of friends in Cambridge, and the idea of studying again at this juncture was appealing. The Div Biz, as we called it, offered a nice array of courses—a little philosophy, literature, history.

Chris, after receiving his degree, never practiced architecture, and I

Kathy's wedding portrait, taken by Chris.
The wedding on Deer Isle.
Chris made the model of Leucothea for the cake.

never practiced divinity. He continued his photography career and eventually started his own film company. I became a teacher, then a curriculum-materials developer and eventually started writing children's books. We had a whirlwind courtship, at least compared to my parents' eleven-year one. Ours lasted three years. On May 30, 1971, we were married on Deer Isle in Maine.

We began our honeymoon aboard *Leucothea,* a thirty-foot Cheoy Lee ketch given to us as a wedding present by my parents. For Chris, coming from that long line of sailors, Grand Banks fishermen, and Nantucket whaling folks, it was a dream come true. For me, from my short line of recently arrived Russian and Polish Jews, it was a nice idea. I knew that cruising in Maine had to be somewhat of an improvement over racing around an artificial Indiana lake in a Thistle with my dad. The fact that the boat did not have a spinnaker was a big plus in my mind. I thought of myself as a bride with the prospect of a lovely honeymoon island-hopping in Penobscot Bay. But Chris is a voyager, and little did I realize that what began as a honeymoon would eventually be extended into an Atlantic crossing, three years' sailing in Europe, and a long voyage back.

PART II

Chris and Kathy sailing down-east in fog.

CHAPTER 8

The beautiful simplicity of rope, wind, and dacron that I had dreamed of in *Three Four Juliet* began to pall rapidly at 48N, 35W. I tried to keep my spirits up by thinking of the dear little Piper Cherokee where Chris and I had struck our bargain in the sky some two years before. I had planned so many fiery demises for myself in fragile *Juliet*. They were of little comfort to me now as we were smashed by forty-five-knot winds with more than a thousand miles of open sea behind us on our voyage to England. This was our second major storm since leaving Nova Scotia. Gale-force winds were hammering us and had been for close to seventy-two hours. My reveries of death in *Three Four Juliet* were supposed to serve as a counterirritant, but they were about as effective as a sore throat during childbirth. Instead, another counterirritant had begun to take hold. The words did not need to be articulated for Chris to know what I was thinking. They flashed in the close cabin air as bright as neon, and an image burned in my mind's eye. There she was, blonde hair flying as she bashed through the Strait of Magellan— Mary Nutt, rounding Cape Horn on a wind surfer. The Nutt on a feverish brain in forty-five knots of wind, just south of 50° N, was one hell of a counterirritant.

Hallucinatory as my image of Mary was, I had no delusions concerning myself. I would never equal the Nutt in terms of sheer guts or enthusiasm, nor was this really my desire. But then again, how had I made the quantum leap from that honeymoon cruise in New England to this bash across the Atlantic, from sea bride to a queasy-but-holding blue water wife within three years?

I was then and still am terribly unsuited for life at sea. I found this out almost immediately on our down-east honeymoon of three years before. We had lovely days, flawless ones of blue skies and spanking breezes that drove us to enchanting islands like Roque, with its one precious mile of white sand, a lazy glorious curve of beach not to be equaled on the Maine coast. We had met interesting people too, not just summer people or cruising folks, but people who had lived year in and year out with the sea, people who knew the toll it took and had come to terms with it. This is perhaps an odd memory for a honeymoon, but in particular I remember meeting two young children, a brother and a sister, on Swan's Island. We were walking into town early one morning, and these two beautiful flaxen-haired children appeared in the road. They were about eleven and thirteen years old. Marveling at our strange accents, they asked us where we were from, also how old we were, and if we were brother and sister. They were just as eager to tell us about themselves, and this was their story.

Their names were Carole and Arthur. They had always lived on Swan's Island. Two-and-one-half years before, a terrible thing had happened to them and their family. It was December, and their father, a fisherman, had gone out scalloping with his buddy Paul. The day was bitterly cold, and the wind was blowing fiercely, but the harbor had not yet frozen up, and it was important, especially since there were seven children, to get in all the fish he could before the ice came and he was locked in the harbor. It was the end of the day, and the men were just coming back into the harbor. The wind was really blowing hard now. Their father had just spoken to their mother on the ship-to-shore radio telling her that he would be home in ten minutes. As he went to get into the punt, he slipped and fell into the icy black water. He went under all the way and did not come up. The radio was still turned on, and at the fisherman's home his family could hear Paul screaming for help. Their father couldn't be found. Soon it was too dark to search and it had started to storm. That night everyone in the fisherman's family was so frightened that they all brought their mattresses downstairs into the kitchen so they could sleep together on the floor. The next morning the fisherman's body was found washed up onshore.

There was something odd about the way these children told the story so calmly, so matter-of-factly. In one sense I had the feeling that it was part of their grieving process and they were reliving and rehearsing one of life's worst possible moments as if to accustom themselves to it. In another sense they were trying to tell us something, too, something about life on an island, a family dependent upon the sea for life and for death.

There are many moments in sailing that others find inspiring. Even during a cruise these often come in the form of self-testing, when we measure our limits in terms of our patience, resources, and adaptability. We either fail or succeed, and we talk about these moments later, especially if we succeed.

There were two such moments on our own honeymoon. Although I passed them quite admirably, I really did not like it and found that they did not increase my own sense of self-worth in the slightest. So what if I had explored a few frontiers previously unknown to me. It didn't make me a better person. As a matter of fact there are certain kinds of self-improvement that I am absolutely loath to pursue.

The first experience is an occupational hazard for all sailors, cruising or blue water, and is so ordinary that one might wonder why I even mention it. The hazard is hygiene. We had been nine or ten days on our honeymoon without a shower. This kind of stuff was old hat to Chris but not to me. I did not find the experience ennobling in the least. When we reached Eastport, Maine, we tried everything short of being arrested as a public health hazard in our attempts to get clean. Upon inquiring for a shower, we had been directed first to a nearby rooming house, where a toothless man opened the door. We described our plight and asked if we might buy a shower. He shook his head doubtfully but called the woman of the house, who informed us that there was only one bathtub and the town marshall was in it. From there we tried two more rooming houses, the Eastport Memorial Hospital, and the police station, not one of which could accommodate us. We did finally get one when we sailed the short distance over to Canada.

I would go without a shower longer than nine days during some of our future sailing ventures. I never grew used to it, liked it, or derived any satisfaction from it. I didn't even thrill to those ubiquitous photographs that appear of people like Sir Francis Chichester pouring buckets of salt water over their heads on the foredeck, giving the impression of salty heroics, but believe me, it isn't. It is itchy and smelly, and the pictures never show the flaming saltwater boils that often develop on one's hindquarters from lack of hot water and soap after days of interment in foul-weather gear.

There is nothing like the image of a brand-new freshly caught husband splat on the deck to fire one's adrenaline. It was precisely this image that spurred me on to another one of those self-tests that was performed but hardly savored on our honeymoon. Since I have a natural loathing for anything resembling salty action, one can imagine my dismay when I found myself dangling thirty-five feet up in the air above the deck, rigging a new halyard. We had been coming back from the Saint John River in New Brunswick and had just entered the bay of Roque Island. A big wind suddenly hit us like a moving wall of concrete. There was a terrible snap from above, and the next thing we saw was the big jenny blossoming to leeward and collapsing beside us into the water. We hauled it in and ducked into a hurricane hole around the corner from the white sand beach.

Chris said he would splice a new eye into the halyard and we would take care of reeving it through the masthead block in the morning. I spent a sleepless night fretting and flexing my muscles in anticipation of hauling Chris up in the bosun's chair. I was not prepared for this kind of responsibility so early in marriage. I was ready to stand by in sickness and in health but not at the foot of the mast with a winch handle and Chris dangling thirty-five feet up in the air. It was very trusting of him, but the sheer physics of the situation appalled me, and that coupled with my proclivity toward panic made the notion of me hauling Chris up intolerable in my mind.

By morning I had reached a decision. I would go up the mast to repair the halyard. I am a notorious acrophobic. I swirl with vertigo on kitchen stepladders, but I was firm in my decision to go up. It wasn't self-sacrifice or bravery. I didn't really think I would die up there. I just thought I would be frightened and nauseous but less so than if the positions were reversed with Chris at the top and me at the bottom. The decision was essentially one of rational cowardice. I was ducking responsibility with good reason. I would be safer with Chris doing the hauling than he would with me doing it. It was as simple as that.

It had crossed my mind that having to accomplish a repair at that altitude might diminish my fear of heights. This was not one of those trips to a scenic observation platform where one was required only to ooh and aaah, exhale and inhale in thin air over the spectacular view. There was a focus here. I had to thread a rope through a block, or something like that. I slung myself into the bosun's chair after Chris had secured the halyard and several tools to it. He gave me a very quick atta girl-type kiss with a pat and commenced to haul. As my toes left the deck, I had a macabre recollection of another kiss, one that John Donne had written about in the poem "The Expiration." Trying to recall the first lines of the poem bedeviled me halfway up the mast, but at about seventeen feet I remembered the first lines.

> So, so brake off this last lamenting kisse,
>   Which sucks two soules, and vapors Both away,
>   Turne thou ghost that way, and let mee turne this, . . .

It was the sucks two soules and vapors part that got me. At twenty feet I could actually feel the sucking on my soul. At twenty-five feet I was feeling rather vaporous. I imagined I saw my soul depart, just kind of float away over the pointy spruce tops. Chris was issuing a myriad of instructions. "You're doing fine. . . . now just take the block and lead the etc., etc. . . . you're doing fine. Good. Good. It's nice up there, isn't it . . . now . . ." I was madly embracing the mast and breathing deeply. The next time I was required to do such deep breathing would be years later when our son, Max, was born.

Chris loves telling about the time I went to the top of the mast. I think he likes recounting the event not just because it is an indicator of connubial love but mostly because it shows how for a brief instant I conquered my fear and nausea. Words like *conquer* and *triumph* are germane to situations like these. Chris perceived the trip to the top as some sort of glorious self-test of my sailing mettle. Unfortunately it had come so early in our married life that I was going to have to spend the next ten years correcting it. My perception of this episode differed vastly from Chris's. If anything I had been vanquished by my ascent. I swore that I would never do anything like that again. My acrophobia was not diminished. It was enhanced.

Although this world of string and wood, spar and canvas, wind and water was for some the perfect embodiment of life's elemental forces and lent a metaphorical dimension to some existences, it didn't do much for me. For Chris, beyond the metaphor, or perhaps before it, sailing represented a kind of complexity that he thrived on. He loved doing battle with the alcohol stove for the simplest meal. He hummed cheerfully to himself as he tried to figure out how to do a wire-to-rope splice on a halyard. His eyes shone bright as beacons off the Point Le Preau fog factory listening for whistle buoys and dodging ships in the Bay of Fundy. For Chris that wonderful phrase of E. B. White's "joy through complexity" was exquisitely appropriate. But not for me. I became impatient and resentful. I was reduced by such complexities, not inspired. In situations where Chris remained as placid as a Buddha, I would become a screaming virago just seeing life's minutes slip away while the simplest functions like eating, sleeping, or keeping clean became complicated maneuvers that wore one down.

I reached my all-time low and came closest to retiring from sailing the

Kathy and a bell buoy in a Bay of Fundy fog.

summer following our marriage. Chris and I had taken the boat to Nova
Scotia. We had almost reached Halifax when it was time to turn around and
head for home. It had been a lovely ten days of sailing with fresh northwest
winds, but on the day we headed back the wind came up from the southeast
bringing thick fog that remained with us for the next two hundred and
twenty-five miles. It became our longest run ever in fog, a nerve-racking four
days during which navigation hung on the compass, watch, Fathometer, and
faith. Sometimes our only landmarks were underwater spits and mounds
which shoaled up abruptly and showed on the Fathometer. Chris scoured the
chart deciphering this invisible landscape.

Fog and nerves go together in my mind like bacon and eggs. Years later
when Chris made a film documenting the 1980 *Observer* Single-handed
Trans-Atlantic Race, I gasped in disbelief when the automatic camera
whirred away showing Phil Weld, the race winner, snoozing while his
trimaran, *Moxie,* hummed across the Grand Banks at seventeen knots in thick
fog. For me it was one of the scariest moments of the film.

I myself had been so frightened during our four-day run in the fog that
for the last eighteen hours on the course between Cape Sable and Mount
Desert Rock I had refused to sleep despite "George," our self-steering vane.
It was our first trip with the phantom helmsman Chris had built the winter
before. I was very wary of George, although Chris pointed out that we were
as blind as the vane in this situation and that George was a more precise
helmsperson than either of us. His ability to shave a buoy at the end of a
forty-mile run without an adjustment from us during the entire course was
truly amazing. But somehow I was not entirely comfortable with the notion
of this plank of mahogany and the small weather vane of dacron sniffing wind
direction on top being in charge of everything.

I had remained in the cockpit all night eyeing George warily and staring
blindly into the fog. We made our landfall on Mount Desert Rock without
ever seeing it, only smelling it and hearing the moan of the diaphone horn.
From there we sailed a fifteen-mile course to a whistle buoy off Swan's Island.
At last in visibility like the inside of a full milk bottle we saw a feeble, pulsing
glow off to port. It was the Minturn Harbor lighthouse, seventy-five feet
from our bow. We continued for exactly two minutes, turned left ninety
degrees for one minute, and dropped anchor in twenty feet of water. I
collapsed a palsied wreck of nerves on the bunk. For four days there had been
no horizon, no stars, no sun. If Chris or I walked to the bow of the boat,
our figures began to fade when we passed the midship shrouds; by the time
we were at the bow pulpit, we had become a disembodied voice to the other
in the cockpit.

Fog blind, cold, and scared, I experienced a kind of sensory deprivation that I had never known. I had never in my life felt so totally cut off. Trying to imagine there was a world beyond that contained within the thirty-foot dimensions of our ketch required an extraordinary effort of the will and imagination. The chasm grew between the world I had known and experienced and the one I was now committed to. Things became abstract to me in a peculiarly threatening way. Perhaps it is similar to when a person has been sick for a very long time and begins to wonder if they were ever really well or did they have a life before they were sick. It was like that for me. I wondered if I had ever smelled green grass or actually stood on Commonwealth Avenue in April and seen the magnolias just opening up or met a best friend for lunch. The oddest thought of all came to me when I was absolutely aching with fatigue: Had there ever been a person like Shakespeare? Had he ever really lived? Had I ever actually read him? I longed for a copy of Shakespeare. I craved it as much as I had ever craved anything. This was really quite strange because I was not the sort to just pick up Shakespeare and read. The last time I had done that was when I had been cramming for an exam in college. But I felt that if I could just get hold of a copy of Shakespeare and read anything, I might be all right.

In that swirling miasma of fog, I was beginning to imagine that Chris and I were inhabitants of a world that was not yet made, some preworld that was before creation, before grass, before magnolias, and before Shakespeare. I didn't like it one bit. I am a sort that needs points of reference, perimeters, and confirmations of sensations, feelings, and impulses. In a fogbound environment it is not just that you get sick of the wetness. You begin to forget what it feels like to be dry, and it is not that you tire of the constant grayness but that you strain and then fail to remember color, and this is the beginning of some serious doubting that can eventually wreak small havoc in one's brain.

This trip to Nova Scotia was supposed to have been our vacation, yet I felt as if I had been subjected to some sort of cunning torture that could have been perceived as fun only by the most bizarre of minds. I did not feel as if I had flunked in any way. There was no tearful demonstration in which I sobbed that I was a failure as a wife, sailor, or whatever. Indeed I felt something almost the reverse—a strange kind of triumph. Chalk one up for sanity, I thought. Only an idiot would call the last twenty-four hours, let alone the other three days, fun. It was one of those rare moments in life when one feels not merely justifiably but certifiably sane. No more, I said to Chris. I calmly announced that I would no longer participate in anything more than a two–day cruise, if that. From now on I would stay home, like a lot of other sane wives, and if he wanted to see more of me he might consider selling the boat. The honeymoon was over!

Calmly, carefully, I gave him all my reasons—very sane, well-founded, understandable reasons. I skipped over the little details like no showers and the fact that interesting molds were probably growing in my crevices after four days of complete incarceration in foul-weather gear. I concentrated on the larger, more significant issues, which involved notions of freedom to think and communicate about things other than immediate survival, something that I thought of as enriched communication. Fortunately I had the grace and smarts not to call it that. Basically it meant talking about things other than fog, and last but not least sex. For days our lives had been led at a thirty-five degree angle as we beat through the dense fog. Our bodies meanwhile had been moldering away in foul-weather gear. The angle, the temperature, the visibility, and the sartorial requirements were hardly conducive to connubial or nonnubial relations, but my God, if there was ever a counteraphrodisiac the Bay of Fundy in fog was it. Planned Parenthood should recommend it as a contraceptive device. I am sure it is as effective as a condom, not to mention foam. Chris listened to me, nodding gravely, understandingly, sympathetically throughout my discourse. He didn't argue or even question. I went to sleep feeling relieved. At least I had told him where I stood.

CHAPTER 9

The next morning I woke up feeling certifiably sane and inexplicably sad. I knew that I could not go through with my promise to stay home. I knew in my heart of hearts that being certifiably sane wasn't any bowl of cherries either, and to look for sanity in marriage wasn't really a value or a goal for Chris or me. I remember thinking about all this as I lay on the bunk and stared out the companionway which was dripping with beads of condensation. The fog had thinned under a struggling morning sun, but misty patches swirled across the view framed by the open shutters. I continued to ponder the connection between sanity and happiness and sanity and love, if indeed there was such a connection, and in my ruminations I stumbled over the first revelation about our relationship: There was nothing rational about it, so why seek reason and sanity within it.

I was not putting us in that category of charismatically crazy lovers like Scott and Zelda Fitzgerald or Hamlet and Ophelia. Nothing as glamorous as that, but indeed sanity as a be-all and an end-all of marriage was not my idea of a fabulous value or goal in a relationship. Besides, it wasn't sanity or insanity that was the real issue with me and sailing. It was comfort, physical and, yes, mental comfort. If I could just be myself and not worry about living up to some abstract performance level that I thought was required, I would be more comfortable. It might even add to my physical comfort too. I decided I was not ready to throw in the towel on sailing yet. Sailing, and sailing across oceans, had been a lifelong dream for Chris. Helping a partner achieve a dream was a value too and more than a value. I was just beginning to realize that this kind of helping might be as much a part of marriage as a current is part of a stream. It is the current that gives the stream life and makes it flow to the river and the river to the ocean. The first dim glimmerings of all this came to me that fog-patched morning in Minturn Harbor, Swan's Island, where a year before I had heard Carol and Arthur's story.

Basically my problem, if I were to continue to sail, was one of identity. I don't like to call this an identity crisis. That implies some sort of lack of focus or definition to one's identity. I was not asking "Who am I?" I knew who I was all too well, and as far as I was concerned there were no precedents in terms of sailing women or couples with whom I could feel any kinship. I began mentally to range about in search of such kindred spirits.

There was another Mary, not Nutt, who would come to bedevil me from time to time and heighten my dread of ocean passages. This one was Mary Patton, who had stepped in quite handily, a century ago, when her husband was struck blind following a fever as they were about to round Cape Horn (what timing) in the clipper ship he commanded. I am not by nature a history buff, but I cannot help wondering exactly what Mary Patton said back in 1882 when she knew for certain that she must take command of *Neptune's Car*. The first mate was in irons for insubordination, and Mary was the only other person who knew navigation. What did the young seventeen-year-old bride mutter when the realization hit her full force that the ball was in her court, so to speak, and the ball in this case was a two-hundred-foot, sixteen-ton clipper ship and the court was Cape Horn. I can only think of one word myself, but history would have to do a sudden splice for nine-teenth-century Mary with her jabot and high-button shoes to utter that expletive. I wonder if she even permitted herself the thought as to how this bugger could have gone blind on her in this of all places. From the reports I could find, delicate Mary (they always mention how tiny she was) stiff-upper-lipped it the whole way, beat around the horn, and sailed *Neptune's Car* on for another fifty-two days until she safely delivered the cargo to San Francisco.

Mary Patton was among a spectrum of women that had begun to hover in my mind. All of them were quite real. Some of them I have met, and one I have sailed with. (In some cases I have changed their names to protect the guilty.) Whether I knew them personally or not, they began to exercise considerable influence over me starting on that foggy morning in Minturn Harbor until our departure on the first trans-Atlantic trip. I was searching not so much for a model as for some kind of soul mate, someone with whom I had enough affinity by spirit, by nature, that I would begin to feel comfortable on a boat with my own decidedly unsea-kindly identity and not be driven to do things that ran counter to my nature or made to feel guilty by my inadequacy.

For example, I cannot tie a bowline. There is something in my mind that prevents me from grasping what Chris calls the simple logic of that knot. I often tie granny knots instead. On a pier once on the Saint John River in New Brunswick, the baroque granny knot by which I had secured *Leucothea* to a cleat embarrassed me so much that I sat on it so members of the Cruising Club of America wouldn't see it. They had just tied up and come over to chat. I was mortified that they might spy my peculiar rope-tying efforts, thus I sat there for fifteen minutes crouched on a cleat with this horrid knot poking at my rear end.

If I were to keep sailing, I simply could not continue to sit on granny knots or be in a state where I was constantly apologizing for myself and making excuses for my shipboard character. I actually considered my character okay, and even if it were not sea-kindly, I did think of it as seaworthy. A Ping-Pong ball is not immediately thought of as having a "sea-kindly hull," an adjective most often reserved for clipper ships or Herreschoff designs. However, they do float—Ping-Pong balls, that is. They have a certain degree of seaworthiness. I saw one out there once at about 50N and 30W, a thousand miles off the coast of England. I too, although not sea-kindly, have a certain degree of seaworthiness. I float. I saluted the little Ping-Pong ball that gray Atlantic morning as it calmly bobbed about in the lashing force-eight gale that had us down to storm jib and contemplating the storm trysail. I shared something with that intrepid little sphere of plastic bobbing about; however, I had been searching for more than a Ping-Pong ball as a soul mate, sea sister, or what have you, and found them to be in scant supply.

One member of the spectrum, Mary Nutt, has been mentioned more than once, and as bright and kind a person as Mary truly is, my imagination slaughtered her daily on our Atlantic crossing. Her stamina, her muscle, her freckle-faced pluck just galled me. Luckily, at the other end of the spectrum was the inimitable Kay Cartwright. It was a fortuitous meeting just weeks before our departure for the first crossing that brought us together with the Cartwrights. We were in Newport, Rhode Island, where Chris was photographing a series of one-ton races. On the press boat I had noticed a big rugged-looking fellow with a deep Texas drawl. I couldn't help overhearing snatches of his conversation. It was about his wife. She had thrown up all the way across the Atlantic, coming east to west, on their honeymoon. That was enough to pique my curiosity, but what absolutely fired it were numerous mentions of another woman who apparently accompanied them. Her name was Rosie, and she was French. It was fragments of conversation like these that made me salivate to know more about this peculiar *bateau à trois* that crossed the Atlantic. "Yeah, Rosie just took off her clothes soon as the sun came out . . . good figure . . . Naw, Kay didn't mind her. She was actually too sick to mind anything. I think what got Kay more than the nudity were Rosie's spices. . . ."

This was getting to sound kinkier by the minute. I could no longer suppress my curiosity. I had a strange sense, prescience really, about Kay. To hell with Rosie; I had to meet Kay. I must have appeared a bit peculiar to Jerry Cartwright, as I apologized for listening into his conversation and then launched into a rather frantic explanation of how within a month I was going on my first Atlantic crossing and how I knew this might sound silly, but it was imperative that I talk to his wife immediately. I needn't have apologized to Jerry. He was immediately sympathetic.

"You've got to talk to Kay?"

"You see, I've never met any woman I really liked who's done this."

"I know what you mean. You got to talk to Kay!" He kept repeating this.

Jerry Cartwright, former croupier turned single-handed sailor, and his wife, Kay, had together sailed back from England to the United States in the company of a certain gorgeous French girl, Rosie, whom they had met on the pier the day before they left. Rosie's sailing experience was extensive. She always traveled, as Kay pointed out, with her own rubber dinghy and sextant. Kay's experience was limited, to say the least. It consisted of one afternoon sail off Falmouth, and she always traveled with false eyelashes. As soon as I met Kay, I knew I had at last found my soul mate, my sea sister.

We were superficially nothing alike. Kay is English, tall and gangly, a Kay Kendall-type beauty with a zany sense of humor and an incredible energy level. She can simultaneously be self-deprecating and pooh-pooh sailing. Kay's article for *Sail* magazine "The French Nudist and Me" in which she describes her trans-Atlantic honeymoon with Jerry and Rosie is a classic example of how humor is as important as navigation at sea. It was this article, which I read before I met Kay, that convinced me that she was my kind of blue-water woman. My descriptions of Kay cannot serve nearly as well as her own words.

The day before the dreaded Atlantic crossing finally arrived I was sitting on deck gazing longingly at land and bracing myself for the worst, when I noticed a small figure with a great quantity of long blonde hair rowing by. It was 4 P.M. and being British to the last, I invited her aboard for a cup of tea. Her name was Rosemary Brubella. She was French and quite charming. She was also a very keen sailor, traveling complete with her own sextant and rubber dinghy.

A few deft strokes of Kay's pen and we have the picture on Rosie. And by the end of this early paragraph in the article, I felt my spirit being drawn to Kay like iron filings to a magnet. I read on:

For the first three days the sky was gray and we were pushed by the winds toward the coast of Africa. I clung grimly to my bucket and just succeeded in doing my watches. Rosie, enveloped in huge oilskins, leapt cheerfully about, hauling in sails and heaving on winch handles. She also did wonderful things in the galley, swinging wildly on the rope attaching her life harness to the grab rail . . . humming a tune and rummaging in a paper bag which contained 101 spices, a part of her kit she was apparently never without . . . the fourth day out I crawled out of my bunk, where I had been dreaming as usual of drowning, and thought I would go up for some air . . . the sun was shining. My gaze fell on the foredeck and remained riveted. Rosie, sitting on a towel and soaking up the sun, had absolutely no clothes on. I was quite amazed. Probably a fault of my English upbringing.

Jerry apparently remained not only cheerfully unflappable in reference to Rosie's nudity but soon decided to abandon his own clothes and to "leap about with nothing on." Kay, increasingly flappable herself, managed with an unerring sense of humor in her article to describe the navigation lessons given to Rosie by Jerry in the nude . . . the two of them pouring over the chart table, working out sights, talking about "hour angles and assumed positions" while she, Kay, clung to her bucket. "The conversation [was] quite beyond me. I did feel however that it didn't fit in with the two bare bottoms perched on the engine housing. . . . Being the only non sailor aboard, I refrained from comment. Seafaring people obviously led a simple, natural life, their minds circling free and clear above convention. I hoped that at no time their minds would sink to more earthly thoughts."

Two weeks out of Las Palmas they were hit by squalls and headwinds. Twin jibs had to be abandoned. Heroic maneuvers on the foredeck negotiating sail changes were left to Rosie and Jerry "[w]hile I being considered completely unsafe out of the cockpit took the wheel. . . . When I did my watch, Jerry always insisted on tying my lifeline himself, not trusting my rather exotic knots. . . . In this way I was lashed for the duration of my stay out there with thoughts of luscious Rosie languishing below. People have suggested to me that this was all highly suspicious. However, I honestly think Jerry was simply ensuring that I would not be carried away by a large wave. At times on watch, wet and cold and buffeted, I found myself screaming at the sea 'I hate you.' Jerry, catching me in the act, was convinced that I should be off loaded to the funny farm immediately upon arrival in Barbadoes. Maybe this was another reason he felt it necessary to tie me down."

Of course both Kay and I really knew who should be off-loaded to the funny farm. Kay had admitted to incompetence, cowardice, and jealousy, yet to me she was distinctive within the spectrum of sailing women. She was a sea princess within that blue water elite. The memory of Kay and her antic charm flashed back to me on that first crossing Chris and I made and sustained me in my dark hours, alleviating my gloom and counterbalancing the hallucinatory heroics of a Mary Nutt that lacerated my brain when I was beset by feelings of inadequacy. Kay Cartwright was the first woman I had met who had done serious sailing and yet did not take herself seriously. Seriousness is an occupational hazard of sailing and something I could not tolerate. It has been my experience that too many blue water women feel compelled to outmacho their men. It is a syndrome I call foreplay, for what better spot on a boat to display one's courage and skill than the foredeck of a small sailing craft pitching frantically in heaving seas while one wrestles with a sail change. I have listened to innumerable accounts of serious sailing couples describing bouts on the foredeck during a gale. They go something like this:

HARRY MACHO: It had been blowing force six all day, but when it cranked up to eight with seas to match, we decided to take in the number-two jenny [already you know that these people are some sort of nuts if they have a jenny up in force eight. What were they doing at force seven?] and put up the storm jib. So I went up there and I was wrestling with this bugger, when . . .

ALICE MACHA: No dear, remember, I went up. You were at the helm. You'd broken your glasses and didn't want to have to deal with Attila. That's what we call our new storm jib because it's made of ten-ounce dacron. I swear it's like sheet metal. It could decapitate you.

HARRY MACHO: You forget, darling, that's how I broke my glasses, up there on the foredeck with Attila. Snapped me right across the face.

ME: You mean you weren't decapitated?

HARRY MACHO: No, I was lucky, just my glasses.

ALICE MACHA: That wasn't where you broke your glasses, dear. It was in the shower at that hotel in Tenerife. Remember? Harry has the worst time (she turns to me). After a few days at sea, when he gets on land, things still rock for him and it seems the worst if he gets into a shower. Something about the space and the sound of the water. Anyway, he stepped out of the shower in the hotel and reached for his glasses, and . . .

HARRY MACHO: Goddammit, Alice, you're wrong. I was on the fore-deck wrestling with Attila.

ALICE MACHA: Fuck you, Harry. Where do you think I got this! With that, Alice hikes her skirt to show a scar on her thigh. (Not since Lyndon Johnson's gallbladder operation, I think to myself.)

ME: Attila?

ALICE MACHA: You're goddam right. Harry was nowhere in sight.

ME: For Christ sake, you were both on the foredeck. Now shut up!

This is very reminiscent of fights between our young son, Max, and his best friend when they both want to be Superman and nobody wants to be Lois Lane. The previous dialogue is a good example of foreplay and the kind of competition that can beleaguer many a sailing marriage. The reverse of foreplay is not aft play. I don't know what you call it, but I can give an example.

It happened one gale-laced night on our southern east-to-west crossing, one thousand miles from Tenerife. I had been standing in the companionway watching in horror as Chris wrestled with our storm jib. I was yelling to him to be careful, when a giant wave broke over our stern and completely scrubbed me off the companionway stairs onto the floorboards. Such were my inclinations for foredeck heroics. I was content to leave it to Chris and wring my hands aft.

That experience (I suppose one could call it aft play) was truly a frightening one, and for days after that peculiarly warm water dashed in my face, I kept thinking of Herman Melville's Pip in *Moby-Dick,* who after having fallen overboard into "the heartless immensity" of the sea and then been rescued went about on deck "an idiot . . . for the sea had jeeringly kept his finite body, but drowned the infinite soul."

Meeting people like Kay Cartwright helped me to be myself on board, to accept myself. I will not say accept my limitations, because I feel that Harry and Alice had their own limitations imposed by their frantic urge to compete on the foredeck. I had no dreams, no aspirations about such things. Foreplay wasn't my game. Because I had no delusions about myself on a boat, this made my transition from the sea bride to queasy-but-holding blue water wife much easier than one might imagine in many respects. God knows I never took myself seriously, or Chris for that matter. It would have been death to the whole adventure and to the marriage. For one who identifies more with Pip than with Slocum, kindred types are scarce. My spectrum offered Kay, with whom I enjoyed a complete affinity of spirit. But she is rare among blue water women, and one is more apt to encounter the likes of a Lucille Pitchpole or an Alice Macha. Lucille Pitchpole is the other half of that engagingly dotty English sailing couple who shows up at the embassy in Rangoon in tux, gown, sneakers, and oilies. They have been circumnavigating the globe for years, writing volumes about everything from force-eleven gales to cream teas in Tonga. Their younger counterparts are Tom and Judy Ahoy. Rugged (to a fault), they make saltwater bread and give birth to babies in the Strait of Magellan.

CHAPTER **10**

It was my less-than-blissful experience to have to sail with one of these couples on a trip from California to Hawaii with Chris and several other people. I'll call them Charley and Maya Albright. Chris was involved in making a documentary film about the Albrights and their many adventures, as they were a sailing couple of some renown.

On land the Albrights were lovely people, lively, intelligent, and humorous, but once they were aboard their cutter Captain Albright's personality took a somewhat diabolical turn and what had appeared onshore as charming quirks at sea became grim defects. For example, Charley's penchant for frugality on land was almost comical. Before setting sail I remember a rather hair-raising but humorous ride down a California freeway. We were northbound in three lanes of traffic, weaving in and out of it, screeching to periodic halts as Charley spotted a lug nut here, a "perfectly good" jacket there, an old tire, some orange road-signal flag there, and assorted other junk. He would jockey the car through the traffic, slam on the brakes, scoop up the roadside treasures, hop back into the car, and tear off, waxing ecstatic about his latest find and wondering about all the dumb bastards who threw away "perfectly good" gear.

Oy vey! *Aloha! The Albrights' cutter under way for Hawaii.*

All of this was tolerable and humorous to a point.

Admittedly, I was less than enthusiastic when Charley arrived on board after one of his evening foraging trips on Route 280 carrying a paper bag dripping with blood and announced "fresh road-killed rabbit" as that night's menu. Indeed, the tire treads were still visible. After skinning it out, Charley proceeded to pop the bunny into a pot with a few bay leaves, canned tomatoes, and onions. To this culinary offering I merely shook my head and said no, thank you as my mother had taught me. This inclination toward frugality on land became in the middle of the ocean something else, and to my mind it became a thing of which mutinies are made. We were not only reproached for taking our fair share, but taunted, scolded, and even threatened, and all this over not such precious commodities as food and water but items like toilet paper. Charley's stinginess concerning the toilet-paper supply finally escalated to a showdown of sorts and offered a superb example of the truly petty mind at work.

In reference to the toilet-paper crisis, it must be understood that there was no head on board the cutter. The Albrights considered toilets a lubberly feature. When one had to relieve oneself, he or she was forced to do so over the stern rail. Before going to the rail, one shouted "Keep a sharp lookout ahead" and then proceeded. There was, however, one soul who was not keeping a sharp lookout ahead. At about the two-thirds mark on our voyage, Charley announced, in what I am sure he considered a most discreet manner, that "some of us" were using too much toilet paper. Given the infrequency with which I used the stern facilities, which I found constipating to both body and spirit, I was sure that I could not be among the guilty. That is until Charley glared right at me and added, "so they'll have to use their books."

"Books, Charley? What do you mean?"

"Just what I said. Pages from those books you're always reading."

I was more than offended. I was outraged. No since Savonarola, I remember thinking, and I have to be on a fifty-foot boat in the middle of the Pacific with this jerk. My reading had always been a source of great frustration for Charley simply because it insulated me against his tyranny. That is exactly what Charley was, a tyrant. Tyrants cannot bear to be ignored, which is what my prodigious reading when I was not on watch allowed me to do.

Charley needed the sea. He did not love the sea, and this is a distinction that must be carefully drawn. Love of the sea, the "sea fever" that John Masefield depicts, is quite different from need of the sea. Charley was one of those persons who needed the sea because he simply could not get along on land. His wife, Maya, was similar. I don't know if she started out this way or became so through her marriage. I have a hunch that Maya basically did love the sea. However, neither Charley nor Maya was really very happy when at sea. They went because they had such a difficult time functioning in society, most of which is land-based after all. Charley could not exercise his strange personality, his needs for constant power, over others on land. Maya, although not a tyrant by nature, had her own peculiarities that allowed her to tolerate Charley's bizarre behavior, not to mention to endure a marriage that most would find impossible. I will not even speculate on the underlying needs that were somehow met in that partnership. Suffice it to say that going to sea with the Albrights was something like a saltwater version of *Who's Afraid of Virginia Woolf?*

Our experience aboard the Albrights' cutter was almost unbearable. I found it of great solace that Chris did not enjoy the trip one iota more than I did, despite some fantastic sailing. Chris really rallied to me—defended my books against the unthinkable, took watches for me when I was feeling sick, and provided humor in a totally humorless situation. I remember his fierce determination to provide a festive dinner for me on the occasion of my birthday. A dorado, a kind of fish that is abundant in the Pacific, had been caught that day. Chris had labored over a court bouillon in which to poach it and then went on to prepare some delectable sauce for napping it. All this, of course, went against Charley's grain. One might expect this would be the case with someone who had cartons of World-War-II-surplus dried prunes in the lockers which he delighted in serving up for dessert.

It was bugging Charley no end as Chris hummed away merrily in the galley mincing carrots, sautéing onions, and reducing sauces. All afternoon Charley kept poking his head in through the companionway admonishing Chris against using too many ingredients. "Who do you think you are, Julia Child?" he'd growl. He never got too ornery with Chris, because after all Chris was making a film that featured Charley and Maya and he didn't want to antagonize him. Actually, by this time Chris had found Charley virtually unfilmable and had grave doubts concerning the entire project. But Chris, who has incredible patience, just kept smiling and saying "Charley, you're going to love this. I haven't had to substitute more than six ingredients."

Charley of course didn't touch the fish and managed to harumph his way through my birthday dinner muttering about "Julia Child sauces." Charley's idea of a gourmet delight was raw sea crabs, the tiny fellows that one could scoop right out of the Pacific waters. He would take a handful of these crunchy critters, as if they were peanuts, and throw them in his mouth, their little feet kicking merrily all the way. He offered one to every crew member as some sort of virility test. Again, I was so pleased when Chris firmly declined.

I have always felt that perhaps some time, not necessarily equal, should be devoted to the study of small tyrants. The biggies like Hitler, Mussolini, Nero have been enshrined in the darker pages of history. But the petty tyrant too must be reckoned with. Although he or she does not plan the extermination of a race, it is the petty tyrant that day in and day out causes the thousands of small deaths of the spirit of the people closest to him or her. And it is these small deaths that wear one down until a person is a mere shell, a husk of a former self through which the wind can moan.

I was not alone as a target for Charley's outbursts. Every other crew member had stories equal to mine. Of course, there is no choice in a situation like this. One is in mid-Pacific with one's life entrusted to this man. He was a good sailor, technically competent, but definitely unstable mentally. It became apparent to all of us that our first order of business in terms of survival was to make sure that Charley did not become totally unglued mentally and do something that would indeed endanger our lives. To a certain extent one had to cater to this completely unlikable human being, which essentially meant never disagreeing with him and never questioning his reasoning about anything.

Charley was also quite paranoid. Small groups of people in conversation on a repeated basis made him extremely nervous. He thought we were plotting against him. Oftentimes we were sharing our griefs and complaining bitterly. Also, any ostensible show of festivity such as my birthday party piqued him. Although there is no choice, given the situation, there are a few coping strategies available that can alleviate conditions for short periods. Reading was one of mine. Chris had the film. A budding affair between two crew members did wonders for their sanity. Maya supported Charley right down the line and seemed to have the same needs to live in an environment totally controlled and defined by the two of them. Yet there was a part of Maya that was quite human, that invited a kind of sympathy even if we did not have the empathy to understand her need to be part of this bizarre relationship. In a peculiar way our sympathy for Maya became a distraction from our own anguish aboard the cutter. After all, our tenure with Charley was limited and Maya's was interminable.

A voyage like this could not end too soon. By the fifteenth day I was definitely at the breaking point. I thought I could not stand it a minute longer. On the sixteenth day I poked my head out of the hatch and saw that there was a shadowy mountain in the distance. There were several squalls, just little ones that would come and wet everything down, then blow past. An incredible series of rainbows arched over the island mountains. Those last few hours were beautiful. I didn't even will them to go any faster. Once I saw land I knew that was enough. Just to know it was there, to be close to it, to have some break in the circle of the horizon. We never saw Charley and Maya again.

It is no small accomplishment to cross an ocean when fit, hearty, and courageous, but to do it when decidedly unfit, scared stiff, yet with humor is a feat of some magnitude. It is the Rosies and their ilk, full of good cheer and guts, who have an easy time of it. But I do feel that it is the Kay Cartwrights of the world who have a perspective on themselves and life that is quite crucial to survival. It has nothing to do with the prefab cheerfulness, stiff-upper-lip, gung-ho qualities that are too often associated with contests of endurance and courage. So on our Atlantic crossing the summer after the disastrous Hawaii trip, while Chris was reading things like Adlard Coles's *Heavy Weather Sailing,* a book with such scary wave pictures that to this day I refuse to read it, I was thinking about Kay—Kay in the day clinging to her bucket while Jerry and Rosie cavorted topside, scrubbing themselves pink in warm Atlantic rain showers, "faces lifted like pagan creatures"; Kay at night, lashed to the helm and screaming imprecations at the sea; Kay nauseous while the fragrance of 101 spices swirled in the close cabin air. Kay with her "little pig eyes." "My God, Kathy, I had to go twenty-nine days without my false eyelashes. I was just too sick to glue them on. I never go without my eyelashes. You know it's rather like those little potbellied curmudgeons without their garters. I just don't go out sans lashes."

If Kay Cartwright is the princess within the blue water elite, I suppose Anne Weld, the wife of Phil Weld, is the queen. Anne does not wear false eyelashes, but she too definitely prefers land to sea. She would never succumb to any foredeck antics, although she has an equilibrium and stamina for duress at sea that I envy. A woman of quiet grace, Anne is given to what I can only describe as alarming understatement in all matters.

I can remember one memorable moment with Anne, my little boy, Max, and myself some months prior to the OSTAR, when down in the Bahamas the three of us had been awaiting Phil and Chris's arrival aboard *Moxie,* Phil's state-of-the-art racing trimaran. Phil and Chris had set sail from Fort Lauderdale some two days before. The purpose of the trip was to test out some of the elaborate film gear that Chris was in the process of designing and would eventually install on eight of the OSTAR boats for the race. Anne, Max, and I had proceeded by plane ahead of them to Green Turtle Cay, where we were comfortably ensconced at an inn. We had told the manager that our husbands would be arriving aboard the swift trimaran sometime during the night of our first day. We were making inquiries about mooring versus anchoring, etc., and of course we advised them that the following night we would need a larger table at dinner.

Well, each night the manager dutifully ordered the two extra places to be set at our table, and each night they remained glaringly vacant. The manager would come over and gently inquire: "No *Moxie* yet?" On the third night, perhaps picking up on our own anxiety, Max had reached a zenith of "regrettable behavior" for a hotel dining room. He was up to his old favorite sport of crawling under tables, tweaking people's toes, etc. To make it worse, it was right at the time when the waitresses had come in carrying trays of hot callaloo soup and were having to dodge this crawling two-year-old. He set up a beachhead under one table in the corner and then from there would make swift little raids out to the center of the dining room floor, just where the waitresses congregated to set down their trays of soup before taking the individual bowls to the tables. Unable to coax or cajole Max from his hideout, I was forced to crawl myself on hands and knees under the table of a very nice family from New Jersey and retrieve my errant son. I removed him, kicking and screaming, from the dining room.

I was absolutely mortified. It was not just the family from New Jersey or the rest of the dining room, but I had only really met Anne a few days before. What would she think of me as a mother? Worse than that, what would she think of her vacation? Here she was in this island paradise waiting for Phil, and she's stuck with me and this bratty kid. It was not a half hour later that I heard someone approaching my cottage. Peering out the door, I saw Anne, elegant in the moonlight, the trade winds stirring her gossamer-weight skirt as she walked up the oleander path bearing a dinner tray for me. There was a look of profound sympathy in her eyes. "You poor thing! You must be starved. But Kathy, I must tell you . . ." I caught my breath waiting for the inevitable good advice from an experienced mother of five. "Kathy, the story of the two husbands on the fast boat is beginning to pall with the management."

Phil tells this story about Anne in his book *Moxie,* which is perhaps the clearest example of this woman's extraordinary good humor and equanimity in a situation.

Though more content on land with her dogs and flowers, she nevertheless makes the best of it aboard, never panics, always uses her head in a crisis. The first full night at sea for both of us, following the start at Cowes of the 1970 Crystal Trophy Race in Trumpeter, found us at dawn down by Wolf Rock Light. The steering cable broke, we broached under spinnaker, broke several battens, and as the shackle holding the topping lift to the boom end shook loose, it managed to bounce off and smash the speedometer dial. Murphy's law at work.

As Bob Harris, Bill Dunlop and I tidied up in the near gale, Anne remained quietly below. When at last we had to drop out and head into Falmouth under jury-rigged steering, I had time to ask her what she was reading.

"*The Yachtsman's Medical Companion,*" came her calm response. "I supposed the mast would go next. I wanted to be ready if one of you got hurt."

Anne Weld completes my spectrum of sea women. I met her several years after our last Atlantic crossing. Her example, although I could never have hoped to emulate it, would have stood me well at sea. In her quiet humor I would have taken refuge. Her ability to serve well, to serve with style, her own style rather than Phil's or anyone else's, aboard a boat, I found extremely heartening.

PART III

CHAPTER *11*

"Harmony," "Communication," "Rapport," and more recently "re-specting one's space" seem to have become the catchwords, the verbal indexes used in assessing the vital signs and general condition of marriage. These words and phrases used positively are representative of the little streams that feed and water the relationship and make it "fertile," "viable," and a "growth experience." Somehow this language and mode of thinking has consistently left me cold. Did Esmeralda say to Quasimodo, "Is this viable?" Or Abélard to Héloïse, "Are we communicating?" They must have been communicating, but I think were concerned more with content rather than process. As much as I eschew the current lingo, I am hardly Petrarchan either in my phrases, and thus I have decided that the catchword and metaphor for our marriage is buoyancy—a search for buoyancy despite three thousand pounds of lead in our keel, and never was the buoyancy more severely tested than in our oceangoing years, which began in 1974 with our first trans-Atlantic crossing to England.

The gap between reality and ideal is dramatic in sailing. Nowhere is the mind more inclined to romanticize and less inclined to realize. I am no exception, and still after long hiatuses in sailing I occasionally succumb to idealized versions of on-board life. I always know that it has been a long time between voyages or even cruises when I start fantasizing about making a soufflé at sea on our gimballed alcohol stove in the collapsible tin-box oven.

I have a strong interest in food on land. I have been a subscriber for many years to *Gourmet,* a passionate reader of Mimi Sheraton and Craig Claiborne, and an absolute believer in literary critic George Steiner's state-ment in his essay on pornography that "there are probably more foods, more undiscovered eventualities of gastronomic enjoyment or revulsion than there have been sexual inventions since the Empress Theodora resolved to 'satisfy all amorous orifices of the human body to the full and at the same time.' " In spite of all this, it absolutely confounds me that to this day after long absences from the sea I can imagine myself whipping up a little Grand Marnier soufflé at 40°W. This hallucination is indicative of the kind of insane idealism that can plague notions of sailing.

The reality is that I can barely boil water at sea and often have to call Chris to do so. The reality is that secretly I have always been most contemptuous of those hearty bake-their-own-saltwater-bread types. The reality is that despite my credentials as a decent cook and outstanding record as a consumer of good food, I truly enjoyed opening a can of Chef Boyardee ravioli and eating it cold in my sleeping bag when it was blowing forty-five knots mid-Atlantic. I enjoyed it every bit as much as the *loup en croûte* I was to have two years later at Paul Bocuse's when Chris and I tied up along the banks of the Rhône less than a mile from his restaurant.

The gap between the real and the ideal began even before we acquired *Leucothea*. When we first knew we were being given a boat as a wedding gift, I applied myself immediately to finding the Ideal Name for our new ketch. With my being a word maven, it was only natural that I began the search by rereading the *Odyssey*. I thrilled in a most lubberly way to the spellbinding cadences and sounds of names like Circe, Amphititre, Calypso. I neatly skimmed and promptly forgot the gloom-and-doom passages about the Land of the Dead and the Rivers of Fear. These passages would come back to me almost verbatim five years later as Chris and I battled our way through the Med toward Gibraltar. However, such fragments of reality, Homer's or others, had no hope against the lively figments of my imagination as I searched for a moniker.

It is a difficult task to name a boat, especially from a woman's point of view. Boats for the most part are named after women. To my way of thinking, there is going to be the suggestion of either something shared or something adversary between the boat's name and the woman who sails the boat, a reflection, whether positive or negative. Even if this is not precisely so, people unconsciously project such a relationship. It begs for comparison. So there is always this peculiar tension that exists between a boat's name and the woman on that boat.

Well, *Calypso* was not a bad name, but terribly common. Every other boat on Long Island Sound is named *Calypso*. Although her promises of immortality for Odysseus if he would marry her were hardly reflective of my nuptial vows, I could manage to live with that image of myself. On the other hand, I kept wondering if all those people on Long Island Sound realized exactly where this nymph came from. Homer did not mince words on this score. Calypso came from the sea's navel, or more precisely "Ogygia, where is the sea's navel." Indianapolis is not great, but it is not that bad either. I just couldn't get over this association, and had we named our boat *Calypso*, I would have been thinking belly button the whole time.

Circe was out from the start. I am not into women with that brand of heavy magic. Turning men into swine is inappropriate on every level from poetic metaphor to politics. They do not need our help. Aside from this, there is a kind of weird sexism going on here—wily sirens entrapping men with their charms. I don't like it one bit. However, this is the siren syndrome and as such is quite prevalent in Homer, so I had to tread lightly as I wound my way through the book.

The sea is filled with boats classically named for gorgeous women who lurk, manipulate, enchant, entrap, sing exquisitely, copulate magnificently— veritable wet dreams for the seagoing male population. It is not that the wives don't necessarily know under what name they are sailing. It is just that they do not take it seriously. I do. I don't take sailing seriously, but words, names, I do. So my search for a name continued. I could almost have written an ad for the "Personal" column:

> Wanted: one sympathetic classical deity. Prefer mature responsible female. Those into growth experiences need not apply, likewise for sirens and sex charmers. Some magic acceptable. Sense of humor mandatory. Ready for gd times, nothing kinky.

I found her, or I should say that Chris and I both found her, when reading our separate copies of the Odyssey. She popped right out of the "salt depths" in the form of a sea mew on the wing, just as Odysseus in one of his less wily and unnautical moments was about to lose his boat. "Poor man," she said to him (note no bewitching voice, just straight sympathy). "Why is Poseidon so enraged with you that he sows nothing but disaster in your path?" (good question even if it is slightly rhetorical). "At any rate he shall not kill you, however hard he tries" (sympathy mixed with confidence, an unbeatable combination). "Now do exactly what I say, like the sensible man you seem to be" (supportive, but no nonsense). "Take off those clothes, leave your boat for the winds to play with, and swim for your life to the Phaeacian coast, where deliverance awaits you. Here, take this veil and wind it around your waist. With its divine protection you need not be afraid of injury or death" (very inventive, quite decent. One can hardly call the proffering of a veil a proposition in any sexual sense, especially when it is discarded from a seagull). But ". . . stalwart Odysseus was left in perplexity and distress." In other words, he did not trust her. He's got this thing about sails. Veils won't do. Who does he want, Ted Hood? Anyhow, a few paragraphs later after much hemming and hawing—I will leave the boat. I won't . . . I will —just about the time Poseidon sends another "monster wave" and Odysseus is left with a couple of planks, he does indeed take the plunge. He scrambles onto one of the beams and "bestriding it like a rider on horseback cast off the clothes that Calypso had given him. Then he wound the veil around his middle, and with arms outstretched plunged headlong into the sea. . . ."

It worked, with a little help from Athene in the wind department. She told it to hush up, or rather in the E. V. Riew translation, "She checked all the other winds in their courses, bidding them calm down and go to sleep; but from the north she summoned a strong breeze, with which she beat the waves down in the swimmer's path. . . ." But it was Leucothea's veil that kept him afloat. And after all his indecision, she had the grace never to come back and say "I told you so!" Definitely my kind of goddess. So we named our ketch *Leucothea*.

Years later, aboard *Leucothea* in Salcombe Harbor, we had an experience that I have come to think of as a rather droll re-creation of the events surrounding those of our mythic namesake and Odysseus. Salcombe is one of the loveliest harbors of the Devon coast. The harbor itself spreads out from what is called the bag into several fingers. Salcombe, a most English resort town, captures its fair share of sun, pretty London families, and a stunning array of roguish boats. The entire town is absolutely batty about sailing. They have races anytime and anywhere. In any case we were staying in Salcombe for several days. One night a forty-knot gale ripped through the harbor. Our sleep was fitful at best with the whine of wind in the rigging and slap of waves against the hull. Suddenly an ominous thunk woke me up completely. I always expect the worst. It is my mind-set on a boat, especially when we are anchored and not moored. As I poked my head through the companionway, my myopic gaze was transfixed in horror as I made out *Leucothea*'s stern nuzzling against a large power vessel, with our mizzen boom stuck at a decidedly rakish angle into their toe rail.

"Chris!!!"

In half a second we were both topside, stark naked, ready to begin our rescue mission. Naturally the electrical panel for the engine had been dismantled the previous day to replace a corroded starter switch and not yet reassembled. So Chris had to try to start the engine by touching the wires together. I stood by, incredulous. The last time I saw such an electrical feat performed was in an old Paul Newman movie about a doctor receiving the Nobel Prize who, just before the awards, revives another Nobel recipient in a Stockholm hotel by sticking cut phone wires to the man's chest. Eureka! It works. "Kathy! What the hell are you standing there for? Get that mizzen boom out of their toe rail."

"I can't. I'm naked." I thought that; I didn't really say it, because I knew the old wizard would electrocute me with his wires. So like a good soldier I marched toward the stern. For better or for worse, the luxury powerboat was lit up like a birthday cake, and down below I could hear the sounds of revelry. Unbelievable as it may seem, nobody on the vessel was aware that we had drifted into them and that there was a naked lady feverishly working to disengage her mizzen boom from their toe rail. Unfortunately the boom was jammed firmly and there was no budging it. Where the hell were those adrenaline muses that are supposed to appear on such occasions? I cursed. Millions of people have lifted cars off millions of bodies. What about a measly little mizzen boom? It should be peanuts for those girls. Between invocations for muses, my mind was working furiously. What would I say if someone came up from the party and found me there doing karate with the mizzen boom? Worse yet, what would be the view if someone peered out the porthole on a level somewhere between my kneecaps and neck? A new version of "The Legend of Sleepy Hollow"? A *Playboy* centerfold run amok?

Suddenly we were free. The boom popped out, hit me in the jaw, and I felt great. But here was the kicker . . . no anchor on the end of the rope. It was cut about fifteen feet from the end of the bow chock. Chris, not one to be undone by such peculiarities, began to shout at me to put up a jib. In addition to the other little inconveniences that were plaguing our evening sail through this gale-laced harbor, there was far too much wind for the roller furl. I was being called upon to actually raise a sail. I was going to have to hank on a jib, put a halyard around a winch, and crank. After months of easy furling and unfurling, this was like going back to a nonelectric typewriter after using a word processor. I never found sail changes easy in the best of conditions, let alone in forty knots of wind, stark naked, and most significantly without my contact lenses. There had been of course no time for me to put them in or find my glasses. Without lenses or glasses I am lost, especially on a dark, starless night. . . . But somehow I managed. Squinting, shivering so hard that even if I could see, everything would have been vibrating beyond any discernible shape, I managed somehow to hank on the small jib and began to crank it up. It rose beautifully and filled with wind, so that we were steadied almost immediately. I in turn was filled with pride. I even stopped shivering. "Kathy!" Chris shouted. "Goddammit! You put the jib on upside-down!"

I squinted upward, barely making out the shape. I scrunched my face until it ached and my eyes were slits drawing into focus the triangle of white. A slow well-I'll-be-darned feeling crept over me. The triangle did look a little broad at the top and narrow at the bottom. It did have a funny curl in it. But we were sailing and sailing comfortably. Much steadier than before, no slapping around. The sail was undeniably doing its job. I mean what did he want, egg in his beer? A veil in a gale? That phrase floated somewhere in the back of my mind. I smiled quietly to myself and looked up into the starless night. The good ship *Leucothea* and I had become soul sisters of sorts.

But there would always be wily Greeks, or whatever, who doubted. The sort who don't take the veil until the last minute.

"It works, Chris!" I yelled back. I will always have this image of Chris scratching his head and looking up at the inverted jib. But of course he could not have been scratching his head as his hands were holding the ignition wires as he steered with his feet. The head scratching was implied, I suppose. He was looking quite skeptical. As for myself, in retrospect I never see myself naked up there on the foredeck, but clothed, confident, and proud—almost smug, but then that would not have been fitting. *Leucothea,* after all, never came back to Odysseus and said "I told you so." I could not help but think as I was standing there and we were sailing smartly through Salcombe Harbor that people really did make a rather big deal over sail trimming and cut. They work quite nicely upside down in a pinch. We finally found a vacant mooring and tied up. The mystery of how a three-quarter-inch nylon rope, brand new, could have been cut remained unsolved. Our best guess was that in some way the strong tidal currents had twisted the line around our prop and it had chafed through during the gale.

The name *Leucothea* had in a curious way resumed some of its classical significance in Salcombe Harbor. The poetic distance had closed somewhat between my earlier idealism and the reality of sailing. Still, I must admit that many times I have wished we had ignored the classics and simply named our boat *Mary Jane* when I think of the time spent explaining the origins of the name, not to mention spelling it over the VHF L—Lima E—echo— U—uniform C—Charley O—Oscar T—Tonga H—hotel E—echo A—alpha.

CHAPTER *12*

This gap between the real and the ideal in sailing does not manifest itself in any uniform manner among sailing folks. With me the naming of our boat and my periodic bouts with gastronomic hallucinations were prime examples. Quite prevalent, especially among women, is indulging in boat decor. I am pleased to say that I did not succumb to this inclination. As much as I love the lively, richly designed fabrics from Provence, the very thought of such curtains in a force-eight gale was enough to unnerve me in the calmest harbor. I could imagine all too vividly their desperate cheerfulness as we pitchpoled off an Adlard Coles-type wave. If one must go to Davy Jones's locker, I myself would prefer to be wrapped in an American flag, or a UN flag for that matter, but not in a bolt of Pierre Deux fabric from Tarascon.

Reading material is another area in which we can observe the gap between the ideal and the real. Paradoxically, I feel that in terms of one's library on board ship, except for the basic first-aid and navigation literature, the less sea-oriented the better. Of course Chris is diametrically opposed on this question. Mid-Atlantic gales might find me reading E. B. White and Chris reading Horatio Hornblower. During a long hot calm off the Canaries, I entertained myself with a little Jane Austen and a guide to the Cotswolds. Chris meanwhile was reading about some odd sort who had crossed the Atlantic in an amphibious jeep and lived to tell about it. It would have been tantamount to suicide for me to even peek at Adlard Coles's classic, *Heavy Weather Sailing,* or read the Baileys' tales of turtle-oil enemas and diets of raw fish as they drifted for some eighty days in a life raft. No, let me read the latest news on twig blight in an old issue of *Horticulture* magazine or marvel over Emma's sweet officiousness as she so royally botches things up with her good intentions in that tiny ordered corner of English country life.

To read about manners and gloxinia while being thrashed about at sea by gale-force winds or broiling in a calm is, although not sheer pleasure, heartening in a curious way. Granted, this is not reality, but it is not that mocking kind of idealism of the gaily printed curtains frisking about the portholes. While strapped in my bunk stiff from the cold and tension of seventy-two hours under the siege of a gale, it is a balm to my soul to read Mr. Knightly's declaration of love to Emma. "I have blamed you, and lectured you, and you have borne it as no other woman in England would have borne it. . . ." This upending of chivalric tradition with the woman having to undergo various tests of moral worth seemed quite fitting to me as we headed for England on our first crossing.

By the time we started serious preparations for this first crossing the real/ideal gap was pretty much nonexistent, but as this gap had narrowed my own anxiety quotient increased. Now, after two Atlantic crossings that did try my nerve, I still can say that the worst part of each voyage was the preparation.

My own work for the first voyage began with the plotting out and measurement of every cubic inch of possible storage space. I became intimately familiar with the dimensions, shapes, and weight of a vast array of canned goods. Our boat was tied up at a city pier, an extraordinary convenience. Because it was right on the subway line between our house and offices, I could stop off morning, evening, and lunchtime for more work on the boat. I became a familiar figure on the Blue Line Subway, toting, along with my office papers, a straw basket filled with "test cans" for trying out new and ever-more-intricate storage configurations in various parts of the boat. My nonmathematical mind became a walking computer on unit pricing for canned goods.

Our lives were monopolized by the infinitesimal details of preparation. We became decidedly less social and even when out to dinner with other people, at any given moment we were capable of breaking into a spirited dialogue of checklists.

"Did the flexible water tanks arrive yet?"

"What about the springs for the winches?"

"Ballpoint pen springs work great."

"Why hasn't the *Nautical Almanac* come?"

"What about the sail-mending kit?"

"Call your Uncle Jack for a tetanus shot. What about the coal? John Lewis says we need five hundred pounds."

"John Lewis is seven feet tall; that's how much it takes to keep him warm. We don't need as much."

"No, no, Chris, we need more. Our bodies don't generate as much heat. We're shorter." Then of course we soon found ourselves in a discussion of body types and Eskimos and heat conservation until I would suddenly remember something else, like Bisquick. "What about the Bisquick. Be sure and remember the Bisquick."

We were indeed living lists, and to the casual observer it must have appeared that we were speaking in tongues. The planning, assembling, and storing of food and equipment represented only part of the preparation problem to me. In the back of a notebook stuffed with jottings on canned goods and where to get instant splints and disposable hypodermic needles, I kept a journal documenting my own feelings and emotions during this preparation period. When I was not doing the Have-can-will-travel routine on the subway, I spent a lot of time doing homegrown psychotherapy: hot baths, warm milk, and prayer. My journal at this time is a fairly good reflection of my state of mind. Even from the more tepid entries one can catch the glimmerings of rampant anxiety.

> March 3, 1974: I think I might be going crazy because I keep saying goodbye to things around the house. This morning it was the underwear drawer: all my sachets, bye, bye . . . so unnautical—all that lace. I know you'd love to see the Grand Banks, but you'll rot and get mildewy. So bye, bye, Bali, Maidenform, and Olga. Hello Duo-fold.

A popular entry was the last-thoughts department, imagining those last images that would streak though my mind as the boat is rent apart in 100 mph winds. I don't go for this business of your whole life flashing before your eyes in the final moments. I couldn't take it. I prefer to categorize my last moments according to topics: great meals, memorable summer nights, favorite newscasters. . . . So a last-thought list could read something like the one I assembled one week in April: "rack of lamb; June 18, 1958; Dan Rather."

Another entry from those predeparture days:

> May 3, 1974: Suddenly to contemplate life without Major Grey's chutney is to think of life with no more sunsets, or babies laughing, or crocuses in the spring. It hit me in the center aisle of the Stop and Shop. God forbid that we should run out of chutney mid-Atlantic.

I bought four bottles of the stuff. I felt the same way about soy sauce, and we had enough on board to entertain an entire Chinese delegation. Nicest of all was becoming the darling of the crew (and this could be hard even though I was the only one without a beard) when I whipped out the chutney at just the proper moment.

"I don't suppose," the dinner cook said, "there is any chutney on board to go with this curry?"

Faster than the proverbial speeding bullet, I dived for the bilges and came up with the coveted condiment. Little did he guess there were three more whence it came. The air was fraught with reverence. Such an action has incredible redemptive value, especially if the bearer of the chutney has not distinguished herself by any outstanding nautical feats and indeed has been throwing up all day.

For the most part, the food-provision list was uninspired—cans of liverwurst spread, corn beef hash, tuna fish, beef tamales, green beans, carrots, puddings, fruits, lamb stews, lasagna, etc. Mundane, institutional, gray food. But unless one wanted to spend wads of money and shop exclusively at the likes of S. S. Pierce, there was little alternative. We did find on our return trip when we provisioned in Gibraltar that the canned goods were infinitely more interesting. In our own supermarkets I did allow myself certain indulgences such as thirty-four dollars' worth of Pepperidge Farm cookies. In those days that meant a lot of cookies. A little exotica entered the larder by way of a trip to my favorite Harvard Square gourmet shop—bourbon balls, Scottish shortbread, plum pudding, brandied pears, and even a can of babas au rhum. I had never had babas before, and when I opened them two-thirds of the way across the Atlantic, I was so appalled by their appearance that I tossed them overboard. They were exactly what I imagined gangrenous toes to look like.

Although I was perfectly capable of eating the entire batch of cookies the first day out, I had plotted in my head what I came to think of as the Pepperidge Farm strategy for ocean voyaging. Latitude 50°07′W, longitude

40°05′N did not simply mean that we had 1,275 miles to go. It also meant that we had finished the first installment of Bordeaux (cookies, not wine) and could now briefly indulge in Mint Milanos, my favorite of the Pepperidge Farm repertoire. The Distinctive line as opposed the Old-fashioned line had cookies that one might consider more sophisticated. The line is indeed distinctive because of the delicate combinations of texture and flavor. It includes such varieties as the Tahiti, the Nassau, the Lido, the St. Moritz, the Barbizon, and of course the infamous Mint Milano. This particular cookie along with the Brussels were the masterpieces of Pepperidge Farm's founder, Margaret Rudkin.

I knew all about Margaret by the time we got to the other side because I had read about her perhaps fifty times on the packages. In any case, the Mint Milano was both voluptuous and delicate. Just the way many of us would like to be. After the Bordeaux run, I permitted myself to consume the Milanos at the rate of three per day until we reached longitude 35°05′W. Of course, interspersed with these could be any of the less-rich nonchocolate varieties such as items from the Old-fashioned line: Oatmeal Raisin, Peanut Butter Chip, or a sprightly Molasses Crisp could set me up just fine toward the end of a particularly dreary and cold watch. The Old-fashioned line had an earthy down-home quality and, as the bag says, "crackle and crunch" when you bite into them.

Upon reaching 35°05′W I would come off Mint Milanos cold turkey and switch to the chocolate-laced Pirouettes with their mere flecks rather than chips of chocolate. The Pirouette is a rather sedate cookie, almost prim, and has nothing approaching the lavish chocolate-minty filling of the Milano. There would be a gradual buildup, and by 29W I would be on Nassaus or Brussels. Then somewhere between 18 and 20 there would be a brief but naughty foray into the Mint Milanos, just for a couple of degrees of longitude. It was a bit like what runners call interval training, which is a method in which intense runs alternate with more relaxed periods of jogging over a specific distance. The final bag of Mint Milanos was reserved for when we saw the lights of England. An unabashed Milano orgy would then take place. I had never been to an orgy, but this was the only one that had any great appeal for me. So with thoughts of Brillat-Savarin, Caligula, and Margaret Rudkin, I ticked off the longitudes and carefully wended my way through the intricate cookie maze that would get me from one side of the Atlantic to the other.

CHAPTER *13*

Preserving the light delicate crispness that Margaret had strived so hard to attain was a challenge. I found the answer in my prevoyage reading of Sir Francis Chichester's classic, *Gipsy Moth Circles the World*. When Sir Francis was not eating his boatgrown watercress or wrapped in his smoking jacket and toasting Sheila with a glass of Veuve Cliquot or just plain sailing, he might have been found dipping into Tupper #16 for a digestive oval or Tupper #13 for cream crackers or perhaps it was Tupper #17 for assorted honeybars. Read the "Stores-and-Storages" appendixes at the back of Chichester's book and you will notice the list peppered with Tuppers. The Tuppers, in addition to containing the digestive ovals and his beloved garlic bulbs, which he felt helped his remaining lung after his cancer operation, held all sorts of sweet, delicate, and crispy goodies. These of course were punctuated by measured but hearty quantities of beer spritzed from the hose by his navigation table and the Veuve Cliquot. It was apparent then that the answer was Tupperware of all shapes and sizes, not only for the quantities of cookies, but also for other things such as matches, bread, sugar, flour, and whatever else needed to be kept dry.

The solution seemed simple enough, or so I thought until I called up the local Tupperware agent, who informed me in no uncertain terms that to obtain Tupperware I must give a Tupperware party. I was absolutely astounded. If it can be said that one broached on the telephone, I did. What did she mean that I had to give or go to a Tupperware party? It was six weeks before our departure. I was in the thick of list-making and gathering activities, not to mention my constant psychoreligious therapy routine. Not only did I not have time to give a Tupperware party, I had no desire to. No problem, she informed me. She could get me invited to one in Needham. I don't want to go to Needham, I nearly screamed, and sit down with a bunch of women I've never seen before and play Tupper bingo and tell Tupper tales. "Oh, you've been to one before." Yes, and I didn't like it that much. It was not my idea of a "keen pack of fun" as we used to say back in high school. "Look, can't I just buy the Tupperware?"

"No, that's impossible. We're only allowed to sell it through the group parties. That's part of the Tupper philosophy."

They have a philosophy? They're supposed to have plastic. Well, I've got a philosophy, I'm thinking on the phone, and it does not include going to Tupperware parties. Would Margaret Rudkin go to a Tupperware party?

Would Margaret Mead go to a Tupperware party? Forget whether they would go or not. Did I really have to go? I tried to imagine myself in this unknown living room in Needham. We're sitting there watching the Tupper lady demonstrate the Tupper burp, a small maneuver for closing the lid during which one presses the plastic in a certain way to expel some air from the container and thus hermetically seal it. These women are imagining the handy ways they can store leftovers or send sandwiches to school or keep freshly baked cakes for days. They are homemakers—makers of lovely, warm, vibrant homes. Immaculately clean homes with scrubbed, well-fed children. Organized homes with well-planned, balanced meals. Cozy homes where cookies are baked for Christmas, salmon, peas, and strawberry short-cake served for the Fourth of July, some of which will find an interim resting place between plate and stomach in a Tupper. Now where would I fit in? Well, I am there because I have to transport forty-seven packages of Margaret Rudkin's finest across the Atlantic Ocean, but that really is the least of it. The heart of the matter is this: When it is blowing force eight and colder than a witch's tit on the Grand Banks and I am shivering from fear as much as cold while I think about the first Levi Knight, who went down on the schooner *Elizabeth* off Bay Chaleur, and after hours of nothing to eat because of a queasy stomach, I begin to contemplate the simple elegance of a crisp Bordeaux, I do not want to remember, hearken back to in any way, the cozy, landlocked living room in Needham filled with women and their laughter and cheerful musings and good common homemaker sense. It is the last thing I want to think about. It would taunt me, mock me, just like the wretched gaiety of those curtains of French fabric. All this passed through my mind as the Tupper lady on the other end of the phone told me that in two weeks there would be a party in Wellesley Hills, if that would be closer for me. The only thing that I think would be closer for me is a Tupperware party on the Grand Banks. But instead I said, "Mrs. Brown, I want to know one thing."

"What's that, Mrs. Knight?"

"Did Sir Francis Chichester have to go to a Tupperware party?"

"Who?"

Within one minute it was arranged. She would send me a catalog. I could call my order in to her and she would include it on the Needham party's order. Once I had explained my reasons, starting with the Bargain in the Sky and continuing through the Pepperidge Farm cookie strategy for ocean voyaging, I got only sympathy. There's actually a lot of support out there for the noncriminally insane. I must admit that not only was it a stroke of genius to mention Sir Francis, but I got a marvelous kick from imagining him at a Tupperware party. I could just see the party, with Sir Francis, Blondie Hasler, and, say, the enigmatic French single-hander, Bernard Moitessier, who just kept sailing around the world in the Whitbread race because he had achieved such communion with the sea.

SIR FRANCIS: I find that one actually can keep leftover Veuve Cliquot in the cylindrical Tupper. However, it is not necessary to give the Tupper burp.

BLONDIE: Of course as a jury rig for the wind sensor of the self-steering vane, one can consider using the base of the Tupper cake plates for brief spells.

(Now Bernard breaks in): Ah-ha, you foolish fellows! You miss zee point of zee Tupperware to zee sailing experience. You tink only in terms of leftovers and parts and "jury rigs," as you say. But the real Tupper experience is something else. For that you leave your hull behind.

BLONDIE: What's that, Bernard?

SIR FRANCIS: Leave your hull behind? You're speaking metaphorically of course?

BERNARD: *Non!* I mean actually. Your boat!

BLONDIE: The bloke's gone round the bend.

BERNARD: *Non! Non,* just round the horn in a Tupper.

SIR FRANCIS & BLONDIE: What!!!

BERNARD: *Oui! C'est formidable.* One senses the, how you say? *La vérité de la mer. L'esprit d'eau en Tuppère.*

SIR FRANCIS: I've heard of *en croûte. Loup en croûte* with a smoky montrachet is quite delicious, but *en Tuppère.* Bloody Frenchmen!

BERNARD: *Ah non,* Sir Francis. *C'est magnifique.* One steps into the Tupper and *pouf! pouf!* (Bernard closes his lips and toots that rather rude sound that French people seem to find enchanting), and one just floats off. *Très simple.*

BLONDIE: *Très* idiotic! It's the salad bowl, not the colander, right, Bernard?

BERNARD: *Oui! Oui!* Blondie. You take me for a fool! *Vive la Tuppère.*

While I was fretting about Tupperware, Pepperidge Farm cookies, and my psychological soundness, Chris was attending to the soundness of *Leucothea.* Six months prior to our departure, Chris had dragged Jerry Blakely out of the comforts and newly found joys of retirement in Beverly, Massachusetts, to build a new mast for us. We knew that *Leucothea*'s mast was not up to an Atlantic crossing, and we wanted the finest wooden one possible. Jerry Blakely had worked with wooden boats all his life, and he had the tempo, grace, and deliberation that it takes to be a master craftsman in wood. In short, he knew how to build a spar of laminated Sitka spruce that could take just about everything that the Atlantic can dish up. In terms of what is controllable on a voyage, this spar was a key element.

It took Jerry a month to complete the mast. While he was building it, and for that entire spring up until the day we left, Chris and I were consumed body and soul with making our boat as seaworthy and safe as possible. The myriad of details to be attended to was overwhelming and included such tasks as installing a Lally column or house jack in the forward cabin, just under the mast, to reinforce it against compression loads from the mast, and adding half-inch-thick plexiglass sliding shutters on the sides of the cabin trunk over the large cabin lights. We had first tried plywood shutters, but they made the cabin so dark we thought we might be reluctant to put them on until it was too late. Chris also rebuilt the cockpit-locker tops on quarter-inch aluminum plate to resist loads of a large wave landing in the cockpit. He added two heavy quarter-inch head stays with roller-furling jibs and a secondary shroud coming into the mainmast between the spreaders and the mast top. All these additions and alterations, strengthenings or reinforcings, I came to think of as the Third Little Pig syndrome. No straw or twigs for us—bricks or the marine equivalent. We were trying hard not to underestimate the strength of the North Atlantic.

We did not have a spinnaker because Chris felt they were too difficult for a single person to handle, whereas the roller furls could be handled by one person mostly from the cockpit, a big safety factor. One of our most physically comforting additions was that of the Tiny Tot coal-burning stove for heating. It could burn for up to twenty-four hours on just two or three pounds of charcoal.

For me the most difficult thing of all to cope with during the preparation for the voyage was all the people who kept telling us we would be lucky if we made it (those were the nice ones); or who said flatly, you won't make it (those were the hard-core nasties). Although most of these people had never sailed, a man I sat next to at a dinner for sailors was absolutely convinced we would not make it, and this represented a real turning point for me in my attitude toward the voyage. I became so mad that I forgot to be scared and began to believe that we could and would do it. The man had been rumbling on about Gulf Stream waves and the design of our boat, which according to him was no more appropriate to cross in than a bathtub. Meanwhile he praised lavishly the capabilities of another type of boat. He

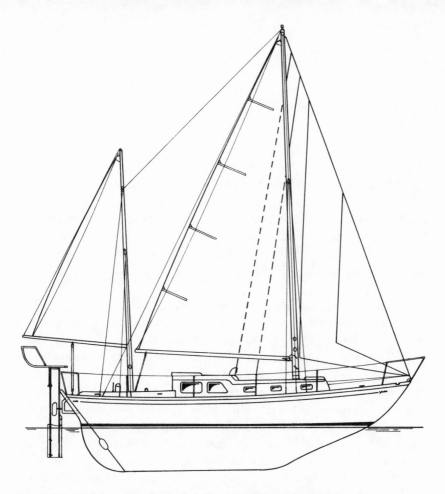

Leucothea and her sail plan before the installation of twin jibs.

was a man who basked in the timbres and cadences of his own speech as if the physical qualities of his voice alone constituted some superior form of intelligence. All style, no content. People like this, in addition to often being wrong, usually are poor listeners, but I turned on this man and unleashed months of pent-up fury.

"Look, sir, we can't afford one of your hundred-fifty-thousand-dollar offshore what's-its. We're going with what we've got, and we've probably put more thought and effort into our ketch than any joker who buys your offshore crossing machine and thinks he's got it made because he's plunked down a hundred-fifty grand. I'm sick of everyone telling us we can't do it. Nobody'd do anything if they listened to you. People like you don't see the human element in all this. You think that all you need is money and a load of equipment. Nine times out of ten the people fail before the equipment, and we certainly are not going to fail."

I came home from that dinner party feeling peaceful for the first time in months.

CHAPTER 14

Chris's father, Pete, was our third crew member. We could not have chosen a better person. Although he had never made an ocean crossing under sail, he was an experienced coastal sailor who knew wind and weather and all manner of boats. His unique blend of stoicism and spirit is a rare quality. He shared his wisdom with grace and cheer and the utmost respect for his son, the captain, and with complete sensitivity for me, his daughter-in-law.

At many of the major crises in my life there has been one special person in attendance, not a relative, but an old and dear friend, Holly Hartley. We met in the fifth grade and have been closest friends ever since. It was at Holly's family's summer home on Cranberry Island that I got my first taste of Maine and sailing in salt water. It was only appropriate that she fly in from New York upon the occasion of our departure for the first Atlantic crossing. Unobtrusive and full of wit, Holly would quietly ease my hysteria and temper Chris's euphoria so that neither of us would suddenly clash in some untoward predeparture incident that would result in a delay or "indefinite postponement," an expression I have heard most often used when a bride has been abandoned by the groom just prior to marching down the aisle. In this case I was the potentially faithless groom, and Holly was there to gently nudge me along that morning out of the house and onto the boat. The "bride" was at the pier, already eager to be off. He had been there since five o'clock that morning. It was now nine-fifteen, and in the last few minutes I had found or conjured up an infinity of small tasks to be done and objects to be found. It became clear that as the minutes slipped by the number of things to be done or located was rapidly increasing. I was having a fit over a lost alarm clock when Holly realized that the moment for nudge to pass to push had come. In her gentle, soothing voice she spoke quietly to me. "Now, Kathy, let's think about this. You're really not going to need an alarm clock at sea. There will always be a person from the previous watch to wake you up. I really wouldn't worry about oversleeping." And with that she guided me out the door.

We slipped our lines at Lewis Wharf and set off at precisely thirty seconds past ten for England, the only thing we have ever been on time for in our lives. We silently waved good-bye to our family and friends. As we powered out of the harbor against a light head wind, I watched these two men, father and son. Their eyes possessed the soft light of fulfillment, of ultimate happiness, of having lived long enough (thirty-one years and sixty-four years) to touch a dream. If they were to die the day after this voyage was completed, they would die with a sense of completion about their lives and not a word about the numbers.

My attitude was somewhat different. I was worried about being cheated of life, of children to be born, houses to be planned, friends to be made. Of course my primary concern was dying not after the voyage but during it. While they sat there feeling complete and euphoric, I was feeling sensations of incompleteness and acute anxiety, and to make matters worse, I actually envied them—their calm, their joy, their sense of wonder. For them this was almost a religious experience, and for me it was merely neurotic. What was wrong with me that I could not appreciate enough, be sensitive enough, be spiritual enough to put aside my fears and feel sheer unalloyed bliss on the brink of this great adventure, this ultimate statement of being free and strong and alive?

Once past the light, we set sail close-hauled. Like avenging demons ten million thoughts whirled through my head as I engaged in a manic inventory attempting to confirm that all was aboard, that we had forgotten nothing. I had to stop thinking about it. As the fog closed in, I promptly excused myself to go below and crump on the port bunk to catch up on sleep—badly

The great departure for the Knights' first Atlantic crossing.
Lewis Wharf, Boston. Chris, beardless, waves; Pete with conch toots;
Kathy, below, prays.

needed after frantic days and nights of preparation. There was nothing more that I could do. The fears, the worry, the haunting voices of well-meaning people would do me no good here. I had done all I could within my realm of responsibility to make us as fit and safe as possible. Put the gnawing demons to rest. Sleep off March, April, and May. Let the salt tang of the Atlantic lick away the devils. Find a buffalo head in the cloud outside the porthole, follow the tracery of a gull's flight, make bets on the breaking points of cresting waves.

"My God! My God!" I sat bolt upright in the bunk. Chris was leaning through the companionway. His face was pale. In the cabin I heard a sickening and rhythmic clunking noise. I looked down and saw everything afloat—floorboards, cans, the tool kit bobbing about absurdly.

"Dad! Head for Gloucester," Chris ordered.

"Chris, what's happening?"

"We're taking water fast. Get up and pump, Kathy."

We put on the electric bilge pump and I feverishly worked the hand one. My eyes were riveted on Cape Ann. I refused to look below as Chris tore apart the bilges looking for, My God, a hole? I mean how, after all these months of obsessive preparation, could we suddenly have a hole in the hull? How could we sink right off Gloucester, three hours from Boston?

Within ten minutes the depth of water was greatly reduced. We shortly were within the breakwater of Gloucester and lowered an anchor. The pump by now had completed its work, and aside from the wet mess of cans and floorboards scattered hither and yon, everything seemed relatively normal. The flow had stopped as mysteriously as it had started. Chris had found no hole, and as we sat below bewildered and still shaking, we began to sort things out in our minds and soon concluded that it must be the pump itself which was the source of the flow. With the heavy load, heeled over as the wind had suddenly bucked up, we had started to siphon a backflow through the bilge pump. There was no stop valve in the U-shaped tube, which normally was high enough above the water level to perform as the stop. We closed the cock immediately. As soon as my heart had left my throat, I had a strange thought. The jerk who said we would never make it, the one from the dinner party. He lived in Gloucester! How convenient of us to nearly sink off his beach. There was no real damage below, but it was a mess to clean up.

CHAPTER *15*

The southeast wind stuck with us like fleas to a dog. The fog socked in tight, and we moved down the coast in one long tack to Penobscot Bay. The weather continued to deteriorate, and it was heading winds, thumping seas, and spray mixed with rain. We finally bore in on Mount Desert Rock and once past it tacked offshore and headed for Cape Sable. A bit of blue sky cracked the fog the morning of June 19 just as we spotted Sable light. By eight AM all was sunshine and we were tied up snugly along the pier at Smith and Rhuland—the world's most extraordinary boatyard.

Soon our boat was crawling with the lanky Nova Scotian shipwrights from the yard, the same men who had built replicas of the *Bluenose* and the *Bounty*. Silently and efficiently, they worked their way through the boat. Chris merely had to point at a problem and no matter how confounding it was or how obscure we thought the vital part to be, the problem was solved, the part provided. Chris looked at me in wonderment as Ernie, a hawk-faced man who spoke in a thick maritime accent, quickly came up with a quarter-inch square porthole gasket, something that might have taken days to find in Boston. "These people are really into esoteric stuff!"

"Chris, ye got a little something to drink?" Even though it was just short of ten AM, I took it he didn't mean coffee.

"You mean something strong, Ernie?"

"Ye'ah. Any rum?"

"No rum, Ernie. How about bourbon?"

"Good enough."

Chris poured a water-glassful, which exhausted a third of our total supply. Ten minutes later he was back at work doing his miracles.

Lunenburg in June is a lovely place to be. The lilacs are still in bloom, and their scent blends well with the salt and tang of the Scots accents to weave a fragile litany of land and sea. It would be hard to leave Lunenburg—this haven with its immaculately tended green lawns and funny erect little houses, all of them absolutely vibrating with licks of fresh paint, often that throbbing red-orange for which Lunenburg seems to have a special passion. We sailed out of Lunenburg on the morning of June 23 with the wind still on our nose! We could not make northing on Sable Island, and after a slow first day, rain and fog began to settle in thickly. This state of affairs continued for some time, right up through the next day, my birthday.

I got up that morning at six for my watch and alone on deck tried to stir up some significant thoughts about having just completed my third decade. For such contemplation the setting was perfect: plenty of sea room for working out any angst—plenty of solitude, and everything one color— gray. What do you say about an environment that offers you twenty-four different shades of that one color gray and just one true white, the down on the underbelly of a sheer water? It was not really a depressing gray. It spoke of peace and an indescribable calm at the heart of life. Anyhow, it was my Atlantic birthday.

CHAPTER *16*

"Nora was eating a piece of cold duck with one hand and working a jigsaw puzzle with the other. 'Find me a brownish piece, shaped something like a snail with a long neck.' "

"Piece of duck or puzzle?"

I broke into hysterical guffaws. Oh, the consummate pleasure and sophistication of it all. Jigsaw puzzles! Cold duck! Alas, I am not in a suite at the Normandy Hotel. We are three days out of Lunenburg. There is forty-five knots of wind dead on our nose, and it sounds like a convention of banshees above. I am reading *The Thin Man* and eating a lemon Pirouette. With the help of the good Lord, Dashiell Hammett, and Margaret Rudkin, I might make it. The Lemon Pirouette is quite a restrained choice considering the circumstances, but I promise myself that if we make it through this storm, I'll break out the Mint Milanos. I would chuck all the Pepperidge Farm cookies, barter various body parts, and throw in a spleen for good measure if I could be eating cold duck in a private suite in the Normandy Hotel in 1932.

"Why can't we be like Nick and Nora Charles?"

Chris looks up from his book, *Hornblower and the Hotspur*. "We're not witty enough. Can't hold our liquor as well. Even if we could, we'd never be able to afford the amount of scotch they drink." He sticks his nose back in his book. I consider it redundant to be reading Hornblower books mid-Atlantic. But Chris, despite his seeming terseness, is pleased—pleased because I have laughed for the first time in five days. He takes this sudden jocularity on my part as a sign that I am relaxing, getting into it. This is not the case at all. In truth I have been vacillating between fear and anger for the last several days. Who said the prevailing wind is westerly? I want to know just who said it. I would never have consented to all this if I thought we would be beating all the way to England. "Chris, this is every bit as horrendous as

I ever imagined," I moaned. Then I whispered a little prayer about going back to minature golf and cornfields.

He overheard me. "They don't have that in Boston anyway, Kathy."

"I don't mean Boston. I mean Indianapolis, where the weirdest thing you can do is vote Democratic and paint a flower on your Volkswagen."

Now he was really worried. When I had spoken of cold duck and the Normandy Hotel, Chris took this as a positive sign: I was moving easterly in my fantasies. But little did he know, as I reached for a bag of Old-fashioned Sugar Cookies as a chaser for the Pirouette, that my fantasies were as midwestern and landlocked as ever. I began to read the copy on the bag. "Remember the cookies in Grandma's cookie jar? Pepperidge Farm remembers. Here they are, with the good taste of old-fashioned cookies that crackle and crunch when you bite them, and delight you with their old-fashioned flavor. That's because Pepperidge Farm bakes these cookies with the same flavorful ingredients grandma used when she baked hers. Pepperidge Farm old-fashioned cookies. They're the sweet memory of childhood for your children to enjoy."

Both my grandmothers had died before I was a year old. However this did nothing to inhibit my memory. Proust had his madeleines and I had my Pepperidge Farm. One bite of the Cinnamon Sugar cookie and the year was 1924, and with a few calisthenics of the imagination, I was not in the middle of the Atlantic Ocean on this boat in this awful storm, but on the back pantry porch of the house at forty-sixth Street and Meridian. As I bit the cookie I recalled the "sweet memory" of my mother's description of making hand-

A mid-Atlantic wave.

cranked peach ice cream on Fridays during the summer. The younger children would sit there waiting with their teaspoons, begging for the first taste, and then finally when she couldn't move the crank another turn she would clear off the ice and remove the cover to reveal the sweet swirl of frozen heaven loaded with nuggets of peaches. Then she would pull out the dasher. The cream would drip off the paddles into the freezer. What remained she scraped into a bowl for the children, who were nearly apoplectic with anticipation by this time. Through a summerful of Fridays she cranked the cream—sweating bullets and churning peaches, scraping the dasher and hushing the kids. That night for dinner there would be fish, river fish or lake fish. They kept kosher, so with ice cream, no meat. The dinner would be served in the octagonal dining room. It would be a lively meal with talk of boyfriends and dances. War Leader Bell and the older girls would help serve. My grandmother, Belle Falender, might mention to her husband, Sam, that she had walked to the corner drugstore and had a cherry phosphate with Mrs. Gordon.

"She drinks Coca-Cola!" Mildi pipes up.

"And I hope you never do. None of you," Belle admonishes in her European accent. "It's very bad for you. It has narcotics in it. Very bad." She was right of course. The two older girls sigh and exchange glances. They know why Mrs. Gordon is drinking the cola. It is Lola McCloud, Mr. Gordon's mistress. But Belle shoots them a glance that is enough to freeze their tongues on this hot August night.

Belle Rosenbaum Falender was a woman of consummate style. The house at Forty-sixth Street was evidence of that extraordinary flair. It was built in 1912, a time when if one did have a sense of style, it could be realized because of the plethora of craftsmen and the abundance of quality materials. It was a stucco house with a double band of arching windows across the front. Every detail from the octagonal dining room to the "Pompeian" sun-room was thought out, sketched, and talked about between Belle and her architect.

In the sun-room a latticelike design, intended to reflect the latticework in the garden outside, was painted on the canvas walls forming arched panels. Framed within each panel was a Grecian dancing lady, each one bearing a decided resemblance to Isadora Duncan, for whom my mother and her older sisters had a passion. My mother must have been about twelve or thirteen when they moved into this house and has vivid recollections of sitting and watching the man as he painted the sinuous dancing bodies. My Aunt Mildi, four years younger, remembers him painting a huge platter of fruit on the wall in the breakfast room and painting in a little Hershey bar in the corner of the platter for her and her baby sister and brother.

On the second floor of the house were the bedrooms and a sewing room for the seamstress who came twice a year to make all their clothes. There was also a screened sleeping porch where all the children up to a certain age were required to sleep both summer and winter. One can only imagine that my grandmother intended this to be a hardening-off process as one does for seedlings to prepare them for future rigors outdoors. The children did not seem to mind, however, and my mother remembers thinking it quite lovely when occasionally she would wake up and find a scattering of snow on her blanket that had blown in through the screens. The only bad part was having to wake up in the middle of the night to take one of the younger ones to the bathroom. On the third floor was a ballroom with a porch off it for serving punch and cake after summer dances, but my grandmother used this more often for making sun preserves.

My grandmother Belle died when I was just nine months old, so I really knew her only through her house and of course the stories parents tell their children about their own childhoods. Because of her style, which was so unique for its time, I have always found her rather intriguing. It is somewhat ironic that people with taste are a dime a dozen but people with style, like my grandmother, are a rarer breed. She had taste, that goes without saying. Taste is easy. When given enough exposure to a certain quality of things, of life, with even a minimum of brains anybody can acquire taste. It is an acquired thing, a convention of sorts. I have no doubt about that. But style is something different. I do not think it is acquired. For example, it seems more appropriate to speak of a woman with taste, and yet in reference to

The Falender women. Left to right, Aunts Franny (holding Marilouise), Mildi, and Beatrice; grandmother Belle, mother Hortense.

style it seems only right to say a woman of style, which suggests that style has to do with something innate or inherent and inextricably bound up with the nature of the person. Whatever it is, Belle had it.

However, it does remain questionable what special qualities the rest of her family, the Rosenbaums from Cincinnati, possessed. They were a peculiar lot according to my mother and her sisters. There were four old-maid aunts, Belle's sisters, who would come on extended visits to Indianapolis in hopes of finding themselves husbands. They were very beautiful but terribly spoiled and would make themselves absolutely intolerable to everyone from War Leader Bell to the youngest child. Once my mother and her older sister Franny were somehow roped into visiting the family in Cincinnati when they were ten or twelve years old. The only thing either of them could remember of the trip was their Aunt Dora and Aunt Ruth taking them to a crematorium for a visit. At their best my grandmother's family was cold and austere. At their worst they were nasty and mean. In the late twenties my grandfather Samuel Falender invested some money in Florida. The Rosenbaums asked him to invest for them too. Like hundreds of others, they lost their shirts in the deal. But the Rosenbaums never forgave my grandfather. They demanded that my grandfather repay them. There was no way that he could as the country was in the middle of the depression by this time. So instead he gave them a mortgage on the house. A crueler plan could not have been conceived. My grandparents and the three youngest children, who were still at home, were forced to move out into a shabby little double house a few blocks away. Forty-six Hundred was put on the market, but there were no buyers as it was still the Depression, or the tail end of it.

My Aunt Mildi, who was working in the decorating department of the local department store, did what she could to spruce the new place up, but it was still just a bunch of boxy rooms—no octagonal-shaped dining room, no Isadoras floating on the walls, no soaring arch windows. My grandmother became very depressed and eventually got cancer. It might have been a year or so after they moved that she was operated on, and when she came out of the hospital my Aunt Franny and her husband, Sam Abels, had provided the best get-well present ever. They had bought back the house at Forty-sixth and Meridian from the Rosenbaums, and my grandmother, grandfather, and the three children moved back home. She never however really recovered and a few years later died. For some unfathomable reason, three of the sisters and their brothers from Cincinnati actually came to the funeral and had the audacity to visit the house after the service. Nobody spoke a word to them. My mother remembers sitting in the sun-room and staring through "the whole rotten lot" of them to the painted lattice panels with the Grecian dancing ladies.

I think it was Sister Parrish, the interior designer, who said that houses are "timeless receptacles of memory." As I was bounced and jostled in one receptacle, I thought of others with rooms for dancing and sewing and porches for cranking cream into ice cream. Beyond my reveries, or I should say above deck of these dreams it was a white world. Troughs and monster waves spewed foam. It was a world run amok, not wicked but willful, and yet at the same time shockingly indifferent. The dreadful noise of blue water making a strike on the deckhouse cracked like the meanest rifle. We lay hove to for thirty-six hours and *Leucothea* rode very well. We soon learned that it was easiest not to look out, except to stick our heads above to watch for traffic and to keep our ears open for any wind and sea sounds that would indicate a change. It was rather depressing going to England at two mph, but there was nothing much anybody could do about it.

CHAPTER *17*

This first storm blew for what seemed an eternity. Just when we felt that surely a wind of such force must moderate soon, it would whip itself into a new savagery. The two things that we needed most, food and sleep, were the hardest to come by. Fixing a hot meal was such an incredibly difficult task that I am sure we used up more calories than we took in. Sleeping, although we were laced in with bunk boards, was a gymnastic event of the first order as *Leucothea* bucked through the confused and angry seas. For me there was always terrible fear as a rogue wave exploded upon the boat and I felt her sudden sluggishness and sickening inertia. I sensed deep in my marrow that this was it. But the boat always came back to free herself from the blue water, to leap from chasm to crest, a lively mad thing on a swirling sea. There were times when I honestly cannot say what I might have given for a moment's peace.

At eight AM, thirty-six hours later, the wind moderated and we put up a jib and started in earnest for England. By the next day the rain had cleared off entirely. The gray skies had cracked open leaving a deep blue bowl, and a northwest wind filled our sails. I got my first good night's sleep. The wind picked up, and it seemed as if everything were conspiring to get us to England smartly. Sable Island was long forgotten, and we headed toward the Grand Banks under incongruous bright blue skies in the foggiest place on

*A Gulf Stream shampoo
for Kathy at 46N 52W.*

the charts. At night *Leucothea* surged along on swelling seas with wind abaft the beam under the cold blaze of a million stars.

There was one particularly unforgettable night for me on the Grand Banks. Moonlight silvered the water off the starboard beam, and slowly, almost imperceptibly, I became aware of a graceful presence. Quite suddenly a magical energy surrounded the boat: dolphins. Looking over the rail, I saw them streaking through the night sea like licks of pale fire, an entire fleet of dolphins, twenty or more, an escort playing off the pressure waves of our bow. Some swam in pairs, others dipped and arced over one another, never so much as grazing the other's fin. To watch these creatures swim was to witness the essence of natural motion. It seemed as if some mystical impulse were sending these tantalizing swags and flashes of light through the water.

Dolphins came back often during our crossing, cavorting madly, showing off, being cheerful masters of Atlantic ceremonies on the bleakest days. They exhibited a genuine petulance and ennui if our speed fell below four knots, for their main requirement was a sporting pressure wave to ride. I much preferred the dolphins to any other living things of the Atlantic community. I exclude my two human companions. After all, we were just passing through.

46N, 52W is a long way to go for a beauty treatment, but it has to be one of the best shampoos I've ever had. At four AM a light rain began to fall. Chris had rigged a bucket to the mizzen boom and managed to collect a few gallons of rainwater. When I got up for my watch, I stuffed a bottle of shampoo and a hairbrush into the pocket of my oilskins and went up top to commence a most welcome and missed ritual. In no time at all the Labrador Current and the Gulf Stream conspired to provide me with a truly luxuriant shampoo. It was quiet and misty. Although I felt strangely encumbered in my foul-weather gear during this procedure, for the first time in a long while the peculiar disaffection I had felt toward my body, sheathed for days in layers of clothing, began to melt away. I sat in the cockpit and scrubbed and kneaded my hair. I delighted in building huge lavish confections of lather atop my head. All on the 52nd longitude.

I have good memories of the Grand Banks. It was not at all the way I had supposed it to be. We had more than our fair share of sunshine. It was chilly but not gnawingly cold, and the wind had settled into a groove off our stern quarter. During these days, when I was off watch and drifting off to sleep in my bunk, I became aware of an enchanting phenomenon. I call it a water nest. It happens when *Leucothea* is running at five knots or more with the wind off her quarter at twelve to fifteen knots. I had to be below for the water-nest syndrome to occur. It is a sort of metamorphosis. The boat becomes a warp, the ocean a loom, the wind and waves together are the woof. These elements then weave a watery cocoon that envelops the near-sleeping voyager in a nest, not of twigs or leaves and clumps of sod and grass but one composed of the most insubstantial things—water rustlings, crushes of sea foam, blue water bubbles, and the rhythm of pressure waves. There is no slapping or pounding as in a beat. The boat is snugly firmed in the sea breast, as secure as a land nest is in the elbow of a tree, and the voyager is wrapped in a glittering, kinetic rustle of speed, sound, and pressure.

CHAPTER *18*

I had just finished the first bag of Mint Milanos, which I had managed to make last until 49N, 30W, about twelve hundred miles out from Lunenburg. In terms of restraint fifteen of these cookies over twelve hundred miles is quite laudable. I should have known as I bit into the last one that all good things must come to an end. The barometer had dropped, and Number Two storm had been working itself into a beastly wrath over the horizon.

Entry from my journal:

July 8, 1974: This trip is just as awful as I ever imagined. We have been under siege for the past three days. Forty knot winds have caused us to run under storm jib for 72 hours. Mega-mother seas rock the boat violently making all activity impossible, except for lying in your bunk. . . . I looked out the companionway 15 minutes ago. The sky was absolutely obliterated by the most enormous green wave I've ever seen, roaring astern. It was almost as if I were standing in a valley through and looking straight up at a mountain. I read Rex Reed's *Do You Sleep in The Nude.* Chris reads *Trafalgar: The Nelson Touch* and he quickly put away something called *The Raft Book* when he saw me turn ashen as I read the blurb on the back cover—"with this book and enclosed charts, no instruments other than a stick and a piece of string, and no previous knowledge of navigation, persons who find themselves in small boats or rafts anywhere, in any ocean or sea in the world can find their way to land"!

The exclamation point is mine, not theirs, or rather his—Harold Gatty. There's just a smug little period at the end of the blurb. After all, what punctuation would one expect from someone who crosses oceans with only a stick and a string and a chart. Harold would not want to share a life raft with me—me and my sack of exclamation points, bags of cookies, Oil of Olay, chutney, Dashiell Hammett. Perish the thought, but what would I grab for in such a situation. We did have lists for such contingencies, and key items had been stowed in easy-to-reach places close to our life raft, which was lashed to the deck. But what if I panicked and forgot to grab for a jerrican of water and instead reached for my mascara. What were the navigational possibilities with a wand of mascara? Did it have another life as a sextant? What was the nutritional value of eating mascara? Or was it toxic? Chris could read me quite clearly as I sat with my eyes riveted on the back blurb of *The Raft Book.*

It was this second storm that brought with it visions of the infamous Mary Nutt on her wind surfer rounding the Horn. It was also during this storm that I began dreaming of flowers, waking and sleeping. I would mentally stroke pastoral images of meadows and English gardens laced with stone paths and primrose. There were long internal dialogues in which I would whisper names like gloxinia, rhododendron, pachysandra, tongue-curling words that became my own peculiar sea chantey. I wished with a desperation usually reserved for a Mint Milano that I had brought a flower catalog with me. I wanted to read about swan-winged tulips or varieties of day lilies or the new strain of paper white narcissus from Israel and the old strain from France. I wanted to read that gentle, sprightly prose of the catalogs that told of "vigorous and abundant flowering," of "fragrances slightly heavier than the well-known English strain but still sweet and fresh," of bulbs of "exhibition size." I wanted to see pictures of a flatcup and a trumpet narcissus, of ligularia and baskets of jasmine, of "flights of butterflies," Iris, and Bristol Fairy.

I became slightly obsessed with dreams of gardens. Once I had written a paper in college on the subject of the cottage garden in Victorian literature,

Forty knots of wind.
Leucothea *hunkers down and*
rides well under storm jib.

but if the truth were told I was in fact a lousy gardener. I vowed then to become a better one. I seem to recall that it was during the very worst of this second storm that Pete, whose profession is that of landscape architecture, described to me a trip that he and Rusty made just after his graduation from landscape school, to study the great gardens of England and France on a special grant that he had received. While being churned in the main cabin as forty-five-knot winds lashed around us, Pete described to me everything from those small cottage gardens, cherished sanctuaries of old-fashioned flowers, to the Duke of Marlborough's Blenheim with its formal water parterre and gardens designed in the classical French tradition by Achilles Duchene. He told me about geometrically patterned herb gardens of fenugreek an hart's-tongue, lavender and leek, lungwort and quince, saffron and sage. I learned about open-knot designs and ha-ha's, the trompe l'oeil ditches that keep cows off the lawn but permit the view from the house to extend uninterrupted from lawn to meadow to woodland. I learned a little about Capability Brown and Gertrude Jekyll. But mostly Pete spoke of the passionate English gardeners, be they the cultivators of the cottage garden bright with flowers or those who traveled to India and back to collect rare species of orchids and Irises and made them flourish in the estate gardens and conservatories.

I became enchanted with the notion of conservatories and winter gardens. In the close damp air of our teak cocoon I dreamed of those magnificent nineteenth-century structures of curved glass and ribbon-thin cast-iron trusses, those domes redolent with the fragrances of exotic plants. Pete told me that Prince Albert and Queen Victoria had once driven in an open carriage through the Duke of Devonshire's conservatory of tropical water plants at Chatworth, which was lit with twelve thousand lamps. A scene began to haunt me. I could picture two young people standing in a domed web spun of light and air. For hours on end I would see these two figures in the fragile light. Finally it came to me: Maggie and Stephen from *The Mill on the Floss.* (There was a moment in the book when they were in a conservatory marveling at the delicate and exotic plants.) " 'How strange and unreal the trees and flowers look with the lights among them,' said Maggie in a low voice. 'They look as if they belonged to an enchanted land and would never fade away.' "

Somewhere between the Fourth of July and Bastille Day, the storm blew itself out into a golden bowl of a sunset, a huge shimmering sphere.

We had hoped to make contact with a ship sometime during the crossing and send word back home that we were alive and well and someplace in the Atlantic. We had had several unsuccessful attempts at message sending. One of the more frustrating of these occurred with a U.S. ship, the *Export Champion,* which veered off her course, cut under our stern, and came within fifty yards of us. After several attempts to call them on the radio, stick and string group that we were, we hoisted the signal flags on the mizzenmast. "Listen on 2182." That is the emergency band that all ships are supposed to monitor. But no contact via radio was made. We looked up and saw several crew members of the *Export Champion* hanging over the rail and shouting through megaphones, "Are you all right?"

The prospect of a small sailing boat out there was horrifying to these fellows. I had always thought that my visage must have been the most worried one on the Atlantic, but in comparison to these faces, I looked "laid back." The merchant seamen appeared absolutely stricken at the sight of us. So we yelled back that we were fine and packed up our signal flags and parted ways. Pete was devastated that these "sailors" could not read signal flags. He cherishes his little bag of brightly colored flags and always has a message of some sort flying from the flagpole at their Deer Isle house. Few can read it, but then most of the folks who come to visit on Deer Isle do not ply the oceans, and explaining is half the fun.

The following day we met a fish of another color in the form of the English vessel *Manchester Crusader,* a container ship that loomed up sketchily four miles off our port bow heading west.

Kathy sleeps through a gale.

Chris on watch.

MC: American yacht *Leucothea?* This is the British vessel *Manchester Crusader.* We read your transmission. Stand by to confirm your vessel's name.

L: Yes, sir. Standing by.

MC: That is L as in Lima. E as in echo. U as in uniform . . . (We definitely should have named her Jane.)

L: Affirmative. Are you the large vessel to port with the black-and-white stack?

MC: Yes, Leucothea . . . (pause) and there's a narrow red stripe in the middle.

L: Ah yes, *Manchester Crusader,* I suppose so. Tell me, can you confirm our position 49N, 30W?

MC: Our fix for 1600 Greenwich was 49° 12'N, 29° 46'W.

L: That's close enough!

MC: May we be of further assistance, *Leucothea?*

L: Yes. We would like to send a message to our family in Indiana confirming our position and approximate arrival date.

MC: Happy to arrange it.

The message was sent with dispatch. My parents received it within two days. We concluded our conversation with the *Manchester Crusader* with a few more remarks about the weather.

MC: Had a bit of a blow about two days ago. Suppose it bothered you more than it did us.

L: We noticed it.

We wished each other fair weather, thanked them, and praised them for their seamanlike style. "Oh, now you're pulling our leg," they replied. And we each continued—*Manchester Crusader* to Montreal, *Leucothea* to Falmouth. For a fleeting eight minutes the grim austerity of the North Atlantic melted away and that vast expanse of water and sky became as cozy as a parlor, warm and alive with the crackle of human communication.

Communication, yes, but I would definitely hesitate to say human intercourse, a word I use advisedly here to deftly introduce a not-often-talked-about subject in sailing literature, sex at sea. It will come as no great surprise to the blue water sailor that the body of written material on the subject is minimal, if not nonexistent, and with good reason. There is nothing to write about. Even weather permitting, meaning no gale-force winds, it is still very cold and wet around 50N. I was for twenty-nine days completely sheathed in long johns, warm-up ski pants, and oilskins. I had forgotten what my own skin looked like. Matters of the flesh seemed rather abstract. I felt like a disembodied spirit. Body? Skin? It was all a dim memory from a vague and distant past. Each time I caught a glimpse of my own flesh, after that first blinding flash of white, it was like trying to place the face of an old but slightly unfamiliar acquaintance. When the first shock of recognition wore off, I always had the urge to yell up to Chris, "Guess who I saw today?"

There is nothing like thrashing about in a cold thrashing sea to dampen sexual desire. However, having a propensity toward making something out of nothing, I began to remember earlier sexual experiences—not mine, other people's, in particular those rumored ones from my high school days when we spoke of fast girls. There were some titillating tales from this era that, although hardly arousing to one in the midst of force-eight winds, were something of a diversion. There was a certain Mimi Gattling who was considered the fastest girl in the school, in fact in our town. She "did it" with every guy. Among others who "did it," not quite so ubiquitously as Mimi and with a great deal more class, were girls that I have come to think of as the Angels, for that was their role in the school's annual Christmas pageant.

The pageant was the same every year. The headmistress sat between the audience and the stage at a small table with a single candle and read the Nativity passage from Luke. Onstage, students silently moved through a series of tableaux that illustrated the various scenes. A student choir in the back of the auditorium sang Christmas songs at certain junctures. Now Luke might have been short on specifications, but not this headmistress. In her schemata of things, angels had blue eyes and blonde hair, while the shepherds were swarthy and had tangles of dark hair—that was me. I was a shepherd for four years straight. Angels wore satin robes girded with golden cords, and shepherds wore dyed cheesecloth tunics and carried crooks. There were four of us, and we slept in a heap to stage left for most of the pageant, and when the chorus sang, "Shepherds shake off your drowsy sleep . . ." we got up and lumbered across the stage, looked with "loving wonder" at the baby Jesus, which was a ratty old doll, and shuffled off stage right.

One year I remember we had a wild trio of angels. They were beautiful senior girls who could have stepped out of a Fitzgerald novel. They were spoiled, lively, and witty. And they drank. The Sunday of the Christmas pageant arrived, and so did the angels, all in inebriate states ranging from tipsy to crocked. The headmistress was also stiff, with anger. Not since

Lucifer got the boot out of heaven had eschatology been dealt such a blow. For Christ sake, one of these fallen angels had already been accepted early decision to Bryn Mawr. Backstage, the headmistress stomped about, the air striped with her anger.

It was immediately apparent there was going to be a draft. The three kings were exempt because they had singing roles and were indispensable, but shepherds were dispensable. God knows how dispensable we were. Here was my chance at last. Swathed in my musty cheesecloth shepherd garb and trembling in the wings while I watched the headmistress's wrath, every Hollywood-Broadway-show-must-go-on fantasy swirled through my mind. I was Lana Turner being discovered at Schwab's drugstore. I was Judy Garland sprung from her trunk at the Palace theater in Pocatello, Idaho! A dishwater blonde and a redhead were chosen. I was sick. If I had known about the B'Nai B'Rith Anti-Defamation League then, I might have complained about what I was beginning to realize was an odd form of discrimination. Screw it, I thought. If that's their religion they can keep it. I stopped saying the Lord's Prayer and singing the Doxology.

Nobody had heard of that peculiar term "sexually active adolescent" in those days, a phrase that makes people sound like pubescent robots. Had I been a Mimi or whoever as an adolescent, hearing myself called a sexually active one would have immediately deactivated me. I was very sensitive to words then as now and took them quite to heart. I find the term absolutely repugnant. On the other hand, when my sister, Martha, came home from her first year at Wellesley and found my friend Holly and I still talking about Mimi Gattling and fast girls, she asked if we had ever considered that perhaps Mimi just had a large "libido." I fell instantly in love with the word. It was so sprightly and rhythmic to my ears. I loved the sound of it rolling off my tongue. I loved using it in all my compositions. "Who knows what Tennyson knew about libido, especially Guinevere's, and to what extent her infidelity . . ." "Range cattle are a far more libidinous lot than grassland cattle, one might imagine. . . ." Luckily my mother edited my writing.

I was still fascinated by the three fallen angels. We were actually all fascinated by them in my group of friends. The angels were a little bit mean. That made them more interesting, and they were fast, which made them absolutely intriguing. They had boyfriends. None of us did. And they did not do unimaginable things with them but delightfully imaginable ones, unlike Mimi Gattling, who did it with every guy—that was unimaginable. There was a rumor that one of the angels had taken the train, "and not the sit up," to Chicago with her boyfriend and , ensconcing themselves in a "roomette," "did it" the whole way to Chicago. I hadn't read Flaubert yet, but the notion of them "doing it" in a roomette on the rails to Chicago was every bit as erotic as that carriage with Emma Bovary and Leon sealed "tight as a tomb" and tossing like a ship in the sea with their mad copulation. A few years later when I was reading *Madame Bovary* and came to the famous passage, my mind was flooded with images of Becky and Henry on the Monon to Chicago. Our ship however was tossing to rhythms other than copulatory ones.

CHAPTER *19*

"There are warnings of gales in Sole, Shannon, Fastnet, Rockall, Irish Sea, Hebrides, Biscay, Portland, Plymouth, Dover. . . . good sailing, chaps." We were south of Ireland in Sole, and that chirpy little voice giving the gale warnings to good chaps belonged to the BBC. Gale-force winds continued to build for the next two days, and before long we were back down to storm jib and still going like a bat. Holed up below we listened to the BBC weathermen reporting gales in every zone they covered and wishing every-body good sailing. A few more days however and we would have "done it," and not the "it" of Mimi Gattling and the three angels, but the trans-Atlantic "it."

For me, the closer we came to civilization the more abstract it became. Had I ever slept in a real bed? Sat at a breakfast table and read the *New York Times*? Painted two thin little black lines on my eyelids and brushed my cheeks with something called Burnt Amber? Hooked an exquisite ring of enamel and silver in each earlobe as part of that almost-sensuous ritual of dressing for an "evening out" with Chris and friends? Had there really been such a time in my life? I seriously doubted it. For twenty-nine days of being "out," there were no evenings "out." There were only evenings "off." You fell off the damn boat, and the most important rings you wore were those clips for your life harness. I kept telling myself that indeed there had been such a time, out of time, and these days would end.

I would discipline myself to believe that in fact I was a person with a past, a civilized past—a past where dinner parties were planned, people were welcomed into our home, where gardens were planted, love was made, blouses ironed, good wine consumed. A past with birthday parties and theater, and movies and Harvard Square, and miniature golf and Swan boats, fresh-picked corn and Wellfleet oysters, Christmas pageants and the Ritz Carleton. Once when I was frantically drumming up my past to obliterate the cloying cheerfulness of the BBC weathermen, an image came to me so crisp and alive that I nearly cheered, and it warmed me all the rest of the way to England. I saw a scene from my childhood, from that time when stockings were made of silk and had seams. I would sit in my mother's bedroom and watch her put on the sheer cotton mitts she used so as not to snag the stockings with her nails. Then with mitts on she would begin to guide those silk stockings up her leg and hook them to her garters. I would watch her and want to have real stockings, silk and sheer, so badly. I wanted them more than anything else in the world, and to have to wait until I was twelve seemed unendurable to me at the time. If they had said wait twenty-nine days, that I could have done. But six years! I did. I became twelve. I got my stockings, nylon by that time and seamless.

However, I had never wanted to spend a month crossing an ocean in a small boat. It had seemed not only unendurable, but unimaginable. Yet now, five times older than that six-year-old, the six- and the thirty-year-old were one and the same person, and this one person had experienced these two distinct, exclusive frames of time. That I realized was the miracle of life.

The wind moderated to force five on the twenty-seventh day of our trip, and the sun started to come through patchily. We had a really good ride. Everybody's spirits picked up considerably, and it seemed as if England were just beyond the next horizon. At twelve midnight Pete spotted it, the light on the Lizard blinking confidently, two points off our bow. I broke out the Mint Milanos and began munching happily. All through the night our hearts soared as *Leucothea* jubilantly sailed toward the blinking Lizard through the same ancient waters and winds that had pushed a most remarkable array of invaders, marauders and seamen all, toward England. All through the night we sailed, each of us only catnapping so as not to miss the dawn. As the sky lightened we did an easy four knots through a wide corridor marked with graceful headlands.

My last entry for the voyage, July 18, 1974: "It is an hour before sunrise. And all the world is keen and England lies green and tranquil before my eyes."

CHAPTER 20

Chris's and my occupations made it possible for us to go away for extended periods of time, which suited us just fine during the three years *Leucothea* was abroad. For the most part we did our cruising in the summer, leaving the boat to fly home for the rest of the year. Joyce Zinno, Chris's office manager at the New Film Company, made it possible for things to run smoothly in his absence. The only writing I was doing at the time was an occasional article for *Sail* magazine and educational materials on a free-lance basis. I was finding the latter excruciatingly boring and was more than happy

After twenty-nine days, a celebration in Falmouth, England.

to write for *Sail* despite my lubberly inclinations and style. I had not yet started to write children's books.

From my perspective, now that the worst part was over, it was time to enjoy the fruits. The fruits to be specific were cruising in Scandinavia and a long meandering sojourn through the canals of Europe to the Mediterranean, continuing toward the Balearic Islands down the east coast of Spain to Gibraltar before jumping off for the voyage home. The voyage home however was a long way off, and I intended to push that out of my mind and savor the fruits that were reaped almost instantly after our arrival. At six-thirty that morning, anchored off Falmouth and waiting for the customs office to open, we enjoyed a wonderful champagne breakfast on board.

The morning was cool and crisp. Falmouth was still asleep. The first living thing to greet us upon our arrival was a lovely swan that glided up to our port rail. Just as I was thinking how charming this was, Chris, apparently suffering from his extended celibacy, leaned over the rail and asked to be taken to its Leda. Now that I have enshrined this pun in print, I hope that Chris will no longer find it necessary to repeat it as he does periodically at dinner parties. Sometimes he feels compelled not only to discourse on the merits of the pun in general as the purest form of humor but to give a small exegesis on this particular pun and how it reaches the highest level of the art with its triple meaning.

To explain the trilevel structure Chris then has to expand upon the context of this pun, which of course gets into blue water sex. At first people are full of anticipation; hostesses shift nervously in their chairs and ask about coffee and with or without, but it is soon evident that the blue of the water is not the blue of movies but a fish of another color. People start to yawn as Chris, oblivious to their reaction, hurtles ahead. Only compulsive punsters are responsive. Our good friend and obsessive punster, Jack Thayer, was so responsive that he managed to get Chris to turn his usual ten-minute discourse into a forty-five minute lecture. In any case the swan swam off faster than the pun.

We cleared customs in Falmouth and by nine that morning went on a brief excursion into town. Falmouth was in the clutches of the summer tourist season, and after twenty-nine days at sea our ears had become acclimated to the rush of the ocean but could not tolerate the cacophony of traffic and people that jammed the streets and sidewalks. We decided instead to sail across the harbor to Saint Mawes, which promised to be quieter from the guidebooks I had read. I had called from Falmouth and made reservations at the Rising Sun, which was described as a "super splurge" in the book *England on $10 a Day.*

Chris had promised me that we could go anywhere I chose for rest, recuperation, and noncanned food. What I really thought I needed was something between Elizabeth Arden's and Menninger's. Saint Mawes and the Rising Sun came as close as any place could in providing just that. The bijou village was perched tranquilly over a little bay in the embrace of sloping green headlands. We stepped out of our inflatable dinghy onto the wedge of beach in front of the whitewashed fishing cottages that belonged to the inn. A gaggle of rosy English girls in bikinis were eating fish and chips a little way down the beach, and farther along two children were building sand castles. Directly across the small street from the beach was a terrace chock-full of hydrangeas and English folks on summer holidays, enjoying the weather, one another, and their Guinness.

The entire village was sunlight and smart breezes and swans paddling over glinting water and children with their lovely accents sounding perpetually delightful and as if they were incapable of ever whining. When I think of Saint Mawes, I can imagine Thomas Mann going there to get over *Death in Venice.* Our first meal ashore that day was luncheon in the inn's dining room, and it consisted of iced consommé, grilled lemon sole, avocado mousse, braised lettuce, and melon sherbet. It tasted like the most marvelous food I had ever had, but I was not sure whether that was just because we had come off canned goods "cold turkey" or if it really was the extraordinary fare it seemed to be. I sat on my gourmet lexicon of superlatives and merely offered an occasional "uummm" and a slightly reverential "delectable." This how-

Kathy, high and dry in an English forest near the River Fal.

ever could hardly describe the heat of my palate's passion, but I didn't want to be caught spoon down so to speak. I had just got off the boat, and what did I know after days of canned lasagna and alphabet soup. I might be saying "yummy" and M.F.K. Fisher or Joseph Wechsberg could be at the next table thinking "richly sauced, but without character."

By our second day at the Rising Sun we had all unleashed our superlatives and generally agreed that it was some of the best food we had ever eaten. I began thinking that in addition to writing an article for *Sail,* maybe I should try one for *Gourmet* magazine. It turned out, however, that *Gourmet* had just visited the Rising Sun the year before and raved about its kitchen.

After the recuperative joys of the Rising Sun, I was not eager to engage in any rigorous sailing, so at my suggestion we headed the mile or so across the bay in pursuit of some low-key "messing about" in boats in none other than that "sleek and sinuous full-bodied river" the Fal, haunt of Water Rat, Mole, and the incomparable Mr. Toad. The river's banks were encrusted with English oak and dented with numerous tiny creeks that chased off into dim leafy woods.

We were walking through a thick glade along the river when we came to an exquisitely built stone wall, high enough and strong enough to rival Hadrian's barbarian preventer in the north. Next to the wall we found a convenient tree with eminently climable branches. Excited and anxious to see what was on the other side, we vaulted up the tree. I was first, and climbing higher and higher away from the forest floor, I could soon see over the wall to discover an enchanted wildwood park on the other side. It would be a fifteen-foot drop to enter. The park, perfect and impenetrable in its magical aloofness, tantalized me from my perch. And looking through the leafy tapestry below, I could hold my breath in anticipation of Pan with his pipes or a unicorn bounding through the wood. I could hear curlews po-tweet, and in a branch I found a partridge feather. It was all so different from the sea.

Pete left to fly home to Rusty, and we continued up the southwest coast of England poking into little sea villages like Fowey and Polperro and larger towns like Dartmouth and Salcombe. Oftentimes we would follow a deep-water channel right into the middle of a town and drop the hook just in front of the local pub. We basically went wherever we felt like, covering in a week what we would have covered in a day at sea.

One pleasant place (once we passed three boats grounded in the nearby mud flats) was the Beaulieu River (pronounced Bewlee). I was below, and we had just rounded a bend when I heard Chris shout, "Guess what's ahead." He had that tone in his voice of restrained jubilation that usually indicates there is a square rigger in our future. But it was no square rigger. It was *Gipsy Moth V*. Sleek, white, and glistening, she rode serenely on her river mooring. And on board was none other than Lady Sheila herself sitting in a patch of sunlight writing. *Gipsy Moth V!* Lady Sheila! It was almost too much for us. Maybe she would invite us on board to toast Chichester. I could check out the Tupperware and bring a little bag of Bordeaux or Pirouettes (the Mint Milanos were long gone). We waved heartily as we swung by *Gipsy Moth*'s port side, but Lady Sheila was deeply absorbed and did not see us. She continued writing while the late afternoon sun still held.

If Chichester was our particular passion, the entire region between Beaulieu and Portsmouth seemed to be nuts for Lord Nelson. At Buckler's Hard, a small village on the estate of a Lord Montague, there is a tiny maritime museum that specializes in Nelson memorabilia—such things as a lock of his hair, an entire set of baby clothes, as well as the autopsy report of his fatal wound including one detail about a gold thread from his epaulette being enmeshed in the bullet. I hope Lady Hamilton was spared that grisly little detail. On the lighter side there was a corridor devoted to Chichester, one display containing a note written by Sir Francis and put in a bottle with hopes that it would reach a certain distillery. In the note he thanked them for some gin they had supplied but regretted that he had indeed run out somewhere off Cape Cod and was facing a "spiritless landfall."

The Nelson mania however reached its apex in Portsmouth with his flagship the *Victory*. In addition to its famous guns, the ship had displayed in its great cabin mementos exchanged between Lady Hamilton and Lord Nelson—a table she had given him, a chair he had given her, more baby clothes, a lock of hair she had given him, and, of course, one he had given her (they both must have been bald by the end), a picture of their little daughter Horatia, various rings and jewelry . . .

Beyond the memorabilia was the untarnished image of Nelson—the boyish, aristocratic admiral, the man whose last message to his fleet was, "England expects every man to do his duty." We found the descendants of those men who did their duty often gathered in the pubs, one of the best being the Old White Hart in Port Hamble, a low-ceiling stone-and-wood structure without a straight line in it. The Old White Hart was a favorite haunt of oyster fishermen of the area. We found ourselves knee to knee or elbow to elbow with as salty and good-humored a bunch of folks as you would ever hope to meet. It was Hogarth come to life.

"How's your head?" The question had been asked repeatedly by each new pub arrival to a weather-beaten fellow with a thick shock of gray hair and grease on his brow. Each time he would nod and say something like "coming along" and sip his Guinness. But when he began to speak of fastening it on with bolts, we began to realize that something other than a normal headache was causing the problem.

"Have you got it to turn over yet?" That eliminated another possibility and led us to understand that he had been repairing his engine. Others joined in and a curious conversation began about past experiences in trying to start diesels when the starter mechanism has failed. Everybody had his own lively account, punctuating it with droll voice sound effects of handcranked diesel one-lungers and other reluctant machines. The tiny oak-and-stone-room was reverberating with the noises of Englishmen imitating engines. For two hours we were caught in the special magic of an English pub.

For over ten weeks, since the time we had left the pier in Boston, we had been messing around in boats, on or with them, and although as Water Rat said, "nothing really seems to matter" in such circumstances, our thoughts did become homeward bound. Was our house still standing? Our business still there? It was time for us to figure out where to put *Leucothea* up for the winter, until we could come back for another summer. Near Chichester we found a small boatyard in the town of Emsworth. We had to wait outside the harbor until the tide filled the inner basin and then we gently bumped in over the mud banks. Three days later, each with a small duffel bag in hand, we walked down the pier away from *Leucothea*. At the foot of the ramp we looked back for the last time until the next summer at the sleek little boat that had served us so well.

CHAPTER *21*

Part of the original Bargain in the Sky was that the itinerary for the next three years was for the most part to be based on my inclinations. During the winters that separated our two summers of cruising in Europe, I diligently researched where we should go. It did not take me long to discover that sailors are not travelers, nor do they write good travel material. With unmitigated practicality they focus on customs procedures, lock maneuvers, anchoring, approaching breakwaters, fuel, showers, fresh water, and of course the costs of provisioning. How much things cost in one port as opposed to another is widely discussed in sailing literature and hums like a drone throughout a large portion of people's conversation. In my early endeavors to plan summer cruises, I would fall asleep over passages such as the following: "On arrival in Germany you hardly have time to bother with a customs flag before you are alongside efficient customs (officers), but you will, of course, have your German courtesy flag hoisted on your starboard side." Achtung! I was asleep. I didn't cotton to the idea of a German flag on the boat anyway. So we wouldn't go to Germany if we could help it.

Another book offered a few cultural footnotes. For example, I discovered that the ship lock in Calais was taken at the end of a fearful siege by Edward III in 1347, who was persuaded not to execute the entire garrison, but to settle instead for "six chieftains, barefoot with ropes round their necks." A bit later as I read the description on the Canal de Calais with its "wide fields of black earth furrowed by rootling pigs," my pulse quickened. Could we be on the scent of some truffles? But a sentence later we are told to turn left or right. Both routes lead to Dunkirk. Occasionally writers would diverge to visit a local sardine factory or describe a particularly quaint village square. But in general the writing in these books could hardly be considered inspiring to anyone who planned to actually get off their boat or barge.

I ultimately turned to more traditional and less water-oriented sources for my research. The Michelin guides and *Gourmet* magazine became our primary means for planning cruises, especially during our third summer abroad. *Gourmet* writers tend to be hyperbolic not only about food but other things as well; however after the dry cruising guides I found it a welcome relief to find someone getting excited over something other than a lock. For example, one winter night in Boston I was reading a *Gourmet* article on the city of Nancy in eastern France. The writer had been describing the wonders to be found in the Musée de l'École de Nancy, a sort of repository for art nouveau objects and furniture. In a moment of unfettered enthusiasm she exclaimed that she would have been completely "undone" by the museum's spectacular grand piano with its inlaid *Mort du Cygne* and contorted legs "had I not been fortified by the most tender *carré d'agneau rôti* with a golden *gâteau de pommes de terre* and a *mousse de marrons glacés*" at the Capucin Gourmand. Although for some this writing might seem a tad much, for me it was all I needed to start the navigational, not to mention gustatory, juices flowing. Soon a summer route was planned that would take us via the Moselle, Meuse, and Marne au Rhin canals to Nancy.

The materials for research were fewer for Scandinavia, but it seemed to be the obvious place to go after England. Its rugged isolation would be an interesting contrast to the cozy but civilized ports of England's southwest coast. Our Scandinavian cruise was therefore planned for the next summer following our crossing. At the end of the first summer, we had left *Leucothea* in what we had felt to be a competent boatyard. It turned out to be other than that. Through some exceedingly slovenly work on our fuel tank done by the people of the yard during the winter, we nearly had our heads blown off as we set sail for Norway. Gasoline began leaking from the tank as soon as the boat heeled. We had two false starts like this before we were able to successfully set off.

It was during our extended stay in the boatyard that I met my first real "boatie," a term we came to use to designate those people who have given up everything to live on boats. The girl, I shall call her Jessica, was Australian and in her midtwenties. She and her second husband had just split up. She had met him while sailing with her first husband, and they had put up in Spain for the winter. He had bought this boat, the one she was still living on, and it was to be their dreamboat. They had brought it to Emsworth to work on together. It was a rather rakish double-ender, and one could just imagine the sweet dreams of harmony and reconstruction the couple had entertained as they imagined themselves sanding her sea-kindly hull, varnishing her wood with loving strokes, caulking, splicing, and polishing the brasswork with ardor. All this of course would be just the prelude to a voyaging life together.

Apparently, however, this was not to be. Jessica fell out of love with her husband and into love with one of the yard workers with whom she was now comfortably ensconced on the boat. Husband number two had not given up claim to his boat, but in the most amiable of fashions it had been worked out that Jessica and her lover, in some sort of peculiar payment for infidelity, would complete the work on the boat. The logic of this defied me and, even though I knew only one of the parties involved, repulsed me. I loathe "amicable" divorces, civilized separations, stylish breakups. To my mind, if people are prepared to leave their partners they should hate them so much that such niceties as might lend a genteel or warm tone to the actual fact should be impossible.

In any case I heard the details of Jessica's separation as I was roasting some meat in her large boat oven to take with us on our run across the North Sea. I had come back a little early for the meat, and she offered me some tea, and as I waited for the meat to finish, she confided in me that she had no intention of staying with her lover. Her real dream was to get her own boat and sail it to Greece and maybe do some chartering around the islands. I was not really shocked by all this (who can be shocked anymore by divorce or serial mates), but I was beginning to perceive the first dim glimmerings of what I came to understand as the paradox inherent to boatie life, or the lives of those people who have decided to forgo all and, in the name of freedom, adventure, or whatever else they might call it, live totally on their boats. I would eventually come to resent bitterly the overused metaphors that equated year-round sailing (I am reluctant to call it voyaging) with freedom and adventure, imagination and courage. Not that these qualities cannot be justifiably connected with seagoing folk; it is just that for a large number of boaties their lives have nothing to do with courage and adventure and that many of them are in fact the least adventurous lot of people I have ever met.

They don't sail; they drift. They don't have adventures; they maintain the boats that keep them adrift. They can perceive little beyond the boundaries of their fiberglass or wood capsules. They are enhulled, so to speak, physically and mentally. They are not voyagers of the world's oceans; they are self-selected inmates of boats, and they might just as well be in a supermarket pushing a cart from produce to frozen foods as on a boat sailing from Fiji to Tonga, because that is largely what boaties talk about: the price of things in one port as opposed to another. One senses after meeting a lot of these types that for many sailing is not a grand adventure but a tedious exercise in maintenance, the boat's and their own. These people could rarely if ever become "undone" over the *Mort du Cygne* inlay of a piano or its contorted legs. If tied up at the quay in Nancy, chances are they would probably not even walk to the town's spectacular centerpiece, the Place Stanislas, let alone visit a museum.

There's an exception to every generalization. Some of the most fascinating people I have ever met are the single-handed ocean racers Chris filmed in the 1980 *Observer* Single-handed Trans-Atlantic Race from Plymouth, England, to Newport, Rhode Island. Bill Homewood, Phil Weld, Judy Lawson, Francis Stokes, Walter Green, Mike Birch, Tom Grossman, Jerry Cartwright, these solo racers have wonderful personalities. Yes, they talk boats, but they talk life. They are true adventurers and could easily go gaga over a piano with contorted legs and a dying swan inlay. It has always seemed a little sad to me that these personalities were so often confined to days at sea alone with only the gulls to appreciate their musings. Of course, for the filming of the OSTAR Chris installed automatic sound cameras, and several of these people became shareable at last in their solo race across the Atlantic. From the film one can see that these folks are not loners by nature but a communicative lot full of ideas about life, sailing, and competition that they were only too happy to share in the middle of the Atlantic Ocean in the worst kind of weather.

Jessica, however, had a rather depressing effect on me. That plus the incompetency of the yard and our prolonged stay really made me eager to get sailing. The prospect of being adrift with only vague notions as to destinations gave me the absolute willies. I wanted to see Scandinavia this summer, not next. We had to be back in Boston by September twenty-fourth. That was when school started. I had been admitted to graduate school in education and would begin work on my master's in reading. This was part of my backup career plan. Being a free-lancer was all very exotic, but standing around with lance poised and not being engaged in "battle" is always a real fear. So I had decided to become a reading specialist to be employable in a more conventional manner, just in case we were caught with our lances down at some future time. I liked to read and I liked kids so it seemed like a wise choice.

CHAPTER 22

We did finally set things to rights with our boat and were able to depart Emsworth. Two days later thoughts of Jessica as well as graduate school were far from my mind as I sat on deck with a glass of inferior wine and had the superior experience of watching a dusty orange sun still hanging in a pale sky at ten in the evening. Punching along gently with force-four winds, we were set on a diagonal course across the North Sea toward Norway.

The sky never became dark that night nor would it for any of the subsequent nights of our crossing. At some indefinable point we had traveled too far for the night to catch us. For a string of rare days we would exist in a fragile color spectrum where light melted from yellow to rose to gray, then back to rose. A day-for-night world. A Nordic summer. During the first days we were kept from enjoying the peace of offshore sailing by the intense shipping traffic churning between the Continent and London off to the west.

Fast cargo ships and ferries appeared on the horizon, thrashed past and disappeared, all in ten or fifteen minutes. They seemed to be in a hurry compared to our leisurely four knots, but we were still winding down from our frenetic activity of readying the boat in England.

We finally cleared the heavy shipping lanes and settled into our sea-going routine, only to have it interrupted by a totally new hazard. Before I saw it, I heard it. An ominous thumping intruding on our relaxation. Soon the entire boat was reverberating, and on the rose gray horizon I spotted unmoving points of light. I watched them intently for fifteen minutes.

"Chris! What the hell kind of course have you charted? We're heading for land!" I yelled down the companionway.

Chris stumbled up, chart and binoculars in hand. "What's that noise?" he asked as he peered through the binoculars.

"I should know?"

He squinted again. "It's oil derricks."

Gene Vance, our friend and third crew member on the North Sea crossing, came up, and within an hour the three of us were sailing rather wide-eyed and drop-jawed through a brightly lit miniature city composed of numerous oil-drilling platforms. We passed close to one AMOCO #49/18A. The twelve-foot-high letters floated eerily above our mast.

I was beginning to get the distinct impression that the North Sea meant big business. And as we sailed around epidemics of uncharted rigs, I realized the romantic phrase "the ocean's vast untapped resources" would not long apply to the North Sea. "Shrinking" and "tapping" was the name of the game. The thumping was to serve as a leitmotiv for the next several days. We encountered myriads of these drilling platforms. Often early in the morning we would see equipment barges being towed up to the rigs. Occasionally we would see a chopper flying out, presumably to pick up and deliver crew. However, we never saw one trace of human life on the derricks.

The North Sea continued to produce numerous paradoxes. Its reputation tends toward the nasty. Because of its exceedingly shallow bottom, a normal storm can become a disaster in short order. There are all sorts of horror stories of cargo ships snapping like twigs under freak waves; boats swallowed up with no traces left; and even a few scant months before our own sail across the North Sea an oil-drilling platform had simply turned turtle during a winter gale with all lives lost. Add to this catalog of horrors a sea floor littered with U-boats and other remnants of various warring North Sea fleets. It doesn't conjure up tranquil thoughts. But since leaving the Dover Straits we had encountered nothing but impeccably blue skies, light winds, and hot sunshine pouring down on an enamel sea. We became becalmed. Bathing suits and shorts were de rigeur deck wear. We tried fishing to no

North Sea oil rig.

avail. Gene, a professor of linguistics and comparative literature, had taken to "going to the office," and each morning arrived on deck with his briefcase for a couple of hours' work as if he were still at the University of Montreal. George, the steering vane, presided over our progress, and I came to think of him as a kind of Club Med *gentil organisateur* who not only steered us but made sure everybody was getting an even tan by deftly moving his wind sensor so the canvas would not block the sun.

Finally a slight northeasterly wind began to increase to the point where we felt it best to turn off our engine even though the wind was dead on our nose. The monotony of beating into a building headwind was broken by the arrival of a special passenger, "Pidgie." There have been many birds celebrated in sailing literature. Chichester had his Mother Carey's chickens, and of course there is Coleridge's albatross, but we of the *Leucothea* had the distinction of playing host to a genuine carrier pigeon. We had noticed him (her?) circling and eyeing us for several minutes trying to decide if we were suitable pigeon terrain. Finally he swooped down and crash-landed, wedging himself between the life ring and the man-overboard pole, utterly exhausted.

Chris in all his pigeon omniscience, garnered from having worked on a documentary film entitled *Bird Brain,* approached the creature and disentangled him from the man-overboard equipment. Shivering from fear, cold, and fatigue, Pidgie was a sore sight. Chris set him down in the scuppers on the lee side and I fetched him some Chinese egg noodles, water, and peanuts to revive him. By this time the wind had picked up considerably. We were beating under our small jenny, with the lee rail occasionaly buried. Pidgie, having no sea legs at all, was continually being swished around in the scuppers. We moved him to the high side, which was drier but windier. Fog closed in.

It was my evening watch, and as I huddled under the dodger my new watch companion and I blinked at one another through the swirls of gray mist. I could not help but be impressed by this creature's remarkably unseaworthy mien. Next to Pidgie I felt like Horatio Hornblower. A most lubberly and urban bird, but in the now-austere North Sea I found Pidgie's presence quite heartening. As great globules of water dripped off everything and the thickening fog drew tighter the circumference of our visible world, I began to indulge in my classic foul-weather therapy—daydreaming about land. Pidgie's mere presence prompted memories of those great pigeon meccas of the world—Piazza San Marco, Trafalgar Square, the Boston Public Gardens. Goodness! I could almost see the Ritz Carleton. I have been known to periodically threaten Chris with moving permanently to the Ritz when I am ninety-five and he is still insisting on this ocean-sailing business. I have very definite ideas about my dotage. I plan to do it on a swan boat and not a ketch.

By morning the wind had shifted westerly, allowing us to just hold our desired course for the Norwegian coast. I finally convinced Chris, who was sleeping below, that the boat was not riding well and that we must reduce sail. We put on a working jib and double-reefed the main, which immediately improved things. Gene, ever-attendant to Pidgie's comfort, decided later that morning when the sun broke through that the bird needed a sunbath. He reached for him, but Pidgie, now sleek, rested, and fat as a cat, flew away. Unfortunately he disappeared in the direction of England, which was now farther away than ever.

We had been out six days. The seventh day came up grim and raw with force-six winds. Thoughts of landfall cheered me immensely. Although Chris had not been able to get any sights during the previous twenty-four hours, the DR showed us to be closing with the coast, and we could hear the radio beacon at Stavanger. We started scanning the horizon about eight AM. Off to starboard Gene spotted a sketchy land contour melting out of the sky. We continued on our northern heading. A few hours later there was another faint gray streak ahead. These two watery brushstrokes in an otherwise unmarked world meant Norway—the headlands of Stavanger. Later that morning we sighted the island that was our intended landfall illuminated in the only shaft of sunlight of the day. Suddenly a world that only an hour before was so vague and awash with nebulous shapes came into sharp relief. We turned into the mountainous coast, entering a rock-studded channel. The trim fishermen's cottages and docks appeared from behind a defense of surf-washed rocks not very well indicated on our American charts. We picked up a channel marker, breathed a bit easier, and followed the serpentine fiord that became the watery main street of Haugesund—first port in our Nordic summer.

CHAPTER 23

"I know an American," said the elderly man in a gray suit and black felt hat who with other townsfolk had lined up along the wharf and been staring at us unabashedly for twenty minutes since our arrival. As a conversation opener this statement was not a promising one, but I didn't want to be impolite; and I also wanted to meet Norwegians, and I would start with this man with his rugged yet gentle face.

"You do?" I replied.

"Yes. Stanley Tannenbaum, the yacht *Doric.*"

Incredible! We knew him. Trygyve Thorsen of Rover, Norway, and I, meeting for the first time in a fairly obscure harbor on the west coast of Norway, discovered we had a mutual friend in Westchester, New York.

"Do you know the yacht *Nina*—a schooner?" He took off his black felt hat and fingered the rim. We had heard of her. "Well," he continued, "I captained her in the Bermuda race." Trygyve, now retired to his birthplace, the island of Rover, had captained a good share of superyachts. We were to learn that many of the great captains for American racing yachts came from this region of Norway.

Haugesund's waterfront was laced by a network of broad water avenues. Old wharf buildings painted red-and-white with orange roofs leaned toward the water with thrusting gables. There was large-scale shipbuilding in evidence. Our boat became a magnet for the townsfolk. Most of them spoke English and were more than ready to give us advice on where to sail along the coast and what to see. They showed us where to find a laundry, showers, a restaurant with fifteen different varieties of marinated herring, and even lent us twenty dollars in Norwegian kroner since the banks were closed.

The following morning we left Haugesund in thick fog for a short sail north to visit some of the nearby islands. We were seeking Espevær, highly recommended by Thorsen and others. Assured by our advisers that there were no significant currents in the area, we set compass courses and arrived in the evening to a pleasant harbor that matched our chart. We tied up between two large rock outcroppings in a deep pine-sheathed granite cut.

There were two huge iron rings expressly for mooring purposes.

The next morning we took a long walk over the island. The beauty here, as we were to see in many Norwegian towns, was a quiet one of subtle colors and patterns, hidden designs, and occasional patchworks of brighter colors. We discovered for example that windows in the cottages were meant for looking into rather than out. They were festooned with white ruffles and lace, and in each pane bloomed a bright geranium or petunia. Beyond the cottages, however, was a stealthier beauty—the pied splendor of a lichen-covered rock with palest pinks and greens, an intricately planted vegetable garden of potatoes, chives, and fancy lettuce.

We came upon an old man mending nets and a young fisherman leaning against the frame of an open shed door to keep out the soft slanting rain. Another man was selling fresh mackerel from the trunk of his car, and we bought several for dinner. Two little flaxen-haired toddlers accompanying their father, who was also buying fish, peered around from behind their daddy's knees in amazement as they listened to our strange language.

We left the island, all the time thinking it was Espevær. But we were wrong. Viewed offshore in the next day's clear weather, it just did not fit right on the chart. We discovered that a strong current had sucked us sideways a half mile to another island and harbor entrance with nearly identical features. This was an embarrassing error, especially after all the enthusiastic recommendations of our friends in Haugesund. However, we decided not to double back to Espevær but to continue up the Bomlafjord, which seemed enticing, with a strong quartering wind and the mysterious current to boost us. We poked in and out of innumerable catgut channels and inlets. For lunch we tied up to a sheer granite face with our bowling to a tree growing from a crack in the rock. Below us was one hundred feet of the blackest water I had ever seen.

After a couple of days exploring these islands north of Haugesund, we turned around and began to head south for the big fjords near Stavanger. The wind turned around and followed us just off the quarter. By this time Gene's wife, Christy, and their two boys, Adam, eight, and Jacob, four, had joined us. We began our fjord explorations with the Nedstrand and then the spectacular Sauda fjord. The mountains on either side of us lay like crumpled green velvet under a flawlessly blue sky. On top, however, there were icy peaks that clawed at the bright blue dome. I remembered legends that the frozen figures of trolls supposedly formed the mountains of the fjords. I was trying to imagine how they grew to be five thousand feet high. We came within twenty feet or less of sheer granite cascades sprigged with firs and juniper. The birds suspended in silent flight against the dark granite faces appeared tiny and white as they rode the drafts. We became a Lilliputian boat

Leucothea *sails wing and wing in Sauda Fjord, Norway.*

sailing through a mythic land. There were clutches of neatly painted cottages nestled in green-lined pockets at the mountain's base. It was a world divided in character: Four thousand feet straight up there was ice-capped austerity, jagged and barren; Below there was a lower world soft and sensuous, one of dark green mountain folds and secret harbors and blind valleys.

For a sailing boat there were almost too many choices, with the infinite number of turnoffs, hidden inlets, and cuts where the most secret lives could be lived. The wind snaked behind us following every turn, curve, and squiggle of the fjord. We found a spectacular site for a picnic beneath a five-hundred-foot-high waterfall. We tied up the bow to a tree and the stern to an Yvon Chouinnard clean-climbing piton brought from Boston and pounded into a crack. The mist of the waterfall swirled around us, but we found a picnic rock beside it in a hot sunny patch abloom with tiny mountain flowers and trimmed in moss. We climbed high to get a better look at the waterfall and its source. It was a great gushing affair with four ropy strands cutting deeply into the rocks. When I climbed back down to the picnic rock, a little one-lung dory came puffing by, loaded with a multi-generational family. Sitting in the prow there was a little old lady with yellow-gray hair. She kept waving at us vigorously, gaily shouting something that we could not hear over the roar of the waterfall. We waved back and shouted a greeting she couldn't hear either, but she smiled happily as they continued on along the cliffs.

CHAPTER 24

"Voor kin tie up?" Chris asked in a barely audible stage whisper of pidgin Norwegian. It was five in the morning. The sun had been up for almost two hours. We had just slipped into the fishing village of Rasvag as quietly as parents tiptoeing into a bedroom of sleeping children. The town was sound asleep—a light cool sleep, because it faces west and most of the houses were still in the morning shadow. A single fisherman was unloading a beautiful catch of salmon.

Rasvag is located on a deeply indented bay. Our approach after an overnight passage from Stavanger was extraordinary. Chris had called me up at four-thirty AM, and I climbed the companionway into a water world of gigantic boulders heaped into islands and mountain ranges illuminated by an unearthly morning light. In the whiteness of the light, I picked out the stunning silhouette of a fisherman in a dory hauling his nets. Chris seemed to be sailing us straight into the rocks, but between the islands were innumerable hidden channels. One led to Rasvag.

The town of Rasvag was actually a maze of several tiny islands with interweaving waterways. Whoever laid out the village had an absolute

Approaching Rasvag.

abhorrence for straight lines. There was not one. The only road in the town followed the contour of the shoreline. It twisted and curved sharply and so did the houses in order to give each one maximum water view and harbor access. Hence the gabled white houses with orange roofs were stacked and packed at amazing angles. At points the sky above the road itself was obscured by overhanging gables. But between the houses, through open shed doors, and where the roofs touched one another to make oddly shaped apertures, one could catch the most exquisite harbor pictures—a wedge of blue sky meeting water, a chunk of mountain, a dory perfectly framed.

We had come as strangers but were welcomed as old friends. At the head of a minifjord that wriggled out from Rasvag, there lived two old ladies in a classic clapboard house. We asked if we could tie up at their pier. They were more than pleased. They spoke excellent English and invited us in to see their home. It was their summer home now but had originally been built by their grandfather, a sea captain, as the family home. On the lintel over the front door, Agnes Soyland, one of the women, had written this inscription. "Vart Paradisio pa jord/for liten og stor." (This is paradise on earth for big and small). She and her sister then led us through a warm sunlit house that radiated love and good spirits. Each door throughout the house was beautifully carved with simple, elegant designs. Each room was a perfect expression of a different mood or character. The living room was a lively gallery of treasured family photographs, many showing the two women as young girls in their Hardanger native festival costumes.

The house went on and on with rooms tucked here and there to stash an extra family member or houseguest. Little sleeping places for children had been built under the attic eaves. The barn had been renovated to accommodate others. There was no electricity, but lovely kerosene lamps and magnificent woodburning stoves in a variety of shapes and sizes could be found in every room. But most impressive were our hostesses; well into their eighties, they were women of natural elegance. They had asked if they could take a tour of our boat and had hopped over the lifelines with a muscular grace. Once aboard they were curious about everything, especially our Tiny Tot coal-burning stove. "All the way across the Atlantic with just that?"

As we neared the southern tip of Norway, we saw more boats and people, although it was far from crowded. The Nordic angst so celebrated by playwrights and filmmakers seemed nowhere in evidence. Admittedly we were there at an "up" time—long warm sunny days, the best summer in forty years. For the most part however, the Norwegians seemed to us like a terrifically healthy and positive lot and quite well-heeled in an unpretentious way. Most of the people had second homes and boats. They especially went in for character boats. A Colin Archer coast guard cutter design had been resurrected and now was being built again with loving authenticity. We saw several old fishing boats renovated and sailing in the best of style.

In Farstad we met a family, the Eks, sailing a marvelous old black cutter, gaff-rigged with red sails. We were invited aboard for a drink and discovered that Mr. Ek, Jens Christian, was the director of the Norwegian State Opera in Oslo and his wife, Meret, was a singer in the opera. They suggested to us several good harbors and spots not to miss, so we continued on southward around the tip of the large spoon shape that Norway makes on the map.

The prominent geological features of this region were the skerries—the networks of narrow channels that lace in and around the rock islands. Locked behind the intricate skerry maze was the whitewashed town of Ny Hellesund—a favorite retreat in the past for Norway's romantic poets. Classic eighteenth-century clapboard houses were set on clusters of tiny islands. All life was oriented toward the water, and instead of sharing a yard with a neighbor, chances were you shared a tiny inlet or postage-stamp bay. We tied up next to a soaring side of granite emblazoned with the royal crests of three Nordic kings. This spot we discovered was famous in Nordic sagas. According to legend, Olaf Haraldsson, an ancient Norsk king, was being pursued by his enemies when he came up against this granite face. The rock miraculously split open leaving a passage twenty feet wide for his escape.

In addition to its legendary heritage, Ny Hellesund was rich in mussels. We gathered a prodigious amount for our dinner. We had been heavily reliant all along the coast on harvesting our dinners from the sea, for Norway's steep prices made grocery shopping and eating in restaurants prohibitive. The rate of exchange at that time for Americans was quite unfavorable. Hamburger and pork chops could be as much as four dollars a pound. There was a scarcity of vegetables because of the poor farmland; thus it was not uncommon to see green peppers or a rare tomato marked as high as sixty cents apiece. We fished whenever possible for mackerel and flounder. A delicious fish similar to rock cod was so plentiful that sport fishermen would think nothing of giving us several pounds of their catch. Our major indulgence was buying fresh salmon, which was not at all unreasonable in price if you had enough people to justify buying a whole one. To fill in the gaps, the rusty cans left stowed from the previous summer's crossing were like money in the bank.

We sailed sixty miles without any open water through the "Blindleia," or Blind Waterway, with short stops in Lellesand, Tvedestrand, and Arendal, where our guests disembarked. The green shores slid by like magic as our favorable wind continued. In Lyngør we ate our second onshore meal at an

Kathy at a wharf restaurant in Lyngor, Norway.

enchanting wharf restaurant where one could tie up a boat practically to a table leg.

Leaving Kragero we had one of our loveliest sails through the Langaarsund, a long narrow channel that divides two islands, Lago and Gumo. On either side were steep rock facings with deep clefts and outcroppings that provided surprises around each twist and bend. Every now and then on a flat rock sloping into the sea there would be a family bathing. They were all friendly and outgoing and would often swim right up to our boat to say hello and get a better look at us. I began to realize that in Norway the idea was to be alone with your family and not on a beach with hordes of people. Even though we had seen an overwhelming number of summer homes in the southern tip region, each house still had been located with isolation and privacy in mind. Trees were left intact, and homes were built in the heart of their dense protection. These summer homes were far removed from conveniences such as roads, stores, and movies. The family alone in nature seemed a strong Norwegian theme.

There was an island just before the Oslo fjord called Malmo. Its harbor enjoyed a rather perfect seclusion tucked away behind a barrier of rocks and protected from the open waters and winds on the other side. Inside the water was like a mirror, but over a low sand-and-rock link one could see whitecaps in the Skagerrak. This type of anchorage has always been a peculiar favorite of mine, where the wildness of the sea is foiled by the exquisite serenity of the harbor. We walked toward the windward side of the island and found the strangest rocks. They had been buffeted and smoothed, worn and wrought into odd shapes like great mounds of rising dough with soft folds and deep dimples. They were glacier rocks, and the strange configurations and texture were caused by the ice scraping over them and smoothing them out. All over these rocks were gull chicks, and the wind was so strong that when they turned to look at us they could not stand up without walking sideways. We couldn't help laughing at these speckled creatures sideslipping across the rocks trying to stare at us.

Oslo! We pulled into a slip at the Kongens Yacht Club on Bygdoy Peninsula. Although a singularly ungraceful city, Oslo possessed a maritime charm. Leaving the Norwegian sweater stores to the tourists, Chris dragged me off on an odyssey of various ship chandleries in the grungiest areas of town. He was of course in ecstasy filling our ship's coffers with an assortment of gorgeous nuts, bolts, shackles, nylon line, stove alcohol, and odd-sized gaskets. I must admit however that it was in one of these half-lit emporiums that we bought two wonderful Norwegian fishermen's sweaters, cheaper and of better quality than anywhere else in Oslo.

A maritime treasure of the world was a short walk from where we were docked—the Viking ships. We went early one morning to the museum and waited until they opened the doors. Just seeing these exquisite black dragon ships took us back one thousand years to the time when Viking seamen ranged the coast of Europe and America. All the elements we had seen on our cruise so far seemed embodied in these boats—the narrow fjords, the superb timber, the ruggedness and the honest craftsmanship of the Nordic people.

CHAPTER *25*

Our friend Eleanor Drew, rechristened the City Mouse for this cruise because of her residence in New York City, had flown into Oslo to join Chris and me for the Oslo-Copenhagen jaunt. Not wishing to shortchange her visit to Oslo, I insisted that she be given an acclimatization day in the city before we set off. There was some minor grumbling from Chris's quarter about how one should grab the northwest wind when one can. City Mouse and I barely heard him as we rushed off to the Munch Museum and then dashed into Number twenty Carl Johans Gate, address of the well-known jewelry store of David Andersen, where we joined hordes of other American women pawing over silver-and-enamel pieces. The only affordable items in the store were some tiny gaily colored enamel earrings set in silver. We each bought several pairs. It was all so lovely after mucking about with Chris in the marine hardware shops in the dimmer reaches of the city.

With purchases discreetly tucked in our purses, we met Chris waiting patiently for us on a street corner with a five-gallon can of stove alcohol in hand. The three of us then advanced to the Theatre Caffeen, where in polished mahogany elegance we lunched on itty-bitty open-faced sandwiches that cost an arm and a leg. We had stuffed the five-gallon container of stove alcohol under the table. As I looked about at the sturdy matrons in Queen Mother hats and elderly gentlemen with homburgs resting on their knees, I caught a glimpse in an exquisite beveled mirror of Chris's distraught countenance. Need I say the wind had shifted to southeast, and even within the cloistered splendor of the Theatre Caffeen, Chris, sea creature that he is, was able to reach out beyond the leather and mahogany, beyond the elegant potted palms and beveled glass, beyond all these lubberly charms of civilization, and detect a significant wind change in the fjord.

Although it was a head wind, we decided to leave quickly while it was still light. One hour later we were under sail, busily tacking out of the narrowest part of the fjord. That evening we put in twelve miles or so down the east coast at a tiny village that, unbeknownst to us, happened to be a busy barge port. No sooner was the anchor down than City Mouse called below to Chris and me as we fixed drinks—"Hey, folks, I think we're double-parked, or something." A frantic symphony of toots lashed the air as Chris and I raced topside. Midst much panting, sweating, and tooting we hoisted our anchor and just escaped being pulverized by a tug pulling a barge. After our reanchoring in a more suitable spot, I began to prepare dinner, our first aboard with City Mouse. As I removed the floorboards in the main cabin and wrested from the Stygian depth of our bilges two precious rusted cans from our crossing the summer before, I saw the color drain from City Mouse's lips.

"What's that?" She asked.

"Dinner." I could read her horror, but after a month's orientation to Norway's astronomical prices we had few choices left.

"Don't worry. They're very safe," I said holding up a can in all its speckled loveliness. "There are no bulges, punctures, or seam separations, and when I open them up you'll see no rust inside. We check them carefully."

City Mouse smiled wanly. "What's inside them?" She asked.

"Ham in this one and corn here."

"Jesus!" gasped City Mouse. "I never thought I'd get trichinosis and botulism in the same meal." A direct hit to the jugular of what Chris and I had fondly begun to refer to as *La Côte Bilge*.

The next morning we were up early hoping to get under way before the head winds built up. No such luck. Our anchor had become snared on something on the bottom, and Chris had to dive to untangle it. This would not have been a remarkable incident save for the fact that the water was so cold that he had to wear a wet suit. After we dug down to the bottom of

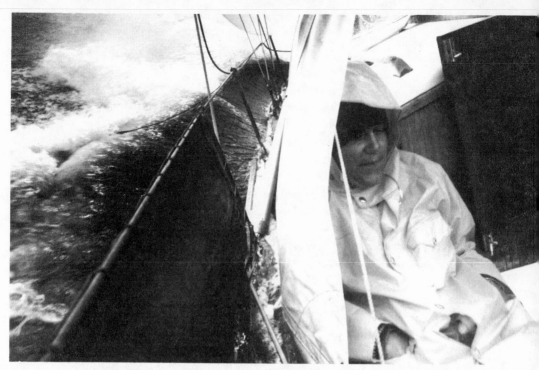

Kathy huddles under dodger beating out of the Oslo Fjord.

the locker we discovered that, when we had left Boston a year before, we had packed my wet suit instead of Chris's. Women's wet suits have built in neoprene mammaries, just to keep things straight underwater lest anyone forget; however, anatomy, even in neoprene, need not be destiny, and Chris, with all his x and y chromosones orderly and attentive, stepped into the sleek black rubber wet suit. Then, looking like a cross between Myra Breckinridge and Barbarella, he dumped himself into the icy waters of the fjord. City Mouse and I cheered him on vigorously, and soon the cantankerous anchor was unsnared and off the bottom and we were sailing double-reefed right into tto the teeth of a due-south wind. We only made thirteen miles that day.

The next day proved worse: rain, racing dark rags of clouds, and generally dirty weather. We put in at Hanko, the king's yacht club on the east side of the fjord. In drenching rain we walked up to the tiny barn red clubhouse to inquire about hot showers and were greeted by some elderly gentlemen who'd been drinking the afternoon away. One fellow with a Band-Aid on the end of his nose approached us with great glee and boomed, "Well, what happened to you?" He had mistaken us for a British boat that had gone on the rocks and had had to be rescued. His face absolutely fell when we informed him that we were not the ones.

The next morning as we left Hanko we sailed by all three hundred sleek white feet of the king's yacht. The deckhands waved merrily to us. Earlier we'd seen a smartly uniformed gig crew bringing the royal dog ashore for a walk. As the yacht became a royal speck in a darkening world, we encountered our dirtiest weather yet and spent four hours ramming our way around a point off a rocky lee shore in steep fast-moving waves. The cold driving rain dug into our faces. City Mouse was very brave but threw up. We had to tie her in with a life harness so she could safely vomit over the lee rail. From under her oilskins the blue enamel earrings gave me a wicked wink. The four miles around the point was the ultimate scary skerry, but once around, the wind jumped to our quarter and we skipped up to the eighteenth-century fortified city of Fredrikstad.

The old part of the walled city complete with moat was fascinating. In a slanting rain we walked the cobbled streets and peered into the delicately proportioned framed buildings, all painted muted sea colors. For dinner we got right into the mood of things and went to a Chinese restaurant, which turned out to be our only bargain meal in Norway. It had an endearing sleaziness to it, with its vermilion flocked wallpaper, plastic tablecloths, and three-foot chrome-plated model of the Eiffel Tower in the entrance.

CHAPTER 26

When the northwest wind finally came, it came cool and clear, waking us up as it blew into our open companionway and over our faces. It was about five AM when I first felt it. I knew that Chris felt it too. We didn't say a word for fear it would go away, but we soon heard it steady in our rigging, a welcome riffling sound. Sure now that it was no whimsy wind of a dream, we roused City Mouse, dressed quickly, had a cold breakfast, and ghosted out of the harbor.

We averaged five or six knots the entire day. Before us unfolded a patchwork of low-lying barren rock islands, pink and smooth—Sweden.

The border between Norway and Sweden is not just a political reality but a natural one as well. The topographical change is dramatic upon crossing over. Suddenly the jagged vertical pine-clad Norwegian coast slips into a treeless world of low pink rock islands that slide with barely a level change into the water. The wind had a blessed northerly component, and we slipped through this silent rock world making hardly a ripple in the waveless sea. All this was hard won after three and a half horrid days of beating out of the Oslo fjord.

Our first port after Strömstad was the rock-island village of Smogen. It sat prim and stone-locked behind a labyrinthine guard of offshore islands

—a sea virgin of the Skagerrak. It was the first time I had ever seen a village built entirely on a rock. All the buildings seemed scaled down in size to match the low proportions of the island. I supposed that this helped to counter a top-heavy effect. Still we had an undeniable sense of things being perched. Especially from a distant perspective, it was odd to see a town virtually popping out of the rock. Without dug foundations, Smogen looked just like one of those pop-up villages found in children's books. As it was very calm, we anchored off to avoid attempting Smogen's bathtub-size harbor jammed with boats. When we rowed ashore I realized that the town reminded me of a miniature golf course with one of those ersatz minivillages. Even the wharf storage buildings managed to have gay ruffled curtains in their windows. I felt I should be putting a golf ball through some opening. Because it is rather hard to grow things on bare stone, there were loads of colorful baskets and pots of flowers in front of buildings.

As the three of us were sitting on the minuscule harborside benches I witnessed one of the most memorable docking feats ever. A fellow in a forty-foot yawl entered the narrow harbor completely under sail. His crew was composed of five children, all under the age of six, and a woman who looked distinctly like a nun standing on the foredeck with a wimple, midcalf skirt, heels, and a boat hook. They proceeded to tack up the sixty-foot-wide channel, backwinding the jib with artful discretion as they headed into a slip. A four-year-old with impeccable timing dropped the sail; the nun in an act of dockside levitation was on the pier with barely a rumple in her wimple and tied down the bowline, while a five-year-old matched her work astern. I had never seen anything so astonishing in my life. They had all the precision of the Purdue marching band.

I knew that this would really get Chris where it hurt. Our dockings recently had been less-than-smart—more like the Bay of Pigs than a marching band. I was neither Golden Girl nor nun in my performance. The more Chris tried to train City Mouse and me, the worse we got. At one harbor along the way I had thrown a temporary line to a German man ashore and had completely forgotten about him when I went below. Fifteen minutes later as we were changing clothes to go ashore, I yelled, "the German!" Chris and City Mouse looked at me with terror not knowing what had happened. I streaked topside to find him waiting there still holding the line, patient as could be, and smiling amicably. "Ja, ja," he said. I tried desperately to apologize saying, "ja, ja" back for this was the only German I knew aside from "mit Schlag."

The wind kept blowing northwest as we threaded our way through the rock islands that characterized this section of Sweden's coast. We sailed through one batch of islands that we came to call the Os—Vallero, Torno,

Salto, Broto. And then there was one perfectly round island covered with houses to its very edge. We sailed so close to the steep-to shore that we could look into people's kitchens and wave hello.

We had set out from Gothenburg with plans to sail twenty miles or so down the Swedish coast to a point where we would take off for a twelve-hour passage to Anholt, a tiny Danish island paradise sometimes called The Pearl of the Baltic. When we were just outside of Gothenburg, the wind was at such a perfect angle for Anholt that we decided to jump and turn a bit starboard so the wind would catch our quarter. City Mouse and I took the eight-to-twelve watch. We endured an annoying evening calm as we were passing through a major Kattegat shipping lane, but no sooner were we across it than the wind freshened and we cranked up our speed to six knots. At ten PM we spotted a lighthouse on the eastern end of the island, then a string of lights to the west. We were a bit low on our course so when Chris came up we had to take a long tack out again to avoid the extensive sandbars around the island.

Soon after City Mouse and I went to sleep, we were awakened by violent motion, a terrible jolting and bucking as if in a bad storm, but there was no more wind than when we had come off watch. The shallow sandy bottom, hallmark of the Baltic, had become even shallower, causing waves to build up steep and close. I soon was completely awake, having been thrown out of my bunk, and had to get out the bunk boards and show City Mouse how to use them. I could hear the hum of the depth sounder. How strange it seemed to be using it in the middle of an ocean. We tacked far out again until the red zone of the lighthouse was no longer visible and we were in the white sector proper for approaching the island. City Mouse and I were called back to deck to assist in landing preparations. I took the helm and was rather alarmed to see the Fathometer indicating in bleeps of orange that we only had eight feet under our keel. Chris and City Mouse organized lines and walked back the big anchor to the stern. We sailed through the breakwater into a U-shaped harbor stuffed with sailboats. Just as light was breaking we tied up next to a handsome Swan 48, and as City Mouse put it so eloquently, out of the forward-and-aft hatches popped "five great Danes" to assist with the lines.

We awoke the next morning to a watercolor world of pale green dune grass, a milky sea, and fragile blue sky. Figures bronze-and-biscuit color walked down a wide beach fringed with sand dunes on an upper ridge. As we came closer to the sun-darkened figures, we realized that none of them wore so much as a stitch of clothing. It was definitely a family beach. All generations were basking in the sun. For those who wished to be more discreet, there were the hidden sand pockets in the dunes screened with tall grass. But all of them, swimmers, bike riders, Frisbee players, grandmas and grandpas, were entirely nude. In a kind of ultimate sensibility reversal we suddenly felt embarrassed by our clothing and stripped down and dived into the cool clear Baltic waters.

CHAPTER 27

The major compensation in leaving Anholt was our magical run to Gilleleje on Zealand, just west of Copenhagen. When we had left that evening, it was hazy, no real horizon, just a milky opaqueness to the summer night. Then quick as a wink I saw the moon roll up so close and quiet to the edge of the water that it seemed to float like a big pale peach just beyond my grasp. It floated up a little higher and nearly slipped away behind low-flying cloud; then it came partway back—a big soft, shadowy sphere. Once more it stole away and returned, hanging up there like a thin wafer, pale and yellow in a not-quite-black sky. We pulled into Gilleleje harbor at two o'clock in the morning.

Next day we arrived in Copenhagen. We had a crew change as City Mouse departed and my parents came aboard, right at the harbor by the Little Mermaid. One of the most pleasant things we did in Copenhagen, aside from Tivoli, was food shopping for the boat. Prices had dropped considerably from Norway and Sweden, and there was a much wider choice. We stocked up on all sorts of delectables for which Denmark is famous. Bacon (almost nonexistent in Norway), chicken, steak, cheeses, wonderful fresh vegetables, and of course weinbrod—Danish pastry. It became a morning ritual in Denmark for the first person up to rush out and buy fresh wienerbrød for breakfast.

Our next port, barely out of Copenhagen, was Dragør, a perfect introduction to Danish village life with narrow cobbled streets lined with pumpkin-colored houses. The influence that the Viking invasions had on architectural styles in England was made emphatically clear here.

Because the wind blew southwest the next day, we tacked across the narrow channel over to Sweden and put in at Skanör, near Malmö. We walked into town and found a wonderful restaurant where we had delicious fish and the traditional lingonberry pancakes for dessert.

Back we sailed to Denmark, this time to the island of Omøe in the Danish Smallands, flotillas of islands south of the large island of Zealand. The minute harbor was a squalid affair crowded behind rock breakwaters. Because it was brimming with boats and we had recently lost our neutral and reverse gears,

Copenhagen's Little Mermaid *gazes on* Leucothea *and oil tanks beyond.*

we stayed outside. The unattractive harbor was no reflection of the village, we soon discovered. We rowed ashore and began our walk toward Omøo following the broad gold fields of undulating wheat, vast expanses of sugar beets, and meadows with sleek red cows. After a mile and a half we came to a charmed village with thatched cottages of painted plaster and dark wood trim. Some of the cottages were white, others blood red. Walls wobbled and roof lines followed suit as there was not a straight line in their construction. Gardens with profusions of hollyhocks, dahlias, and cosmos sprang up around the cottages, the riots of blossoms floating prettily at windowsill level. These cottages with their charming angles and wobbles, steeped in clouds of blossoms and attended by hundreds of white butterflies, were uncanny reminders of the illustrations from classic fairy tales. How often had such an abode housed a witch or a kindly woodsman in children's literature.

From Omø to Præstø we sailed and then through the Bogstrom channel, straight and wide and flanked by low velvety green fields. It was an absolutely windless day thick with heat. Long strings of fluffy white swans floated in the distance, and we began to notice that on most boats we passed the crews had slipped into something more comfortable—nothing. We exchanged friendly greetings with nude helmspersons.

We stopped for a picnic at one point, tempted by the shade deep in the luxuriant green fringe of the channel. We rowed ashore and got caught in what we took to be bulrushes. Chris and my father had to get out and wade ashore pulling my mother and me, who were still perched primly in the stern of the dinghy. I was having flashes of *African Queen* and two Humphrey Bogarts as Chris and Dad hacked through the bulrushes, but my father muttered that he hadn't been in these since being abandoned just after he was born, thus confounding my metaphor. Halfway through this swamp I began having doubts about the suitability of our proposed picnic ground. Things got worse. Once out of the bulrushes and on to firm land, we were confronted head-on by four bulls. "One for each of us," my mother commented weakly. They were not particularly bullish on us, so after we had crossed two electric fences we at last found an idyllic spot which, midst mountain ash and weeping willows, provided a sylvan setting straight out of a Claude Lorrain.

We made a special effort to stop in the village of Troense just outside of Svendberg as we had heard about an outstanding privately owned maritime museum. It did live up to its reputation, since Captain Holm Petersen, the owner, had acquired an amazing collection on his travels all over the world as a merchant marine captain. There were a lot of old sea dogs living in Troense, and as we walked back to our boat, a particularly salty-looking man with a tuft of snowy beard practically danced a hornpipe up to us and asked if we were "the Boston ketch." Yes, we were. "Well, Captain," he addressed Chris in his soft accented English, "have you ever seen a ship called *Pan?*" His faded blue eyes searched our faces. "Yes, the *Pan?*" he said again and fingered imaginary pipes in a lovely gesture.

"How much water do you have here, Chris?" And just in sync, forgive the pun, we ran aground on the mud banks of one of the two harbors of Aerøskøbing. It became a point of great debate whether my father's question was issued as a warning or an exclamation. We finally got off by setting out an anchor, running a bowline ashore to some people on the pier, and sending Chris and my father crawling out on the boom and bouncing wildly while we all screamed profanities at one another.

Aerø, scene of our fiasco, was one of the larger islands in the archipelago south of Fyn, and the town of Aerøskøbing on the island provides one of the most perfect examples of an old Danish village. To walk through the dollhouse streets of Aerøskøbing is to pass through a time warp into the eighteenth century. Tiled-roof cottages painted ice cream colors and carved doors, each one a masterpiece with beading, wheat, or ribbon design, porches festooned with roses, all combine to make Aerøskøbing an enchanting village.

CHAPTER 28

"It is a game—like any other game. It is directed by superiors. There is little choice for the rest." The professor spoke rapidly. The countryside slid by outside the train compartment window as we chuffed from Hamburg to Kiel. We had to put into Kiel for a couple of days to let off my parents who were to fly home. I was not anticipating with any great joy our two-day layover in this German town. My prejudices were such that I was disinclined to get off the boat and explore or spend any money in a town that has U-boats for municipal monuments.

Bad weather had delayed our sailing plans, and I had finally succumbed to a day trip to Hamburg. And now, in the close air of the tiny compartment, I seemed to be paying for it as I listened to a German physics professor who taught at Vanderbilt University and was now back to visit "the Fatherland." He had been talking about the game of war. He took the metaphor seriously but not gravely. He took it seriously with the same kind of satisfaction and sense of descriptive rightness that any mathematician must feel in setting up a formula and making the calculations that, when they work, describe a particular piece of reality. The professor had played the game of war as a child in a village outside of Hamburg. We have just been treated to an animated lyric description of his life as a small boy during the war years. He and his little schoolmates in their blue smocks would go every day to a cornfield on the edge of their village and play a game in which they would collect unexploded incendiaries.

He spoke very fast, each word a stroke in the pastoral image he painted for Chris and me of this wartime village with its little blue-smocked children in golden fields. "The Americans," he continued, "after the war understand better than we do. It is the only way to fight communism. So after I complete my mathematical studies I went to Huntsville!" Where presumably he worked out his calculations with Von Braun and waxed equally lyrical over the beauty and simplicity, the elegant balance at the heart of these solutions for larger war games.

Chris, who had chosen the peace symbol as our house flag, tried arguing with the man, but it was useless. He believed the metaphor of war as a game. He worked out formulas to describe it; calculations to compare it to reality. I sat there silently in that chuffing train and grew more fearful as the miles flew by and thought of other trains and other journeys that had been made on German railroads and Polish ones, and I stared at this man full of numbers and solutions. I had not heard of young Stephen Hawking then, the Cambridge cosmologist. Had I heard of him I would have realized or perhaps been able to articulate what Hawking has always known to be the crucial question: Numbers can only describe, but as he once told an interviewer, he wants to know why. Why does the universe exist at all? But for the man on the train to Hamburg, it was all a game, and his skill as a mathematician did not deepen the mystery as the same skill does for Hawking. It merely made it possible to calculate smug solutions. I finally had to excuse myself to go to the bathroom. I had just met my first killer, and I wanted to throw up.

We finally did get a break in the weather and were able to leave Kiel and sail back toward Denmark. We eventually made a complete circle of Zealand, coming up along its western side and then turning east toward Copenhagen, where we decided to put up our boat for the winter. We had originally planned to go much farther that summer. There had been talk of Amsterdam, the canals, down to the Mediterranean and on to Spain, but we would always say "just a few more days here," just a week more of this fragile northern light; thus the best-laid plans disintegrated. Come September, as we worked cleaning out La Côte Bilge and taking down spars, sunshine quickly slipped away as night began to catch the days of the Nordic summer, and the winter light stole into the harbor. We packed our duffels and prepared to fly home for our own winter of work and study.

CHAPTER 29

The longest period of time we ever spent continuously aboard *Leucothea* was five months, and it began during our third and last summer of the boat's European stay. We planned to head *Leucothea* home now. The voyage would begin in August with a long meandering putt through the Dutch, Belgian, and French Canals, which would lead us southward to the Mediterranean. We wanted to be in Gibraltar by early November and cross to the Caribbean by Christmas. Preparing for five months away from home and a trans-Atlantic crossing loomed as a monumental task. Our previous crossing of two summers before had not done that much to assuage my fears despite Chris's constant refrain that this southern crossing would be a "piece of cake"— sunny, clear skies, and gentle trade winds the whole way! But I was still nervous. Five months away from home—away from the comforts and rhythms of home!

The boatyard in Skovshoved, outside of Copenhagen, where we had

Leucothea *under twin jibs.*

left *Leucothea,* was an excellent one. Our Atomic 4 gasoline engine, more suitable for tractors in Nebraska, had been replaced by a brand-new Volvo diesel during the winter. We arrived that summer in Copenhagen via London looking like a traveling circus carrying sail bags with new sails, jerricans which we had stashed in London two summers before with friends, and assorted paraphernalia for five months of boat living and a crossing.

Somewhere between the baggage area and ground transportation my back went out, and by the time we arrived at the boatyard I was a total cripple. Naturally the boat was still up on the cradle, where it would remain for forty-eight hours. Without a crane I did not see how I would ever make it onto the boat. Chris eschews hotels on general principle, and in addition he wanted to work day and night on the boat so we could be off as soon as possible for the canal trip that I had so diligently researched. He promised me that I could remain supine and that he would serve me hand and foot. So with the help of a yard worker and Chris I was raised like an old wreck and installed in the starboard bunk, where I remained with barely discernible movement for almost three days while Chris worked furiously to set the boat in order. It must be understood that Chris has always left the absolute minimum for a boatyard to do, preferring instead to minister to every detail himself. He basically loathes yards, even good ones, and feels nobody really knows our boat as he does. He is probably right, but it makes for frantic times.

Any sense of order that life had previously possessed was quickly destroyed with the onslaught of getting the boat ready. Geraniums in windowsills, fresh-picked lettuce from a garden, cooking a special dinner soon were remembered as the most extravagant luxuries as my world, viewed from the bunk, became one of oilcans, exotic fiberglass rubbing compounds, buckets for urinals (remember we were still up in the cradle—dry dock), gear in soggy boxes, tools and more tools. All this was spread out over thirty linear feet, only twelve or fifteen of which can be used for living space anyway. I was in a locked state both mentally and physically. I lay in my bunk dazed in this topsy-turvy world. Under my pillow I found a nest of allen wrenches. At my feet was an old bottle of Jack Daniels, regrettably empty, with a moldering label. To make matters worse, Chris was disgustingly cheerful. But for me everything was unmitigated misery. Everything that was normally difficult on a boat was now twice so. I was overwhelmed, and languished in a depressed state; however I panicked as I realized that a first draft of my third children's book was due. I had promised the editor that I would send it from Denmark. Writing, and the promise of a good meal at the end of a short sail to Skanör, where we had visited last summer, seemed to restore me finally.

We had some nice sunshiny days of sailing in Denmark, but we were again going to have to pass through Kiel in order, this time, to enter the canal system in Holland. So under what else but leaden skies we sailed into the port. We were there for just twenty-four hours, and this time we really did not leave the boat even for a meal in town.

Apparently our sentiments were shared by a neighboring sloop that flew a Norwegian flag. At about nine AM on the morning following our arrival, there was a call from the pier.

"Hello! Hello! American boat . . . May I invite you aboard for some breakfast." We came topside to find a lean, striking-looking Norwegian man in his early fifties. "Come for French toast. I just learned how to make it from my American visitors. They just left. I think this is quite funny, don't you? American specialty—French toast!"

Thus we met Arne Brun Lie, one of the handful of cruising folks I am interested in ever meeting again, and the one that indeed we have had the good fortune to reencounter and see on a somewhat regular basis. He had put into Kiel to drop off his guests and with better reason than either Chris or myself was reluctant to spend time or money in the city. During the war Arne had been in the Norwegian resistance and had been captured by the Germans. After being beaten and interrogated, he was declared a *"Nacht und Nebel"* prisoner, which meant that the Nazis planned that he would be dead so soon that bureaucratic details like giving him a number were unnecessary. Instead of being summarily executed, he had been sent to Dachau and Natzweiler extermination camps, where he somehow managed to live for three years as most of the others around him died. However we never learned any of this on that first meeting in Kiel. It was only some years later that we heard his story.

That morning in the snug cabin of his lovely *Très Belle* we enjoyed the results of Arne's newly cultivated skills in making French toast. The previous guests from whom he had learned this were Tom Winship, editor of the *Boston Globe,* and his wife, Beth, the advice columnist for teenagers. Chris had just finished a major slide show for the *Globe* a month before. It seemed to be a rather uncanny coincidence, but boats can become small worlds in the best of ways too.

The following day we prepared to enter the Kiel Canal, one of the busiest artificial waterways in the world, which cuts across the base of Jutland between the Baltic and the North Sea. I was extraordinarily nervous confronting our first lock, particularly as I noticed a large tanker and container ship lining up at the entrance too. Just before the locks opened we were informed by a British petroleum tanker that there was another entrance for pleasure craft. The *Baltic Pilot* book, for all of its charming details ("keep to the right and let the devil take the hindmost"), had neglected to mention this second entrance. The lock, however, was a very tame one. The water level only changed three inches. We moved out of the lock, officially entered the canal, and began cutting right through the heart of Schleswig-Holstein, rich fertile farmland dotted with snug little cottages. There was a good deal of traffic—tankers and container ships sailing under flags from everywhere —Turkey, Russia, Poland, Greece, China, Liberia. But the canal was wide and the navigating easy. We stopped our first and only night on the canal in Rendsburg, a lovely old town of cobblestone streets and ancient houses that was Danish before World War I.

The next day we completed our passage through the canal, exiting at Brunsbüttelkoog in the mouth of the Elbe River estuary. We were now sailing along the Frisian coast, the low sandy islands and the coastline of northern Germany and Holland that were celebrated in Erskine Childers's book *The Riddle of the Sands.* Our own first riddle came in the windswept Cuxhaven yacht basin, which consisted of a maze of piers, swirling crosscurrents, and precious little maneuvering space for our long-keeled *Leucothea.* After successfully negotiating a docking in one of the vacant slips facing into the wind, we were accosted by the harbor master, who insisted that we move to a much less accessible spot swept by a strong crosswind. Of course we were blown sideways, fouled our prop on an underwater line, and snapped the flexible couplings to the engine.

We lost a day waiting for parts, but a sympathetic yacht-club member took us on a "grand" tour of Cuxhaven. The highlight of the tour was an ice cream parlor serving twelve-inch sundaes. We left the next day near noon, anxious to get on our way. There was still some current against us, but by two o'clock it turned favorable and we scooted by the dread Scharhörn, the submersible island, which was part of the diabolical plot to kill the hero in *Riddle of the Sands*. The weather was bright and sunny, the wind perfect. We had everything up—twin jibs, main, mizzen, and briefly the mizzen staysail.

Rather than much about with this tricky coastline, we decided to stay well offshore for an overnight sail, thus passing the perilous "roogs"— Wangerooge, Spiekeroog, and Langeoog, as well as Baltrum and Norderney. The wind was good on my watch that night, and I was busy checking the heavy shipping traffic streaming in and around the Elbe delta that leads into Hamburg and other North Sea ports. To complicate matters, although offshore, we still had to be aware of currents that could suck us into the sandy shoal areas. These waters were certainly among the most dangerous anywhere. God forbid I should ever see them in a gale, but the night was calm and the clear black sky pricked out with stars. When I saw that many of the ships were not moving but appeared to be anchored, I turned on the depth sounder and saw that there was only sixty feet of water although we were out of sight of land.

CHAPTER *30*

Of all the landfalls we have ever made, none was more peculiar than Holland. As we approached Delfzijl anticipating our first bit of Dutch coastline, all we could see were miles of beveled concrete walls sloping into the sea at clean angles. One had the sense of approaching a grand fabrication in every sense of the word. Images of chubby-cheeked children in wooden shoes, dairymaids, delft tiles, and sailing barges gasped for life. There seemed to be nothing except for endless miles of beveled concrete dikes. Not even a crack for Hans Brinker. It was a country under concrete wraps, and the only variation of the infinite stretch of dikes was provided by the cubicles for power plants and some large cranes that scratched at the sky. For two hours we chugged up the Eem River toward Delfzijl without a sign of land, trees, or people except for one sailboat that had gone aground on a mud bank. Then behind a breakwater we spotted a thicket of masts. We motored into the grimy little harbor, tied up, changed our clothes, and set off for town. We passed through the concrete curtain via the town water gate that led us down several flights of steps into our first Netherlands village, alive with people, trees, and loads of bright flowers carefully hidden from the sea.

There is nothing so cozy as a Dutch canal, especially when dirty weather is brewing. Now safely and literally "entrenched" away from the sea, Chris and I felt the gale winds at half force, and the thirty-foot fetch did not allow much chop. We could smell a sea scent, but it was incongruously mixed with that of grass, cows, and newly mown fields. Some leaves fluttered onto the surface of the canal, which reflected the cattails, tall grass, and trees that fringed its edge. The banks of the canal were just a foot above the water level, and beyond the banks, visible through openings in the trees, was the sunken farmland, the dikes, and beyond the dikes, the North Sea battering the dangerous Frisian coast we had just escaped.

"There are warnings of gales in Dogger, Forties, Viking, German Bight . . . German Bight force seven to eight north."

For the first time I could listen to the BBC man with some degree of equanimity. I need not smolder as he wished everybody in Viking and German Bight good sailing from the cushy refuge of his broadcasting studio. Chris and I would be in these canals for the next eight weeks as we "sailed" *Leucothea* across Europe to the Mediterranean. So much for weather forecasts, gale warnings, and the Beaufort scale. Bring on the fresh milk, good restaurants, and European scenery. I prepared to navigate strictly by the Michelin stars from here on.

That first morning in Delfzijl we were up early and off to Datema, a paragon of a chandlery shop we had spotted while walking the previous evening. The only chart in our possession was in fact a Michelin road map of Europe and some sketches in guidebooks for the canals. Except for a vague notion of which countries lay between Holland and the Mediterranean, we had no definite plans or ideas of how one got "there" from "here." So we stood in the chart room of Datema, an elegantly simple space bright with the luster of hardwood floors, polished brass fixtures, and sunlight, while Captain Lukas de Vries charted a suggested course for us from Delfzijl to Belgium. We would be able to go as far as Amsterdam with our masts up along this particular route. And we could count on some good sailing where the canals opened up into lakes.

From Datema we went to a string of food purveyors. The wind had turned cool, the skies gray and squally. We were loaded with charts and cheese and light on guilders, so it was time to leave. We boarded *Leucothea*, passed through a lock, and then a tiny drawbridge lifted and we turned our backs on the North Sea, which was ready to snarl. It was August 26, the day the BBC man predicted gales for German Bight.

"Let's have some hot chocolate, Kathy, and listen to the rest of the weather report." I went below. Our gimballed stove sat there steady as a rock. What a delight. This was definitely my kind of sailing. I came back up with the chocolate just as we began to pass through the main street of Groningen, one of Holland's most classical cities in terms of its architecture. Curves of old brick row houses lined the canal banks. Occasionally there would be a break in the row; space would open up; and a stately Dutch mansion guarded by a sweep of willows would appear. Numerous drawbridges spanned the canal, and often two in succession would be handled by the same bridge keeper, who wore a crisp black uniform and cap and would ride a bicycle from one bridge to the next. There was one instance when we threw a bowline around a lamppost by the canal side as we waited for the bridge keeper to peddle the quarter mile between bridges—urban sailing! The Dutch canals kept a fairly leisurely schedule. All locks and bridges shut down between twelve to one PM for lunch and four to five PM for dinner. After eight it was lights out and nothing moved.

The next morning we woke up into a world suffused with that limpid light of the Dutch painters. It silvered the water reeds and made the canal glitter like a tinseled ribbon. A windmill was perfectly framed in our companionway. After a tall glass of the best milk ever, we were off to explore the tiny village of Garnwerd, where we had tied up the night before. We walked up the canal bank and down the other side into a brick village. The brick streets extended right to the edge of the brick houses. There were no sidewalks, nor was there any soil for planting in front of the houses, although the backyards had been turned over entirely to gardening.

We continued later that morning from Garnwerd, and though we were miles inland from the North Sea we found ourselves heeling about fifteen degrees under bare poles. We figured that it must have been blowing at least forty knots at sea. We decided to spend the night in the town of Leeuwarden

Leucothea *tied up on a Dutch canal in the village of Garnwerd.*

tied up along the grassy banks of the public gardens with our masts sticking right up into a huge willow tree. That night we walked to an elegant restaurant a few blocks away and feasted on a spicy turtle crab soup and excellent beef. To return to our boat that evening and then lie in our bunks and listen to the susurrus of the willows rustling in our rigging was a special memory, the full irony of which would be realized only months later during our southern crossing.

There was more sailing as we crossed the Sneeker Meer. We spent one night in the ancient fortified town of Sneek and then headed for the IJssel-meer, formerly the Zuider Zee. Our first stop on the IJsselmeer was Hin-deloopen, which Captain de Vries had marked with two stars and an exclamation point. A tiny doll-scale village as snug as a wooden shoe, this old town was a busy seaport in the sixteenth century, sending out flotillas of the tubby, gaudily painted East Indiamen to Java in the great days of the Dutch East India trade. The town was built mostly of yellow brick, and in the interiors of various homes and stores the walls of this brick juxtaposed beautifully with the jewel-colored tile floors. Laced with canals that were spanned by minia-ture footbridges, the village was a Dutch maze. We walked through it all morning discovering miniature sailing barges, tiny canals painted bright with the reflections of cottages, flower gardens, and trees. Over one arched bridge clomped a young Dutch family, and everybody down to the two-year-old wore wooden shoes.

We had not planned to spend the night in Hindeloppen, but we did and the next morning set off with a following breeze on a diagonal course across the IJsselmeer toward Enkhuizen, where we spent the afternoon wan-dering through the Zuider Zee Museum, which has the definitive collection of sailing barges. One could trace the squat lines and pudgy contours of the East Indiamen directly to the barges, which were clearly designed to spend a lot of time sitting in mud and shallow waters. Shortly after leaving Enkhuizen on our way to Hoorn, we passed through a set of locks that marked the entry to the inner IJsselmeer, which is completely separated from the outer one by a long dike. The water here turned much smoother, and a following wind chased us into Hoorn with our twin jibs pulling mightily. It was a fantastic sail, one of our last before we would have to pull our spars.

Hoorn awaited us in all of its fifteenth-century maritime romance. As we approached the little bridge, we spotted fifteen or more of the most authentic old sailing barges we had seen so far tied up along the massive brick jetty wall. At a bend in the wall loomed a medieval tower. Chris and I did a double take as we caught sight of three Dutch boys in old-fashioned pantaloons and sea caps perched on the wall looking out to sea over the spars of the barges. They were not real boys but bronze ones cast directly onto the brick wall. It was an immediate and involving piece of sculpture in which time collided and reality and art overlapped in a fitting tribute to a seafaring town. Nowhere else did we sense so clearly the direct links to that golden age of sail, navigation, and trade with the Spice Islands than in this ancient town. We might have speculated for which of Hoorn's dazzling inhabitants the bronze boys were scouting the horizon—Willem Schouten, Abel Tasman?

The headwind we had leaving Hoorn gradually shifted around to our quarter. We were going fast, really fast, and as usually happens when we approach full hull speed *Leucothea* started to hum—a high-pitched whine. If you're sitting in the right spots, you can feel all sorts of delicate flutters tracing up through her rudder and spars. We wanted to remember this last sail for several months, as we were just a few miles from Amsterdam now.

CHAPTER *31*

The lock leading into Amsterdam was a horror show, but thanks to the good seamanship and gentility of the barge captains we somehow managed to survive the ordeal. We were packed in with three other barges, each one hundred feet long. We were the last ones in the lock and somehow got turned backward by the prop wash of a barge. While the water was draining out, we were busy throwing lines to people who maneuvered us around again, but we were still not in a great position, risking impalement on the lock doors, which sported a pattern of sharp protuberances resembling something out of a ninth-century torture chamber. This danger would become imminent with the prop wash of all three barges as they started their engines to exit. Chris decided that the only safe answer was to be towed out of the lock by the barge directly in front of us, which really shocked me as Chris had always been adamant about the absolute perils of towing.

"It's get towed or get . . ." and he made an obscene gesture while nodding toward the lock gate eighteen inches behind us. When the fatal moment arrived we braced for the worst. Instead of a deafening roar as the three barges revved up their props, there was only a purr. The word had been passed among the bargemen not to cause undue turbulence. When our tow barge started up, it was with all the gentleness of a mother lion tugging at her cub. Even after we had cast off the lines, the barge pulled away with great restraint, not opening up until he was a quarter mile away.

The drama was not over. Upon our arrival in Amsterdam, we would have to take out our masts if we were to continue on our canal course through Europe. Chris's aversion to boatyards stems I think in part from an experience he had in one near Boston that put in our spars the first year we owned the boat. They managed to curl the top portion of the mizzenmast into a slight C shape by reversing two stays. Ever since this unfortunate event he has stepped both mainmast and mizzen himself. I loathe this activity of doing it ourselves as much as Chris loathes boatyards. Most often I can escape the task because with a good crane and a second person I am not needed.

Unfortunately there was no good crane in the place we were tied up in Amsterdam. This did not faze Chris in the least. We would simply take the boat over to "that bridge" and rig our own apparatus from the bridge and in Chris's words "Lift 'em right out!" I looked at the bridge. He couldn't mean that one. He did mean that one. It was at this moment in our marriage that I realized what a complete nut I had chosen as a mate in life. There was, for starters as my favorite food magazine says, a traffic jam on the bridge. There were cops and stop-and-go lights, and an ambulance trying to get through it all. It was a major artery into Amsterdam, and he was planning to pull out our spars on it. There was no arguing. I made it emphatically clear that in no way, shape, or form were the spars going to be pulled out in this manner. Chris succumbed. I can be compelling when I have to be. He said he would jury rig the broken crane at the spot where we were tied up, but I would have to help and so would Holly, our friend who had arrived that morning, the very same Holly who had pushed me out the door ever so gently for the first crossing. She was staying at the Hotel Gran Krassnapolsky until we got things arranged on the boat for her to move aboard. I called her up.

"Hi. How was your flight?"

"Fine."

"How's the hotel?"

"More krassnapolsky than Gran, but OK."

"Want to come over and help us pull spars?"

"Sure," she replied with cheery innocence. How could I be doing this to my friend?

The best that can be said about our mast-pulling activities is that there were no broken bones, cracked skulls, or hernias, and the masts were not flawed or marred in any way. But for what seemed like hours, the three of us were staggering around like drunks under the weight of the spars. I have an indelible memory of Holly, who is short and not very strong, seeming to sink directly into the ground as we swung the butt of the mainmast onto her shoulders. Luckily a well-set Dutchman walked by and volunteered his services at a crucial point. He and I were wrapped around the mainmast in a passionate embrace while Chris loosened the shrouds. I was tempted to whisper something to Chris about his being a sexual provocateur by choreographing this entanglement with the Dutchman, who was quite attractive, but I was fearful that he would drop the shrouds and the Dutchman and I would be catapulted into oblivion. So instead I asked the Dutchman his name.

Leucothea left Amsterdam in a much-altered form, with both masts reclining horizontally on sawhorses placed amidships, an X-frame on the stern, and a crossbar lashed to the bow pulpit for the butt ends to rest on. We felt in case of collision it was better to have the heavy ends of the masts pointing forward. We had ample head clearance in the cockpit and would still be able to slide easily under the lowest bridges as we measured only three meters in height from the water surface. Our first day out of Amsterdam we spent motoring through lovely residential sections. The canal was quite narrow, and more than once the spinnaker pole enjoyed a whole new life as a barge pole when we sank it into a mud bank and heaved to dislodge *Leucothea*.

On the chart the area we had entered appeared as a latticework of canals. In actuality it was a maze, and instead of shrubbery hedges there were thick bands of river reeds. We were in a nature preserve midway between Amsterdam and Utrecht. It was a place of rarest beauty and exquisite peace. We had pulled into one of a thousand watery alcoves and used our arboreal mooring system of casting a line over a hanging branch. A creeping thicket of raspberries nudged our port rail. There was an inviolable privacy to this one-boat anchorage. We made a dinghy journey to explore the marshland maze and found several other boats tucked away in various cul-de-sacs and offshoot passageways. We returned aboard to enjoy a sunset drink in our cockpit as a flotilla of swans cruised nearby.

One by one we passed under the low arches of the ancient brick bridges that led into the heart of Utrecht. In the darkness of the underpass we would see framed before us in the arc of the next bridge a stretch of canal lined with houses. It was as if the city revealed itself to us through these crescent segments that offered successive but separate views of the old town: a bend in the flagstone quay, a sweep of willows, a waterside café, a cathedral spire against a curve of blue sky. We tied up alongside the quay by a chestnut tree near the center of the city. While we had our dinner on board, the liquid notes of a flute player floated down from the street above and every hour the city clock chimed "Pop Goes the Weasel."

The barge traffic and the number of locks had increased significantly in this southern region of Holland. We became increasingly friendly with the barges and the families aboard as we shared successive locks. In the very early morning, if we were in a lock tied up next to a barge, we might see

Leucothea *approaches the quay in Utrecht.*

the sleepy faces of tiny children peering through the inevitable lace-curtain windows of the stern cabin as father stood at the wheel. Mother, in thick knee socks, housedress, and heavy gloves, lassoed bollards and jumped between barge-and-lock platforms with skill and grace. One day we had to pass through a series of ten or twelve locks and went in the company of a small armada of three barges.

All the locks were rising ones as we were approaching the Dutch-Belgian border. After the gates were closed and lines secured, there would be a turbulent surge as the lockkeeper let in the water. We would brace ourselves, fending off with boathooks and spinnaker poles, guarding with great care the projecting butt ends of our masts.

After the lock had filled, the gates would open and the middle barge, usually the longest, would pull out, allowing the others to file out in sequence. As we became more relaxed about lock maneuvers, I began to notice how well tended the lock areas were. There was always a trim cottage where the lockkeeper lived with his family, and along the flagstone quay were lovely gardens planted with flowers and herbs. One time, while the lock was filling up, I noticed the keeper walk over to the vegetable garden alongside his house and begin to dig potatoes. I cleated the line, climbed up the ladder built into the wall, and bought a couple of pounds of potatoes.

By the end of a ten-lock day, we were quite friendly with our lock-mates. One barge called *Victor* was run single-handedly by a young fellow no more than twenty-five years old. He was a bachelor with no crew at all and amazing to watch in action as he sprinted the one hundred feet from bow to wheelhouse and back again while maneuvering his barge in and out of locks. He invited us aboard at the end of the day. We walked down a short companionway from the wheelhouse to an old-style cabin paneled in rich dark wood with beautiful molding details. The cabin was very reminiscent of the captain's quarters on the *Charles W. Morgan,* but his extensive collection of rock music tapes for whiling away hours at the helm struck a more modern note.

We had by this time switched to the Afgedadmaas, which we thought translated into "dammed-up Meuse." The landscape did change as the broad river swept through rolling countryside in a more natural way, unlike the straight lines of a dug canal. We passed through one lock where we experienced our greatest change thus far in water level, at least six to eight feet, and we began to get the definite impression that we were climbing a stairway into Belgium.

Maastricht appeared ahead of us on the river wrapped in a veil of soft rain like some silent dream of a city. We tied up at the quay just before the ancient bridge that spanned the central portion of the river. The eastern portion had been blown up in World War II by the people of Maastricht in a vain attempt to stave off the Germans. We crossed the bridge to the west and walked into the center of the city, into a swirl of frantic late-afternoon Saturday shoppers. There were myriads of elegant stores and chic women. A street fashion show blossomed out from the glass canopy of a dress shop as spectators formed a ring eight deep to admire the mannequins—Indonesians, Africans, and lean Dutch milkmaids. The broad cobbled pedestrian way whirred with activity. Charcuteries and pâtisseries swarmed with people making last-minute purchases of delectable foodstuffs.

By this time Holly and I were salivating for the stars, the Michelin stars. We had suffered a humiliating rebuff in Amsterdam when we showed up at the first starred restaurant on our route. It was a rainy night, and we arrived in foul-weather gear. The Dutch maître d' with all the arrogance of a French one could not be convinced that under the dripping oilskins were three appropriately clad persons with wonderful palates and great enthusiasm, charming yachtspeople who had sailed all the way from America. Perhaps not directly to this restaurant, but still. It was no deal. He claimed it was because we were without reservations; however, the place hardly appeared to be overflowing, and Holly and I blamed Chris for lacking a tie with his Norwegian sweater.

We planned ahead now. We had called that morning from a town

Holly and Kathy contemplate the next pound.

before Maastricht to make our reservations at the one-star Au Coin Des Bons Enfants. We had carefully plotted our entrance so that in spite of the rain we looked as elegant as possible in our foul-weather gear, and Chris held a last-minute briefing about hiding the flashlight in a handbag. A liberty scarf artfully poked out from the neck of my oilskins. Holly and I had left behind our sea boots and tottered over in heels, which were now soaked but still were serving their function of making us appear tall and "land-dressed" as opposed to squat and foul-weathered. Chris had donned the unthinkable— a tie and jacket. We were greeted, accepted, but Chris nearly was overcome with shock when I asked him to hold the flashlight while the hostess took my coat and Holly refused to part with her blue rubberized wrap. He felt these were unpardonable gaffes considering the pains Holly and I had gone to rehearse everyone for this event. We felt that he overreacted, once our orders were safely placed. The food was excellent, particularly the Norwegian smoked salmon served with a savory horseradish sauce, but the service was rather perfunctory and Mimi Sheraton would have taken them to task in this department.

The next day, Sunday, we wandered through the great stone church of Maastricht, which was a mixture of Romanesque and Gothic and to my mind was not all that satisfying architecturally. That which was Romanesque had been undermined, in spirit at least, by someone who was nuts for barcolage and had been given carte blanche with his paintbrush and gilt to do his thing on the lovely curved arches. Thus the repose and serenity that is so pleasing in Romanesque architecture was shattered by the garish painted decoration.

The effect was jarring. Imagine if those wonderful heavy-bodied, rather monumental figures by Picasso had been dressed in sequins and frothy cascades of lace rather than nothing or the simple chemises he painted them wearing.

Also at Saint Servatius there was a splendid exhibit of priests' robes. Silk thread had been worked into incredible nuances of skin tones so that Christ and many of the apostles, etc., had been depicted in an almost painterly style directly in the cloth. There was the usual display of relics: so-and-so's toenail, a bone chip from Saint Somebody. It is not that I am totally irreverent, but I cannot help but be struck by the peculiarity of the mind and spirit that seeks out and guards this religious memorabilia. And I have to admit that once past the surface grizzliness suggested by such objects to the non-Christian, to wit myself, I am impressed by a certain mysterious beauty of the mind and heart that can make through its faith what is perhaps a chicken-bone fragment into that of a saint. I believe that this kind of faith can perhaps attain a certain level of truth, not necessarily sublime. I mean the earthly day-to-day variety, the kind of truth that propels some through life or if need be across an ocean in a small sailing craft. Keep your pants on, Jerry Falwell, Oral Roberts, and the rest. I am not ripe for conversion at all. I am still Jewish, but in terms of ritual I think of myself as a religious eclectic. So along with my Pepperidge Farm cookies, a few little relics might help, if I could really believe in them.

I could almost see Harold Gatty, the *Raft Book* man, wincing as I stepped onto his life raft with, in addition to the obligatory stick and string, the cookies and Hammett, the mascara and guide to the Cotswolds, I now say, "Just a minute, Harold! You think you know it all; you think that even without any previous knowledge of navigation you can get us to shore. Well, Harold, I've got news for you. Before there is 'previous knowledge' there is something else—faith, buddy." Harold, of course, looks at his stick and string, then at me. I hold up something remarkably similar. "Stick and string?" he asks. "No. Harold, different strokes for different folks." (Not being able to resist a visual pun, I put an oar in the raft's oarlock.) "A piece of hair and a femural shard—relics of Saint Mary Ecstasia Dementia." Harold of course blanches and falls into the open jaws of a shark that's been circling the raft.

Such were my thoughts at Saint Servatius, and Gibraltar and the southern crossing were still miles and months away! I must have given some indication of my mental state to Chris because upon his suggestion from the reliquary we repaired straight to Chez Jacques, a one-star restaurant that was within easy walking distance. Holly and I had entertained the notion of writing an article for a food magazine. In order to be able to sample a variety of dishes, we urged "our companion" to depart from his customary crème caramel for dessert and try the ginger Chantilly. The waiter had described it as candied gingerroot in a sweet cream. It sounded lovely. It looked lovely. As Chris bit into the first chunk, Holly and I watched, ready to hear his response, my brain busy searching for savory accolades. My companion turned pink, then pinker, then vermilion. My companion detonated. His eyes ran with copious tears. He gulped his water, then mine. By the time he was halfway through Holly's, she and I were frantically signaling the headwaiter for a pitcher of ice water. Thus ended our attempts at food writing, blown away by hot ginger. As a postscript I might add that the inspiration for the dessert came from a lady at the next table, a fiftyish porcelain duchess in a Chanel suit who had been eating these seemingly innocuous creamy boules de gingembre with what I can now think of only as frosty equanimity. *"C'est délicieux, Maurice,"* she said and popped another little *boule* into her mouth.

CHAPTER 32

It was fairly easy to repress the specter of an Atlantic crossing within the insulated confines of the canals. Still, every now and then there would be some sort of a reminder or foreshadowing of what was ahead that I found immensely unsettling. It was not long after we had left Maastricht that a little tendril from an Atlantic gale found its way to us and managed to titillate my imagination to force-seven anxiety. We had tied up for the night along an unprotected spot of the canal and in the early morning began catching a lot of wake from passing barges so Chris roused Holly and me from our bunks as he planned to move the boat. As I crawled out of the companionway I felt a definite winter set in the weather. Soon a freezing gale began nicking the air like splinters of glass. When Chris could spare me topside I went below to excavate our North Atlantic heavy weather gear. Not since the Grand Banks had we seen this stuff—red long johns, sweat suits, watch caps. Chris was turning blue in the cockpit and called to me to fetch some additional line from a locker and to come up and steer. While I was steering, Chris, his fingers stiff with cold, tied extensions onto the wheel lines that lash the rudder when we are using the self-steering gear. But the self-steering gear had been in hibernation on deck for weeks now.

I was initially puzzled, but things became clearer to me as I watched Chris thread the line through little bronze half rings farther forward in the cockpit. "Okay," he said as he seized the lines, "you can go below and get warm now." I went down to my bunk and stuffed myself into the arctic sleeping bag—the first time since the North Atlantic. Chris sat comfortably in the companionway, his legs swinging down into the cabin warmed by our stove, his head protected by the dodger, and in each hand a steering line— a set of reins suitable for canals. The Tiny Tot stove was stoked and burning. The radio reported that it was blowing a blistering force nine in the Bay of Biscay, and here we were in a rainy Dutch canal, Holly and I tucked into our sleeping bags sipping freshly brewed tea and eating croissants. She was reading *Sense and Sensibility* and I was wrapped in *The Alexandria Quartet.* There were no locks for a long, long time, and the next day Belgium. I had never felt safer, cozier, more insulated. I put down my book and took a sip of tea. I had just finished reading a description of twilight in the city of Alexandria that was so stunning in its beauty that it was hard for me to believe that anyone could write that well. I put down my book to think about it, at least that's what I thought I was thinking about. I took a sip of tea and looked across the cabin at my good friend Holly. "I'm so scared." She looked up. I didn't have to tell her what I was talking about. She knew.

We continued along the Meuse. After Maastricht there was a stretch where we passed through a gorge thickly encrusted with trees and sided with steep cliffs. It was the most romantic landscape we had seen thus far, and on occasion elegant stone châteaus loomed up on granite promontories. However, as we approached Liège things became abruptly less romantic, in fact downright ugly. One might even say "satanic" and be tempted to hum Jerusalem at the sight of the cement and iron-ore factories that lined the banks and belched lurid clouds of smoke into the air, giving the sky a peculiar, jaundiced appearance. There was a spot along the river where the air was so foul that when I ran my tongue over my lips I could feel a film of fine dusty particles. For the next half mile Holly and I both held scarves over our mouths. The last two hours before Liège the trip was absolutely stygian as the shore was lit with fires from a string of blast furnaces casting a frightful glow over everything.

It became obvious that there were absolutely no pollution controls in or around Liège. The elegant old buildings were black with soot. For the first time we started to see many Communist party posters plastered about. It was quite different from an article we had been reading with the enticing title "The Lures of Liège." In fact the lures were quite few and countable on one hand: the Walloon Museum and a restaurant, Au Vieux Liège. There was also a quaint red-light district where Liègian women sat in thinly curtained windows on the ground floors of buildings. There would be a sign on the front door that said either "ouverte" or "fermée" depending on whether work was in progress or not.

The river went on, and we kept following it eastward. We rounded a mirror—smooth bend, and the citadel of Dinant appeared ahead as if magic rock gates had opened. Late afternoon sun gilded an onion-domed cathedral snuggled against the cliff flanks supporting the fortress. *Leucothea*'s trusty diesel throbbed echoes off the rock walls as we swung around into a three-star mooring spot a few steps from the cathedral square and directly in front of a patisserie that could provide the next day's breakfast. A bed of geraniums bloomed outside our portholes. Holly departed in Dinant to return to home and we continued on our easterly course.

"*Passez! Passez!*" With an unceremonious flick of his hand, the Belgian customs officer flicked us into France. He did not even open our passports or look at the vessel's documentation papers. At Givet, on the French side, it was another story as we encountered the notorious customs man celebrated in Irving and Electra Johnson's book *Yankee Sails across Europe.* It was this particular man who sent them on a two-hundred-mile taxi ride to Brussels for their missing carnet de passage. We were ready—armed with this carnet and a formidable array of documents, enough to titillate the Gallic mania for bureaucracy. However, it was five-fifty-five PM, and the customs man was just piling on his bike with its neat little saddlebags to peddle home. Chris ran up to him. "*S'il vous plaît . . . Je vous en prie . . .*" The entreaties were to no avail. The man pointed to his watch. He could not possibly stamp us in before his dinnertime. We would have to wait until Monday morning. It was Saturday. But that was impossible, Chris exclaimed. Look, there was no place one could even tie up safely here for that long. All right, tomorrow morning at eight, the man said. Not now? Chris asked again. The man held out his hand in a gesture that Chris interpreted as good evening. So he shook the hand limply.

By ten-thirty the next morning the customs man had still not shown up, and Chris was mad. "The hell with this. Let's go." I felt Chris was being quite rash, tempting the French bureaucracy in the worst way. In the United States we had spent weeks writing for all the official documents required for bringing a boat into France; we had posted a three-thousand-dollar bond to guarantee that we would not sell our boat while we were in this country. I protested loudly that just leaving was dangerous and illegal. I didn't like it. We would be *mouillés dos.* Chris, allergic to bureaucracy, said, "Let them find us if they want to see the papers."

Within ten minutes after casting off our lines, my anxieties had evaporated. We had begun the most startlingly beautiful portion of our voyage across Europe—a magical three-day journey through the French Ardennes. Above the river's still surface streaks of mist were suspended, and I kept imagining that we were traveling across the sky rather than up the Meuse. But gradually the fog melted into a milky morning light that blurred detail and reduced the world to the simplest shapes and forms. It was as if we were looking at the mountains and valleys through a gauze screen. It was a quivering world of white shadowy outlines. As the day brightened the screen lifted and the river caught the reflections of the valley's reality. Villages and clouds danced a trembling dance in the black water around *Leucothea.*

The liquid ribbon of a river uncoiled and for three days we followed its winding course through this green-gold bowl of the Ardennes. At dusk we slipped in and out of dark patches where mountains would soar abruptly to paint out the sky and where we were held tightly in the grip of the ridge's shadow cast upon the water. This region was an absolutely enchanted one and for me has always been the most memorable and perfect part of our European cruising: the weather impeccable, the scenery as if painted, and the solitude and peace incorruptible. I remember it as a time of incredible closeness between Chris and myself and as a time when I wrote copiously in my journal contemplating all sorts of heady philosophical matters. I would often discuss what I was writing with Chris. It was the closest we would ever come to being Will and Ariel Durant.

For some reason the shimmering reflections caught by the water and the movement of the river triggered all sorts of ruminations on reality and illusion. From looking at my journals, one would have imagined that I was back in my old undergraduate poetry course steeped in Wordsworth, Yeats, and Eliot. There are in fact little Yeatsian diagrams showing interpenetrating gyres done in my wobbly hand with legends that read river = movement; valley = stasis, followed by a cryptic question: What are valley reflections in river? And then there is a little exegesis on it all. "If you have two interpene-

The liquid ribbon of the Ardennes.

trating motions, there becomes a stasis point at the center so all appears still; thus, on the river, although we keep moving we have an apparent stasis. Is apparent statis reality?"

It amazes me now that I am knee-deep in diapers and car pools that I ever had the time to contemplate reality and illusion while gliding down a river eating pâté. However, what amazes me even more is that in rereading my journal I can perceive things much more clearly, and in reading between the lines I see that what I have always thought to be a string of halcyon days of peace and meditation was not precisely so. I could write all I wanted to about shimmering reflections and the philosophical implications of stasis and movement, but the subtext here had to do with terror and anticipation, with states of suspension and inexorable movement, for ahead lay the ocean, and it was toward that end the river moved us. I desperately wanted to stop the river, halt the boat. This was heaven, says the text. Or was it (as the subtext suggested) a nasty little joke instead, the punchline being the trans-Atlantic crossing? Would the golden image of our days in the Ardennes come to mock me in a gale with a vicious gaiety like the patterned curtains that I had refused to hang. At the time when I was writing in my journal, this was all deeply buried, but when we reached Gibraltar the ten-thousand ugly little heads of my anxiety would have reared and be tossing maniacally. I would be more nervous than I was before our first crossing and full of resentment toward Chris.

The enchantment of the Ardennes ended abruptly at Charleville, birthplace of Rimbaud. I could see why he left. A drab industrial little town, it was a bitter pill to take after the splendor of the valley. Sedan, a few kilometers down the river, was equally lackluster. But even the dingiest French towns have their compensations, and in Sedan we purchased an array of goodies at the charcuterie for a most marvelous picnic that included a creamy pâté de Champagne the texture of velvet. The French pâtés were addictive, and this was the beginning of a 250-gram-a-day habit. It was not hard to ascertain that we were nearing one of the major *gastronomique* regions of France, and indeed when I looked at the guide map Sedan was shown to be not too far from the Vosges, the mountain range that cuts across Alsace and Lorraine.

We were still on the Meuse, also called the Canal de l'Est in this section. We stopped one night in late September at a spot just after the Lorraine town of Inor. The canal carved a lovely half-mile curve at this point. Along the canal on either side were elegant plane trees planted at fifty-foot intervals as far as you could see. On our right was a vast green field where holsteins were grazing and thousands of lavender blooms were scattered across the green. On the left was Inor.

From the distance Inor appeared like a cubic jumble of red-tile roofs and ochre buildings. But early that evening when we took a walk through the village, we discovered that almost everything was new. The couple of buildings that were old had gouges and pockmarks in their walls, and it became apparent that this was one of the towns that had suffered a lot of damage during World War II. As we walked we noticed that Inor seemed to have a certain blankness to it. Streets seemed a bit too wide in proportion to the size of the houses, and the houses had a strange anonymity and facelessness to them. I remembered reading in the Michelin guide that the first invasions of this region by the barbarians occurred in the third century A.D. From then on for the next sixteen centuries, there were invasions as regular as clockwork. There were Huns, French dukes, political bishops, and others. Louis XV had even given Lorraine as a gift to his father-in-law, an old Polish king. As we walked through the tiny town of Inor, its facelessness suddenly made sense and seemed to possess a certain ironic eloquence. It was as if the town desperately sought a kind of anonymity to serve as some sort of protection. It did not want to be noticed. I began to wonder what the children's history lessons in this town consisted of. Did they learn about what their town was like before 1940? 1914? 1870? 1766? 1552? 840? Did it matter?

The blankness was split with a sudden skidding and screeching of tires. There were wild whoops and hollers. A fan of gravel sprayed Chris and me like bullets, and out of the dust swirled a little demon boy on his bike. He was skidding around us, popping wheelies, sometimes riding with no hands, incising the street with wildly carved turns, in short running the entire gamut of an eight-year-old's repertoire on a bike. *"Madame! Madame! De quel pays êtes-vous?"*

We continued through Lorraine. We endured our first real scrape with a barge since entering the canals in Holland. *Leucothea* was sitting with her tail firmly implanted in the mud one hundred yards from a lock entrance while we were waiting for the lock to disgorge a barge. We were within the *limite de stationnement* by a few yards, too close, in other words. When the barge exited at full throttle, the strong current that flowed back from its bow as it passed us swung our bow out into the middle of the canal, while our imbedded stern acted as a pivot. I watched in fascinated horror as *Leucothea*'s bow moved in a steady sweep toward the midships of the barge. The butt ends of our masts, resting on sawhorses, were aimed squarely at her. There was a bump . . . another bump.

A torrent of blistering French came from the bargeman as he blasted out of the wheelhouse. A third bump knocked down their clothesline. Chris and I madly tried to fend off the black leviathan from our masts with our absurd little boathooks. Both of us, meanwhile, were torn with fear of having lost our "ticket" back across the Atlantic. Imagine being dismasted in a French canal! Maybe we could call it an emasculating war wound and rename our boat *The Sun Also Rises*. After an agonizing minute that seemed like five, the collision was over. Chris was at the helm. I feebly made my way to the bow to examine the masts. Not a scratch! Just a curl of black paint scraped from the barge. Next time both ears and the tail, I thought. On to Verdun.

CHAPTER *33*

Seven kilometers outside of Verdun there was a deep lock with a change in water level of ten feet or more. In such a case you can never see much of the world above until the water has risen three or four feet. The water began to gush in. We felt the familiar surge backward and then the line went taut. *Leucothea* began to rise out of the dank slimy chamber. The peak of the lockkeeper's house appeared, then the attic window, a door; a few shabby potted plants sat at the base of the house; then beyond the house a row of little white crosses marched into view. The more we rose, the more crosses appeared until the low hills and land seemed to be undulating with an ocean of these white crosses. They lost their definition entirely and became strange chalky ciphers on a blank landscape where hundreds and thousands of men had died during the World War I siege.

We had dinner that evening at the Hotel Bellevue, possessor of one shaky Michelin star. I had truite au champagne, which although perfectly acceptable was not outstanding. The country pâté, however, was texturous and redolent. I had been scouring my brain for appropriately descriptive phrases when I saw a lady two tables away order it for her companion— a Pekingese, the canine variety as opposed to a human resident of Peking. The single star in the Bellevue heavens started to shake violently for me. The dog, dressed in a little knitted jacket and a pink bow in its bangs, or whatever you call that fur that flops between its eyes, apparently found the pâté as redolent and texturous as I did. Her mistress ordered her (him?) seconds, something my master did not do, with extra *cornichons,* which she fed to him (her?) by hand. Chris didn't do that either.

We had our own *petit* siege of Verdun. We had tied up next to a lovely city park by a walking path. There were no other boats tied up there, but it seemed quiet and pretty, clear of barge traffic, and was walking distance to the restaurant. Sound asleep in our bunks after dinner, we were awakened by voices along the path. It sounded like several young fellows who had had a night on the town. They paused beside *Leucothea* and in loud voices talked about our boat, wondering where we came from and what kind of boat it was. We lay very still in our bunks, and although they could not see in, we could see their legs through the cabin windows. I counted five men in khaki pants and boots. They continued to talk very loudly; they were obviously drunk. They walked a few paces, stopped, then rapped sharply on the doghouse. "*S'il vous plaît!*" shouted Chris. They laughed harshly. I saw a leg swing over the lifelines. The boat heeled over. They were aboard. Or at least one was aboard. We felt incredibly vulnerable. Chris hopped into his pants and stuck his head out the companionway. I listened frozen in the bunk below.

Chris: *S'il vous plaît. Nous voulons dormi.* (Please, we are trying to sleep.)

Boarder: *Dormir.* (Leave it to the French to correct your grammar at a time like this.) There were a few more exchanges. The voices of the men became harsher and filled with a cruel self-assurance. I could hear Chris's voice constricting in quiet rage. Things were escalating.

"*Va t'en!*" (Get out) Chris repeated.

"*Combien de vous?*" (How many are you?) countered a voice. It was the lead-up to a challenge. What the hell would he say? "*Je ne comprends pas.*" (I don't understand.) They repeated the question. The stalling technique could not go on forever. Chris had picked up our kitchen knife behind his back. I started thinking furiously. Another leg swung over the lifelines. "*Monsieur!*" Chris packed a lot of rage into a word that naturally sounds mushy. It became instantly clear. I would go up and absolutely blitz them to distraction with my execrable French all delivered very sweetly. Bad French was not hard for me, and it seemed to be their Achilles' heel. My hope was that they would become consumed with trying to understand my French, shot through with my Hoosier accent and spoken only in the present tense. After a couple of drinks I've been known to speak only in infinitives, failing to conjugate verbs altogether. I hopped into my jeans.

"*Ah, bonjour!*" (It was *soir.*)

"*Bonsoir, mademoiselle,*" responded one thug.

"*Madame,*" quickly corrected the other thug. There was not a trace of harshness. I knew we could win. In a small whispery voice I delivered my speech: "*Je ne comprends pas beaucoup francaises et votre pays plaît-moi très. Et aussi les francaises et cette bateau est nôtre maison et maintenant passe minuit.*" (I don't understand much French and I like your country a lot and also the French people and this boat is our home and now it is past midnight.)

They were having to bend over to hear me. I had to repeat things, but it didn't really matter. They were mesmerized by the sweet jumble that issued forth. One leaned toward me. "Listen, Madame," he said in French and continued to explain drunkenly about how they were in the army and had only five days left. *"Cinq jours, c'est fini,"* he repeated. And it was *"fini"* all of a sudden. We sang the "Marseillaise." We shook hands all around, and they trotted off into the darkness. Chris and I slumped onto the bunk below, then proceeded to sit bolt upright for the rest of the night, hermetically sealed into the cabin with every hatch battened down tight. It was awful.

All one day we had spent descending into the Moselle Valley. There was a lock almost every two hundred meters as we stepped our way down to Nancy. But it was a three-star city in the Michelin and not to be missed, thanks to the building passion of Stanislaus Leszczyńska, father-in-law of Louis XV and dethroned king of Poland. The canal did not cut through the city but skirted the east side, which was rather industrial and served barges. We tied up near the coaling station at Saint Catherine's basin. From here it was a short walk to one of France's most elegant cities.

The centerpiece of Nancy is the Place Stanislas, which one enters through magnificent wrought-iron gates festooned with gilded curlicues. Five grand Palladian buildings flank the immense central space, each one gleaming white with appliquéd pilasters and heroic statutes soaring from their cornices. The fronts of the buildings are embroidered with wrought-iron balconies. There was a marvelous geometry and balance to the place with no monotony. It was so very rich and elegant that as Chris and I sat in the sidewalk café I felt as though I were in the midst of a phalanx of wedding cakes.

Nancy bears the imprint of the art nouveau movement. Sinuous lines and convoluted forms crop up everywhere—building façades, windows, grillwork, furniture. Even the pastry shops seemed to have adapted the art nouveau motifs for decorating cakes that were glazed luxuriously and then inscribed with delicate scrolls of chocolate. We visited the Musée de l'École de Nancy, which I had read about in my winter's research in *Gourmet* magazine. The museum was a fascinating repository of the very best of art nouveau furniture and objects. There were breathtaking examples of pastel stained glass and unbelievable furniture with ornamental work that can only be described as painting in wood. The craftsmen had managed to incorporate all the sinuous organic forms of nature using small slices of inlaid wood. Whole stories mostly based on mythology showing gods and goddesses, horses and satyrs, clouds and lightning had been not carved but inlaid with contrasting kinds and grains of wood so that at first glance a piece might appear to have been painted until one looked closer and realized that the swirl had not come from a painter's brush or a chisel but the grain of the woods itself. All of the furniture had an unexpected lightness. Supports for a desk or tabletop would often be slender curved legs or elegant parabolas of wood that allowed the piece to almost float in its space.

Unlike the author of *Gourmet*'s article, it was not the piano with its *Mort du Cygne* and contorted legs that "undid" me. It was the bed in the master bedroom, a piece called *L'Aube et le Crépuscule*. The headboard was inlaid with a giant moth of sleep that hovered over the occupants' heads dusting them with inset jewel fragments—the dust of drowse. The swirling wood grain provided the clouds, with a suggestion of a village or landscape beneath in a contrasting grain. It gave the effect of the multiple overlay images of dreams. The foot of the bed showed dawn with a great candy-colored opaline, set in a sunburst of inlaid wood. I liked the master bathroom too. The tub was set on an altar of sorts, and the whole thing was decorated with a scramble of glazed terra-cotta forms—cupids, bosoms, leaves, and fannies ran riot.

We followed in the *Gourmet* writer's footsteps to the Capucin Gourmand and enjoyed our most memorable meal thus far en route. We had a velvety duck soup followed by rack of lamb and finally a walnut-and-chocolate génoise cake that was (to hell with *Gourmet*) orgasmic.

We were getting plumper and plumper. However, I knew that the world's most effective reducing spa lay in wait for me in the Atlantic, six weeks from now.

From Nancy the Marne-au-Rhin Canal began. After the soda plant just outside the city, the scenery once again became quite rural, with lovely broad green expanses of clover. Far in the distance across one of these fields loomed the flamboyant Gothic twin towers of the grand Basilique of Saint Nicholas.

Leucothea *on the Marne-au-Rhin heading toward Strasbourg.*

I was becoming quite attached to this business of sighting Gothic towers in the morning mist rather than whistle buoys in a Bay of Fundy fog. The peaceful river rhythms with the wonderfully quite landscapes and locks at decent intervals were for me. One morning I noticed that a spider had spun a web around our masthead where it rested on the sawhorses. Had *Leucothea* really forgotten the sea? I had not.

CHAPTER 34

Climbing up and down mountain ranges in *Leucothea* during our travels thus far in France, we had encountered some truly remarkable navigational oddities. For example, at the town of Liverdun we traveled in a canal bridge filled with water suspended over the Moselle River. At another point we tunneled in darkness through a mountain one-and-a-half miles while I sat on the foredeck with a flashlight, bouncing the beam off the walls and calling off the clearances to Chris. He steered by lining up the masts, which rested side by side on the sawhorses, with the pinprick of light at the tunnel's end and forming a kind of rifle site. There was no other point of reference in the darkness.

But by far the most wondrous sequence of navigational events awaited us at the summit of the Vosges before descending to the Rhine. First we came to what appeared to be the end of the canal with a mountain spanning across it presenting an eighty-foot face of solid granite. "What do we do now?" I asked. Chris was busy looking at the charts to see if we had taken a wrong turn and had entered a dead-end section of the canal. But then, when we were within three hundred feet, a little black door appeared smack in the middle of the mountain wall. When we were within fifty feet, the black door silently swung open, and there beyond was the Wizard of Oz. No, but I would not have been surprised.

Interpreting the open door as a signal to enter, we putted into a chamber that was totally black with slime. The walls soared to an astonishing fifty or sixty feet. There were no other boats and no lockkeepers visible. The doors swung shut, and just as I was beginning to think that we had discovered a new circle of Dante's *Inferno*, enormous black bubbles began to gurgle up around *Leucothea* in gentle profusion. We were being lifted to the top in some sort of gorgeous hydraulic dream. At the top was a tiny lockhouse, not visible from below, from which a little man leaned out and waved, his face full of merriment, obviously enjoying our stunned countenances over this fantastic trick that he played daily. *"Bonjour. Vous êtes arrivés!"* We had

In a moveable bathtub,
we slide down
the inclined plane.

indeed arrived at the summit. For several hours we putted through the canal, which followed the mountain crest. To port was a sheer drop of three hundred feet into a valley. We were actually more than six hundred feet above sea level.

At the end of the summit we passed into another lock—a gigantic bathtub with an openable end suspended on the side of a mountain. When the gates were closed and the signal given, away we went, sliding down the inclined plane in our movable bathtub at a gentle parade pace. We got off *Leucothea* during our two hundred-foot slide, walked on the sidewalks of the tub, looked at our boat, waved to each other, and watched the mountain rise up to starboard as we slid into the Alsatian Valley below. We spent the night in the village of Lutzelbourg, which looked more like a Tyrolean ski village than a harbor town.

Two days later we arrived in Strasbourg, winding our way through the ancient city with its lovely canal buildings of stucco and half timber. For the first time since entering the European canal system in Holland, we could feel a fairly strong current under our keel—a hint of the Rhine. We turned right off the main canal into the smaller river Ill, passed the twin-spired Saint Paul's Church to starboard, and tied up at the side of a former lock where there was a lawn and lovely flower beds. It was at this very spot that we met one of our all-time favorite boatie families—the Craig Hoods from Vancouver, British Columbia.

Craig Hood and his three young daughters (Tammy, Tracey, and Trixie), all of whom helped us tie up and get settled, were going through Europe on an enormous power boat that resembled a floating tennis court more than anything else. We were invited for dinner that night, which was quite delicious and prepared by Tracey, age twelve, with the aid of Tammy, age ten. Trixie was on shore collecting chestnuts from a nearby tree to sell to unsuspecting tourists. Craigie held forth on deck in a somewhat raggedy upholstered wing chair and explained that the peculiar vessel upon which we were now enjoying the cocktail hour was only a means to an end. They had spent the previous winter in Guernsey on their sailboat, which he had fixed up so nicely that someone made him an irresistible offer. He hoped to get another sailboat once out of the canals. In the meantime they were quite content with their present mode of travel. "The girls do the cooking, and I drive the boat and keep the tricks of this canal navigation a deep dark secret." At midnight we all tiptoed off to see a water rat that Trixie, the six-year-old, had spotted.

We spent three days in Strasbourg, where my parents joined us to continue the rest of the way through France to the Mediterranean. After leaving Strasbourg and entering the canalized Rhine, which would take us to the Doubs Valley, we encountered the toughest part of our cruise so far. We were on this particular segment of the Rhine for two days, and it proved to be a real horror show: fast-moving current, many immense barges, and the gigantic locks. Neither the lockkeepers nor the barges were used to small boats or yachts, and we had several close calls. There was a good deal of screaming between us and recalcitrant or blithely ignorant lockkeepers and barges who knew nothing about the handling of small boats. Some turned on their props full blast in our faces as we tried to enter crowded locks or insisted that we would be perfectly safe exiting a lock simultaneously while scrunched between two-hundred-ton barges.

During one death-defying incident we were sucked into the flanks of a barge which refused to turn off its 800 hp engine while we were entering the lock. We managed to get free suffering only a squashed stanchion, but we were immediately swung crosswise in the lock between the props of both barges on either side of us. We yelled and screamed at them to turn off their engines to no avail. We had no way to control the boat against the tremendous force of the two prop washes. People on all the barges were shouting instructions to us in a mélange of French, German, and Dutch. No one, however, thought of turning off the offending props. The lockkeeper, some thirty feet above, came out of his house and made a symphony of totally incomprehensible gestures that mainly consisted of flailing his arms about and alternately hugging himself. Finally, in a fit of angry self-preservation, we turned ourselves about and left the lock. We were furious over the schizoid instructions. They then began to address us in German over the loudspeaker. In an attempt to put me ashore on the sloping concrete banks to visit the lockkeeper and negotiate, I slipped and fell into the river. I managed to scramble up the bank and slogged my way up to the lockhouse. My first announcement was "speak French." We then sat down, and I explained to them the impossibilities of our entering a lock safely in a boat our size with everyone else's engines churning away. At last they understood and were most courteous. They promised to order all engines off when we entered.

Everything went fine in the lock. The exit, however, was not so smooth, as they decided that the barge whom we were tied to should exit first. Somehow we managed to untie ourselves from them before they dragged us off. We tied up to another barge that was still stationary as the exiting barge's propwash struck, and we proceeded to fend off madly on all sides. It was like square dancing with elephants.

By the time we got out of the lock, it was dark. It looked bad ahead for tying up as all the banks were concrete slopes swept by wakes. The night was thick with fog and the huge leviathans chugging by us. We finally found a barely adequate place alongside another barge. We were all aching with tension. I was almost crying, and yes, at last actually yearning for the open sea.

The next morning we were up at the first turn of our host barge's diesel and were off for another day of calisthenics on the canalized Rhine. It was not so horrible as the first day but no great fun by a long shot. We finally finished this portion of the Rhine when we turned off at Niffer and went through a smaller lock with a lockhouse designed by Le Corbusier. The gang at the lockhouse was a charming bunch. We had to clear customs here as the canalized Rhine went through parts of Germany. Luckily nobody asked about our original entry into France. The customs man was a Rabelaisian fellow who wanted to see *"tous les papiers."* He adored our international registration for our Hong Kong–built Cheoy Lee, savoring every figure that indicated the boat's measurements, date of construction, etc. *"Oooh, la la!"* he would exclaim as he came upon some fascinating little detail on the form —a real gourmand of documents. He reveled in the seals and the embossed stamps on the orange US Coast Guard documentation form, read aloud the small print, the typed-in information, letting exotic words like "oil screw" and "fiberglass" roll off his tongue. He looked up at Chris to ask his name. *"Votre nom, monsieur? Ah, voilà!"* he said, looking on the form where *Leucothea* was built: "Kowloon. Monsieur Kowloon."

CHAPTER *35*

We were now in the smaller canals once more, and for three days we traveled through freezing-cold rains, glad only that we weren't in the Bay of Biscay, where a severe gale was reported. The towns slipped by: Mulhouse, Dannemarie, Valdoie. We had been in a section known as the staircase of the Jura mountains. Every one hundred meters there was a lock, and rain was pouring down. This was tough going, especially for Chris and my father, who insisted on doing all the work at the locks while my mother and I stayed dry below. In one day we went through thirty-one locks, but it got us to the Gorge de Doubs.

The fields that next morning were quivering platinum with dew bright in the light. The rain had finally stopped, and we were on the river's way early with a three-knot current sliding us down the black liquid ribbon from patches of white sunlight to dark shadows cast by the mountains. The terraced fields climbed up at gentle angles to port, and to starboard granite cliffs curled around the river's bends. In our guidebook I discovered a one-star Michelin restaurant at Baume-les-Dames, a perfect stopping point for the night. We tied up in a beautiful rural anchorage just walking distance from the little valley town. At the restaurant that evening we enjoyed one of our most splendid meals, which included *terrine des escargots* and *poulet Bresse* in a sauce of *morilles*. My mother had quenelles as a first course, and they were exquisite. It was all served expertly in cozy but unpretentious surroundings, and when we left, the chef came out to shake hands and thank us for stopping by in our boat.

Our lazy voyage through the Doubs Valley continued, and I found this ironic entry in my journal: "The Gorge de Doubs is spectacular this morning. The river valley twists and bends with all the curves of a chambered nautilus. Why do I use this sea image in the midst of this pastoral perfection? Am I secretly yearning for the sea in this green pocket of tranquillity? Hold onto your hat, journal, here comes a labored metaphor: Am I the oyster in need of a grain of sand to make the pearl? I better stop writing this stuff, or I think I might throw up."

We stopped at the elegant citadel city of Besançon. It was a city of extraordinary charm, with narrow streets and tall ancient buildings of simply but elegantly dressed stone. It was a city I loved immediately. The proportions were just right, the width of the streets to the height of the buildings, the way the cool gray shadows would bathe one street and then around the corner there would be blinding white light where the sun had pierced between cupola and spire to light a tiny square. There was a cool green park where we had tied up. My mother and I took a memorable walk, just the two of us through these streets. We came upon an irresistible patisserie. The windows were enchanting, with pewter bowls filled with chocolate. Inside, the shop itself was like a chocolate mosaic with its dark wood paneling and coffee, white, and brown tile floors. There were small wicker baskets on one counter displaying chocolates and wrapped candies. In one corner there was a tiny cold cabinet with pineapples and oranges stuffed with ice cream. We ordered coffee and pastry—a little fig-shaped confection the outside of which was green-tinted almond paste, the inside crème pâtisserie. Mother and I ate them savoring every bite, and we talked about food and an old boyfriend of my mother's from the year 1924.

From Besançon we continued on to Dôle and then Saint Jean-de-Losne, where the Doubs ended and the Saône River began, which would take us south into Lyons.

Saint Jean was our first town in the Burgundy country. The architecture began to look more Romanesque, and in the hot brilliant sunshine Chris declared that he felt "something Mediterranean" in the air. A hint perhaps of the perpetual summer we expected to be following from then until Christmas and our landfall in the eastern Caribbean. My father, however, sniffed another bouquet in the air—wine. We were only thirty-five kilometers from Beaune and Nuits-Saint-Georges. One hour later we were whizzing

M. Moillard welcomes us to his vineyard. Nuits-Saint-Georges, France.

through the wine country with M. Moillard, owner of the Moillard vineyards, at the wheel of his Mercedes. On the left we could see the expanses of golden vines that flared in the bright October sunlight—the celebrated Côtes-de-Nuits, also called the Côtes d'Or for their golden color. M. Moillard stopped the car in front of some big iron gates and officially welcomed us to his little piece of this gold—eighteen hectares of the most valuable vineyards on earth. From the vineyards we went to his plant, driving through the slopes of vines and passing such hallowed names as Romane Conti, la Tache, and Richebourg. At his plant, we began our tour of the caves, which culminated in a visit to one located beneath his office that was three hundred years old. We were led through labyrinthine corridors, dank, cool, growing with mosses and the most grotesque fungi. Finally he led us up a staircase to his office. "Now what can I offer you?" he asked in French: "Champagne, burgundy, cassis?" M. Moillard left briefly and then returned with a dusty unlabeled bottle of 1950s burgundy resting in a wicker basket and five goblets. The wine was unforgettable.

Winding down the Saône, we were proceeding toward the center of France's most famous gastronomic region. Just outside of Lyons we found that the best local tie-up spot was directly across the street from France's most celebrated chef's restaurant—Paul Bocuse. A twenty-minute drive from here was the restaurant of Alain Chapelle, and within twenty-four hours we had formed a constellation in terms of eating—six stars. If we had our choice we would not have aspired to such astronomic gastronomy in such a short period, but it was the middle of October and we felt it essential to get to the Mediterranean as soon as possible. We had a date in early November to meet our crew for the southern crossing at Gibraltar.

At Lyons we would join the Rhône River and descend with it to the Mediterranean through the Midi country. The Rhône is still a turbulent untamed river for the first sixty kilometers below Lyons, so we decided to take a pilot familiar with the route rather than risk damage to *Leucothea* on rocks that had never seen salt water. Careful reading (sometimes between the lines) in Electra Johnson's account, *Yankee Sails across Europe,* convinced us to avoid a well-known pilot and the hazards of any form of towing.

Our pilot planted himself firmly behind the *Leucothea*'s wheel and lit up one Gauloise after another. Chris explained our "ground" rule of no towing and that we would handle the boat in docking and lock maneuvers. After a few uneventful kilometers Chris asked the pilot how he came to know the river so well. He replied, "I was born on it." Pressed for further details, he said he had been on boats all his life and showed us a hand missing a finger to prove it. The current became stronger, and soon we were whistling down through the Rhône wine country at eighteen kilometers an hour compared to our normal ten. Although beautiful the countryside did not feel particularly friendly as the banks were rocky and swept by current, offering no cozy spots to tie up and explore the intriguing châteaus and Roman-looking towns. About lunchtime an empty barge swept past us. The skipper seemed to wave in a strange way to our trusty pilot, who let go the wheel to make a series of gestures back. I gathered that the people of the river used some sort of sign language as it was impossible to hear over the throb of engines.

Around the next bend we spotted the same barge tied up headed upstream. Our pilot announced that we were to pull alongside the barge, allowing him to get aboard it, and that they would tow us for the next thirty kilometers to the end of the wild part of the river. Chris stared at the pilot waiting for his French to catch up with his anger. He reminded the pilot that we had hired him, and that we would not allow ourselves to be towed. The pilot replied that the man on the barge had never been down this stretch of river before and needed help. A compromise was agreed on allowing the pilot aboard the barge with *Leucothea* to follow, not under tow, and the barge to maintain a slow speed so we could keep up. A strong wind was blowing, and the current was almost equal to *Leucothea*'s cruising speed, making the transfer difficult, but the pilot disappeared over the rail of the barge complete with beret, Gauloises and his paper-bag lunch. We kept cruising power on, heading upstream, but we were gradually swept down by the current as we waited for the barge to get under way. He pulled into the current but was unable to turn downstream because of the weathervane effect of the wind on his unloaded hull.

We were swept around a bend out of sight. A constriction in the river appeared below us, a small rapids made by some construction on a new dam. We were approaching it backward. Chris decided to forget about our erst-while pilot, turn around, and continue down the river using the charts we had. His experience in white water kayaking proved useful in spotting the fast water that is usually deepest. We relaxed as the dam project was astern and we were swinging down the river at a pleasant pace. We consoled ourselves that at least we hadn't paid the pilot in advance. A few miles before we reached the end of the tricky section, our pilot and his barge appeared again. We followed them for the last few miles until he rejoined us, collected his fee, and hopped off at the next town. We were glad that no other pilots would be needed on our voyage home, unless we detoured through the Panama Canal.

The next day's run to Arles was very long with no good intermediate stopping point, so we were up before first light. Looking out the hatch, we saw that thick fog had settled in the valley. The first arch of the bridge overhead disappeared into nothingness twenty-five yards away. Chris figured that it would probably burn off, but if we didn't start now we would be caught by darkness before Arles. The first ten miles looked easy enough on the chart with the channel marked by posts about one hundred yards apart and a lock at the end. We set off with the engine running dead slow and my father acting as lookout up on the bow. Compass course on a river! Moisture dripped from our foul-weather gear as we peered nervously ahead. The bridge disappeared astern. After endless minutes the shore appeared dimly to starboard, and we followed along to the first marker, passed it, and plunged into the mist again. The markers were too close together to plot a separate course for each, so Chris estimated each course until the marker melted out of the fog ahead. Our summers of Maine cruising paid off.

After about twelve kilometers the sun broke through from a swirl of mist like a Turner painting, and a gasoline barge churned past heading upriver. The rest of the day went like clockwork, with a larger French yacht sharing each lock with us. He was faster and arrived first at each lock so that the gigantic gates would swing shut promptly after we pulled in behind him. At the highest lock in the world we passed our camera to one of the Frenchmen so we could have a picture of *Leucothea* dwarfed by the ninety-foot vertical drop. Our feelings toward France and Frenchmen improved from the nadir of the previous day's problems as we admired the futuristic engineering of the lock and chatted with the keeper who bicycled out to talk with us. We were pleasantly close to Arles as the sun set. Medieval and Roman ruins caught the last golden rays, and the Mediterranean was only a single day's run away.

After the rigors of the Rhône we spent a couple of days recuperating in Arles and the environs. We rented a car and drove through the wild Rhône delta area known as the Camargue, where herds of white horses run freely over the wide plains. We also visited Nîmes and attended a bullfight. We lasted one bull. But after two days, and knowing the Mediterranean was within striking distance, we took off. At Port-Saint Louis-du-Rhône, we stepped our masts and became an honest sailing boat again for the first time in over eight weeks. We had a brisk sail to Marseilles, and even I had to admit that the old familiar forces of the wind's interplay with us were welcome after nearly two months of the diesel's throb.

Marseilles, which has been celebrated for everything from its bouillabaisse to its prostitutes, I did find undeniably exotic, although its metabolism was a bit frenetic after the serenity of the canal villages. We shopped in the outdoor market that offered the bounty of Provence as well as the redolent spices of North Africa. We ate in restaurants with names like Café

New York and Hanoi, and we scoured the ship chandleries for needed equipment.

My parents decided that as long as they had come this far, they would make the hop with us to the Balearic Islands. We all set off from Marseilles under bright blue skies with a lively northwest wind. By three that afternoon it had increased to gale force and we were quite uncomfortable, yet the skies in some sort of perverse defiance still smiled brightly. We braced for a hard night. I was tense and very worried about the weather and my parents, who after all were almost seventy.

We soon discovered an inordinate amount of water in the bilges. While Chris explored the source of the leak, I looked back at Marseilles. Her chalk cliffs appeared through the spume. The harbor was fifteen miles away dead against the wind. Ahead was open sea; to the east Cassis was a twenty-five-mile beat. Some choice on a darkening afternoon. Chris found that the source of the leak was the flaps around the rudder quadrant where water could squirt through in heavy seas, which we were definitely having. The added weight of the new diesel made the stern ride lower than it had on the northern crossing. This was a relief to all of us and we kept on top of it by pumping every hour.

The wind increased, and the seas mounted stupendously—a very touchy place, this Mediterranean. The wind force, which was six or seven, did not warrant waves of the magnitude we were seeing. Chris and I sat in stunned silence looking at these creatures. They were not at all like the giant Atlantic rollers but were short and steep and came at all sorts of weird angles to ambush us. They had a strange period with no rhythm and built up fast. It was really dangerous on deck. My dad and I shared the evening watch while poor Mother lay strapped into a bunk below, quite sick. I went down to peel her off the bunk and help her to the head as it was so rough she could not make it by herself. Being below did not improve my health, and soon Mother and I were sharing a bucket for our seasickness, passing it back and forth between the head and the main cabin. I finally went up and promptly got sick again over the side. Remembering the fabulous bouillabaisse I had enjoyed less than twenty-four hours before, the sudden irony of this moment struck me full force as I recalled a florid piece in *Gourmet* in which the author described the true Marseilles bouillabaisse as having "all the flavor of the incoming tide." You'll have it tomorrow, I thought.

The wind continued in shrill determination all night like some raging Mediterranean virago. At four AM it finally lessened. We had a clear day of reasonable breezes. That night the sky was webbed with starry configurations. Toward dawn the wind shifted to southerly and increased. We were in for it again, with a rapid unaccountable buildup in the seas. We had picked up two lighthouses of Minorca, and at about ten AM we rounded the headlands in very choppy waters and slipped into one of the world's most magnificent natural harbors. We followed a fjordlike cut over which Lord Nelson's dark red villa commanded the view. It was easy to understand the appeal the harbor held for Nelson, not to mention my mother, who was still feeling weak but relieved. After I had helped her topside for some fresh air, she turned to me and said: "Kathy, remember the time you were a little girl and threw up in my pocketbook at Niagara Falls? Well, I forgive you."

CHAPTER 36

"My God, you guys don't look so great!" That was what Nat Barrows, our third crew member for the crossing, said as Chris and I staggered into his room at the Rock Hotel in Gibraltar. Nat and his friend Ann Bradshaw who was to go with us as far as the Canary Islands, had been waiting several days for us to get in. It would be a few more days before we could continue as there were a myriad of details needing attention before we set off on the thirty-seven-hundred-mile Atlantic crossing ahead.

It had been a bad two and a half weeks. We had left the Balearics and my parents to sail down the east coast of Spain and had encountered nothing

Mal de mother. Hortense feels the mistral.

but headwinds, high seas, and fluke storms. On three separate occasions we had been blown back fifteen, thirteen, and twenty miles. One afternoon, an example of how weird things got, we had just made a point against a light headwind and were turning inward to cross the four-mile stretch of water into the port of Almería. The first icy tendrils of the wind curling down from the snowcapped mountains served as teasers. Chris cast a wary eye. "Wind's picked up slightly. Glad we made that point. Would you get my jacket?" I went below to fetch it. Just as my feet hit the cabin sole, I felt the boat nearly stop and then begin to rock as we lost way. Within five seconds, forty knots of headwind had exploded in our faces. Smashed against a wall of icy wind and rain, *Leucothea* staggered like a dazed contender in the ring with a heavyweight champion. The avalanche of frigid air crashed down from the icy Sierra Nevadas, whipping the water white around us. Within thirty seconds we were both soaked. As we squared off for the confrontation, Chris shouted for me to dig out the safety harnesses. Things were looking mean. The sky had darkened into a big purple bruise; the seas foamed up like mad dogs. Slamming into each wave, *Leucothea* moved slowly through a tunnel of frigid spray. We were going to the "Land of the Dead" where "the river of flaming fire and the river of lamentation unite around a pinnacle of rock."

"That's what Homer called this part . . . the whole run from here down to Gibraltar. Remember? When we were reading the *Odyssey*. It's all called the Land of the Dead in here," Chris offered. I remembered, all right. Wonderful, I thought. These delightful sobriquets for where we now were did little to lighten my spirits. I grumbled something to myself. "What?" Chris was trying desperately to keep the conversation going in the face of this new onslaught from the elements. "What?" he yelled. "What did you say?"

Yelling over the noise: "I said Penelope was no dumb bunny."

"What do you mean?"

"She stayed home."

"Well, I suppose that's one way of looking at it."

I couldn't believe that Chris still wanted to talk. He was going to come back with some perky rejoinder. "Look!" I growled. "I don't have to talk to you. This isn't some goddamn cocktail party. Now just shut up. I'm too cold to talk."

"My child, how did you come here under the western gloom, you that are still alive. This is no easy place for living eyes to find. For between you and us flow the wide waters of the Rivers of Fear, and the very first barrier is the ocean, whose stream a man could never cross on foot, but only in a well-found ship." That is what Odysseus's mother said to him when he arrived at more-or-less Gibraltar. So when Nat told us we looked awful, I

Southeastern coast of Spain.

knew what he meant. But he couldn't know how glad we were to get there.

The forbidding southeastern coast of Spain had been less than inviting, its landscape scarred with Miami Beach-style development and interspersed with little villages desolate and exhausted. There had been few harbors where we could put in so we had to plan on a day's run of forty to fifty miles against the wind. Once in a harbor, a visiting yacht could expect to find that the "host" yacht clubs, for the most part, were social gathering spots for the Spanish elite and there was very little sailing. We were permitted to shower and to take on water for a stiff price, but we were never permitted to tie up at the dock. At one of these clubs I nearly gave a woman cardiac arrest when I walked into the ladies' room wearing oilskins. Fur-lined raincoats and high elegant leather boots with matching handbags were de rigueur foul-weather gear at these yacht clubs. Our entire trip down this eastern coast had been an alienating experience.

There is an entry in my journal that simply reads—"Garrucha—makes Milford, Indiana, look like San Francisco." Garrucha was where I reached the absolute nadir of my sailing existence. We had been four and a half months on board; four and a half months of missing friends, house, the *New York Times,* and movies. It had been all too easy to quickly forget the idyllic canal passage during our brief time on the Spanish coast. It was as if for the last two weeks some vile wind god had been shoving a fist in our faces and saying, "You're not getting out of here, folks." I felt trapped, preempted, and angry. Chris and I had been married five years and postponing children. Why? So we would end up being insulted by arrogant Spaniards in their yacht clubs or whipped by a dust storm in a pathetic little town with a name that sounded like a bronchial cough? It was my anger and Chris's listening and his sense of humor that saved us. I had suddenly realized one thing, and to make my point I shouted it over the forty-knot winds that belted through the harbor.

"The point is this, Chris: The alternative to *Leucothea* is not some monochromatic suburb with a colonial house and a sprinkling system. It is not me joining the La Leche League or you coaching Little League. There's got to be something between this boat and that suburb, Chris!"

He listened very carefully. No points needed belaboring. I didn't have to say any more. We became calm and in accord. We just had to get across now and then no more voyaging—or perhaps it would be "voyaging" of a different nature. This was an important point that we had discussed and come to better understand and articulate during our long talk in that miserable town: Adventure was not precluded by a more land-based existence. *Leucothea,* although the obvious vehicle, was not the only one for a voyager. And I had never considered myself anything less than a voyager. It was irrelevant whether it was done with a boat or not.

I felt better after our blowout, but I was still shaky. After all, we had to get across an ocean before we could explore what was between Garrucha and Wellesley Hills in terms of life-style. The specter of the crossing still loomed large as ever. The beating we had taken coming down this coast had not only worn me down but made me less than certain just how much of a "piece of cake" this crossing would really be. Besides, I had no cookies. Ever try to buy Pepperidge Farm cookies in a place like Garrucha? Forget it. A fresh lettuce leaf was unheard of. In the one tiny grocery all that was available was canned goods. The only fresh item was some particularly awful-looking goat meat abuzz with flies. Our own provisions by this time were severely depleted, and although Chris, with his cast-iron stomach, palate of steel, and culinary wit can survive the most outrageous concoction the bilge or a town like Garrucha might offer, he in fact felt so terrible about my state of mind that he did something astounding.

In a burst of unprecedented extravagance (for him), he hired a taxi from a nearby town (Garrucha did not have a taxi) and had the driver drive us two hundred miles over the Sierra Nevadas to Granada, where we feasted on garlic soup and calamari and saw the Alhambra. Over our dinner we talked about the future some more, which was to include not only children but a small vacation house, not by the sea but on a granite slab in Vermont on land we had owned for some time. We drove back that same night to Garrucha. I felt not only better but as if I just might make it across even without my cookies.

It was fun shopping for provisions in Gibraltar. The local supermarket, Lipton's, was completely adapted to provisioning oceangoing yachts. It had

*Departure
for the Canaries.*

the best selection of canned goods, especially meats, that I had ever seen. They gave a substantial discount for orders over a certain amount and delivered to the boat. Shopping at Lipton's was a fascinating experience. I figure in my days as a housewife I've tracked a few thousand miles in supermarket aisles. Seen one, seen them all, or so I thought until I walked into Lipton's. The aisles were crowded with men, crew members from other yachts, padding along softly in thongs, cutoff jeans, and bandannas tied pirate style on their sun bleached heads. Pushing their carts piled high with canned goods, they would stop to exchange recipes and buying tips. A utopian scene from a feminist's notebook.

What Lipton's could not provide, I found in the bustling back streets of Gib. I waited in bakery lines with veiled Moroccan women and cool English beauties. I bought a crate of oranges from a fellow who managed to deal with me in English while speaking a mélange of Spanish and Arabic with another customer. Midst all these preparations I was, of course, very busy cranking up the old anxiety quotient in anticipation of the crossing. My fear, at least the really debilitating form of it, usually reached its peak on land and then would begin to diminish as we sailed. Indulging in an exotic blend of both rational and irrational thinking, I was as busy as a Zuni shaman reading animal entrails before our setting out. Everything became a portent. No action or event could just happen and be free of double or triple stratas of meaning and interpretation. Each event or action existed on a heady level of symbolism that would have immediate and direct implications for our survival at sea. I threw an apple core at a trash can and it missed, rolling into an open bilge instead. Uh-oh!

This predeparture period was a classic one. Gibraltar was no exception.

If anything, it exacerbated all my fears because it was absolutely necessary that we wait for perfect weather conditions, meaning northeast or southeast winds and calm seas, to clear the potential lee shores of Africa and southern Spain. This particular section of the Moroccan coast down to Casablanca had a high incidence of onshore gales and very bad seas. These weather anomalies, coupled with ledges and shoals off Cape Spartel, made it advisable to clear the point in daylight and to have it well behind you by evening.

We left at ten-fifteen on Saturday, November 13. The date did little to reassure me, but at least if the numbers weren't right, the wind was: light and out of the northeast. There were no seas to speak of, but the straits were punctuated by little boils and swirls of current. The Pillars of Hercules receded behind us. To port, the Moroccan coast was a thin, sketchy line, and to starboard was the Spanish coast. This section of it, mercifully untouched by resort developers, appeared much as it must have in Roman times, with stone watchtowers and a few cottages wedged into the green hillsides. At one-thirty we met up once more with the Atlantic for the first time in almost two and a half years. Chris gave a Bronx cheer as we left the Mediterranean. Good-bye, Homer. Hello, Columbus.

> The Captain General's simple seaman-like plan for the voyage en-sured its success. He would avoid the boisterous headwinds, monstrous seas and dark unbridled waters of the North Atlantic. Instead he would run south before the Northerlies prevailing off Spain and North Africa to the Canary Islands and there make, as it were, a right angle turn.
>
> —SAMUEL ELIOT MORISON

Skip the right-angle turn. Something less acute is sufficient and gets you in the trades more quickly. Columbus would learn better in subsequent voyages, but for the most part our captain's plan and Columbus's were almost identical. By five-thirty we were in complete darkness as these short winter days were barely twelve hours long. The wind had freshened and we were doing a brisk six and a quarter knots. We commented lightly on the fact that there was no evening calm that night. Little did we realize that we would never experience an evening calm again until we were snugly tied up in a lagoon in the Caribbean. Like some sort of macabre clockwork, at six o'clock every single day except two for the next 3,786 miles we would be subjected to what came to be known as the evening schmozzel, a term that had endeared itself to us years before when reading Chichester. The schmozzel would range in intensity from fresh to downright vicious, making dinner preparations a lethal task, cocktail hours torture, and all of the usual evening amenities almost impossible.

However, everything was relatively decent these first two nights as we clipped along at a sprightly five and a half knots under just the genoa. Chris was a bit disgruntled that the westerly wind eliminated the possibility of our twin jibs. After so many weeks in the canals with our masts in a supine position on deck and sails virtually mothballed, not to mention our more recent slam down the coast of Spain, he was very anxious to hang up all the finery. After all, we were bound for the trades, and what were the trades without twin jibs, or some such. I was quite happy though, never having been a fetishist about sails myself. I was disappointed about the west wind for entirely different reasons. Rumor had it that when the east wind blew in these parts, a spectacular red dust would rise up from the Sahara and loom in the east, tinting the entire sky such a brilliant color that it was visible even at night.

The west wind backed a little to the north. We were able to put up the twins, but there was no red dust in the east. The nights were black, and we were spinning through the darkness in a world without boundaries—no desert, no dust, no continents implied. Alone on watch at night my boat world became an increasingly abstract one. We were but a pinprick of light, the sails floating up like wraiths newly freed from earthly bodies. The boat seemed hull-less in a peculiar way. There was wind; there was the sound of water; there was blackness. There was the thick slumber of the crew below, no longer part of my reality. It was a world strangely dispersed, full of sensibility but without meaning. And if there was any pattern at all, it was one of movement, for we were moving at a spectacular speed, accomplishing an unprecedented (for our boat) twenty-two miles every four hours. The Kenyon log never went below five and three-quarter knots and occasionally leaped to eight or eight and a half. Things seemed to exist in a state of overwhelming diaspora—wind, light, sounds, people. I had to quickly will it into something more. Below, I heard a stir, and I peered down into the teak cocoon of honey light surrounding the sleeping people. Chris was bent over the chart table. He looked up smiling. "Casablanca's two hundred miles abeam."

"Gee, that sounds exotic," I answered.

"Time for you to go to bed. Come on below. You look kind of spooky."

The winds did not abate but continued to build. Ann and Nat were extremely uncomfortable, and as Nat so aptly put it, we had officially entered the Barrows Barf latitudes. The two of them could often be spotted draped languidly over a lee rail, wondering, most likely, why they had ever ventured away from Stonington, Maine. At noon on the fourth day out, we passed within three hundred yards of the cargo ship *Pauline C.* Her decks were completely awash as she hammered through the waves. Meanwhile, aboard

Leucothea, we all sat topside, uncomfortable but dry as could be. We talked to the ship by radio and confirmed our position. They were on route to Surinam to pick up alumina. The whining wind blew even harder, as impossible as that seemed. It took me an hour to make two cups of tea and two of bouillon and to serve bread with butter. We would not enjoy a real meal for another twenty-four hours. Chris promised that these were not the trades.

Six days after we had left Gibraltar, Pico de Teide, a 12,200 foot volcano, appeared through the haze only fifteen miles away. Later as darkness settled on the rugged coastlines of Tenerife in the Canaries, the lights of Santa Cruz twinkled ahead, and looming larger and larger was the flare stack of a refinery. We rounded the breakwater of the fishing harbor and tied up next to several yachts.

CHAPTER *37*

The highlight of our short stay in Tenerife was meeting a couple who had built their own Herreschoff 28 called *October.* There is nothing more relentlessly exuberant than a conversation, or perhaps one should call it a seminar, between two Herreschoff freaks. Chris and Adolf, the owner of *October,* crawled together over each other's boats, the latter noting with particular glee where the Cheoy Lee departed from the original Herreschoff. Esoteric bits of information were swapped and stories told. I was particularly impressed with Adolf's account of being in Bermuda and recognizing *Ticon-*

The Pauline C *sited in the Barrows Barf latitudes off the Moroccan coast.*

deroga by the tangs on her mainmast just before she glided out from behind a point of land that had obscured her hull. He possessed an intimate knowledge of Herreschoff hardware as he had cast his own replicas for *October.*

We invited Nat's friend Ann to come with us all the way, feeling that anyone who could be as cheerful as she was under the onslaught of the Barf latitudes would make a great addition to our seagoing community. And she did deserve to be treated to more than five days of gales. After all, the piece of cake was about to be served. So Ann wired her job that she would be back "later" and joined *Leucothea*'s crew. Space and provisioning for a fourth person aboard our thirty-foot boat did not prove difficult, a mitigating factor being that in these sultry latitudes we did not need the voluminous cold-weather gear that we did on the northern crossing, which had taken up an entire fourth bunk. And there was an important bonus that came with Ann's presence: She was a registered nurse. I, in particular, was enchanted with this idea.

We departed Santa Cruz on November 23 with light headwinds and under power. By six o'clock Punta Roja was abeam and so were our dinner bowls and spoons as Ann had inadvertently thrown them overboard while washing dishes that evening. Improvisation was to be the name of the game for the next twenty-three days. We began a diverging course with the island and our dishes, but there was not a breath of air. The monotony from steering under power combined with my exhaustion from departure preparations and the usual tensions made my watch difficult. I began to doze off. It was hazy all around, and when I would jerk back into consciousness I would find myself disoriented. I called Chris to take over.

We had devised a new watch system for this crossing. During the day each of us took a three-hour watch. At night Chris did not take a watch, and Nat and Ann and I took four-hour ones, but Chris was on call for sail changes or to take over if someone was not feeling well. By morning, when I came on watch again at six, we were still under power on a glassy sea. There was not a hint of wind, and as our diesel chugged along, I began to be wrought with anxieties over using up our fuel supply and being becalmed indefinitely with food and water dwindling. I reread Hiscock's chapter on the northeast trades. They had experienced calms and had made only five hundred miles the first week. They told of one couple who had endured twenty days of calms!

Later that morning I detected a slight ruffle in the liquid mirror. At nine Gomera, the island on which Columbus's mistress had lived and had thus warranted a stop for him, pulled a beam. A very light wind came out of the southeast. We set sails, and it promptly evaporated. I was being driven absolutely bananas by the calm. For hours on end I would mentally rehearse the different ways I remembered winds having come up: the slight rifflings and darkenings of the water's surface; the funny little hiccups of the ties slapping furled sails; the clink of wire against wood; and, of course, the wonderful light licks of winds on the back of one's neck or earlobes—definitely the most erogenous zone for a helmsperson ensnared in a calm. But wind becomes an abstract thing, and one ceases to believe it exists after forty-eight hours of waiting.

Finally, in the early evening of Thanksgiving Day, a wind came up out of the southeast and soon shifted to northeast. Nobody commented for fear we would scare it off, but after seventeen hours of thrumming steadily along at five knots, someone ventured to suggest that indeed this did resemble a trade wind. We had skipped any Thanksgiving activities in spite of my having purchased whole canned chickens in a Riesling wine sauce when we had been in the French canals six weeks before. Ann and Nat were still experiencing active seasickness, and Chris and I, though ecstatic about the wind, did not feel confident enough to tempt fate with an out-and-out celebration. I, instead, thought a great deal about the ones at home, remembering vividly the miniature handmade feather birds that ornamented my mother-in-law's table every Thanksgiving.

In the late afternoon of the following day, the winds increased and seas built to a point of discomfort. It was blowing force five or six and would continue to do so for the next few days. The evening schmozzels had returned with renewed vigor. We were now in what might properly be called the heart of the trade-wind belt. We sailed a bit more southerly at this point than the prescribed routes in hopes of avoiding the lengthy calms endured by so many. But after thirty-six hours of force six, we had had more than enough wind in this square of the chart that indicated that it averaged force four; if this was a force four square, who knew what a five square would offer. So we jibed the big genoa to port and the other to starboard and switched our course from 240 to 270. By evening we were down to the small genoa only, holding the course and making five knots. It was awfully uncomfortable below with this rig. Chris likened it to trying to sleep in a cement mixer. In the next couple of days we did experience some "sunny periods" as the folk at the BBC weather stations put it, and during one sunny period we all stripped down and took saltwater baths, which was quite refreshing. As I was sitting on the foredeck scrubbing away, Chris pointed out a Portuguese man-of-war sailing by at a leisurely pace. From Chris's great fund of nautical trivia he came up with this rather intriguing bit of information concerning these creatures: Their bubbles shift tacks depending on the hemisphere they are born in; thus this one was sailing on a starboard (?) tack on its voyage

Nat and Ann in the forward cabin.

Bucket bathing near the Cape Verde Islands.

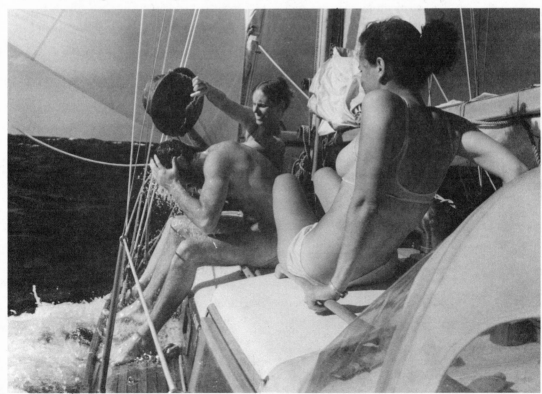

across the trade winds. This mindless blue bladder probably knew more about ocean sailing than I did. I stared at it hard. It probably spoke Portuguese too, for God's sake!

By November 30 we had been out a week and put in a neat 850 miles toward our goal. For four days the Kenyon had not dropped below five and three-quarter knots. The last two days of the first week had been full of bright sunshine. We had indulged in much sunbathing and all the other stuff you are supposed to do on a southern crossing. At night we would roar along. Skies would build up with monumental cloud structures that would suddenly clear off so that we could see the stars swaying in the companionway or the rigging. We had a waxing half moon so evenings were lighter. During those two charmed days I worked industriously on one of my minor goals in life: an allover tan. The barometer had made a spectacular ascent to 30.7.

But on the morning of our seventh day out, a schmozzel came up and matured into a near gale that besieged us for three days. Upon careful observation of the chart, we noticed that we were indeed in a square of force-five winds and not four as we had thought. The fifth little tail of the square's flag had been neatly obscured by a magnetic line. By evening we were quite miserable and standing watch from below by sitting on the galley counter. We were running under the little genoa lickety-split at five and a half knots. From my perch on the counter, I looked out the porthole and saw a herd of dolphins knifing through the water right beside our hull. Their black fins glittered in the moonlight. Sitting there almost eye level with the water, I felt a terrific sensation of speed as *Leucothea* and the dolphins slid down the waves together. In retrospect it seems more romantic than uncomfortable, but rereading my journal for that night is enough to stand my hair on end.

Dec. 3, 1976: There is a lot of tension because conditions are not clear-cut and we're trying to figure out what to do about sail. The boat is riding well now, but we are on a fine edge. Seas are moving fast and there is a good amount of wind. Ann and Nat cannot stand watch below without getting sick, so Chris and I divide up their watches. Neither of us really sleeps when we're off. Despite the hum and constant tossing, I keep waiting for Chris to say with all the tension melting out of his voice, "Well, I think it's blowing itself out." He doesn't say this. At 0200 things get worse. No longer are we on a fine edge. We've crossed over, and it's a livid gale full of rage. Chris and Ann go up to change sail—the storm jib. The spreader lights come on lighting up the deck like an operating table. This eerie illumination midst the howling black seas is so peculiar. Chris on the foredeck appears like a solitary figure on a stage . . . the jenny straining madly behind him. He is in just his shorts and his life harness

Kathy—halfway across.   Chris—halfway across.

shouting orders. His hair, a startling white under the lights, streams straight out behind him. A stage Odysseus. No. This is no stage. This is it: five knots bare poles. I am standing in the companionway so afraid he will fall overboard. Ann is on the starboard winch. . . . I hear it; then I see it off the starboard quarter. A mammoth black shape nearly as tall as the mizzenmast racing toward us. It drops its black jaws into a death grin of white spikes. There is a horrible grinding sound. I scream to Chris to hang on as the freak wave breaks on us. I see him fling his arms around the mast. But it is Ann and I who get the brunt of it. I am scrubbed right off the companionway onto the cabin sole. The cockpit is half-full, and below all the bedclothes are drenched. But it drains quickly.

Only a fool of the first order would stand in the companionway with the doors flung wide open, leaving the cabin vulnerable while yelling at her husband. But indeed this trip was becoming too much for me. Some piece of cake! We ran for a day and a half under the storm jib. And these days became excruciatingly boring. It was too rough to be on deck, and down below, while we were hot and sticky in our bunks, rectangles of sun danced across our faces teasing us to come out. After what seemed like endless days under just the storm jib, we set a small genoa along with it as conditions became somewhat, but just barely, more tolerable. This was a new downwind partnership but it seemed to work tolerably well. We began to make brief forays topside into the fiercest sunlight I had ever seen. We continued under this odd-couple rig for two or three days.

One evening on Nat's watch, a legion of line squalls accompanied us on the port flank. Although there were no direct hits, whenever one would pass we would feel it, and the boat would begin to careen and hum madly. Ann came on watch and hadn't been up two minutes before a sea caught us from behind and pooped us quite royally, filling the cockpit to the brim and drenching Ann once more. Chris called Ann quickly out of the cockpit to lessen the weight astern, and we all advanced forward below. The cockpit drained efficiently despite the fact that Chris had not taken off two of the drain strainers. The night was laced with squalls. Within one thirty-minute period we had to change sail three times: first down with the little genoa as the wind came up southeast and was driving us straight for Miami; then the wind changed once more, so up with it again as a howling squall struck, and in a most unholy act of levitation, I felt *Leucothea* leave the water and become airborne! It was as if time had frozen. I was once again perched below on the galley counter when I felt this unimaginable sensation of flight. I looked out the port porthole and all I saw were sheafs of white flying by. There was nothing but the white foam. I looked out the starboard porthole—all white. I looked again to port—the same. We were virtually flying through a tunnel of white foam for what I figured to be a full five seconds as we surfed down a twenty-foot wave. All night long the squalls came and went. The seas grew in confusion. We tried to keep an especially good lookout because we were approaching the New York-to-Cape of Good Hope shipping lanes.

We were finally given respite from all this with a three-day patch of twelve-to-fifteen-knot breezes and gentle seas. We spent these days sunbathing and rinsing down with buckets of seawater and getting some of our first good night's sleeps, although the voyage was more than half over. The evenings were lavishly starry, and Nat was treated to a meteor shower on his watch, while Ann had the extraordinary experience of seeing a piece of the heavens doused in the sea miles off. This must have been some sort of omen, for the next morning it was squalls once more and rolling seas.

My patience was being tried to the limit, not to mention my bruised and aching body after sixteen days in the cement mixer. Shipboard life had become torturous. The amenities I had envisioned for a southern crossing had long ago evaporated. Sunbathing or just stretching out topside was difficult to the point of not being worth it. Chris and I made several attempts to go to the bow for a sunbath. Gripping stanchions and forward stays with everything but my teeth, I would realize after ten minutes that I was not only extraordinarily uncomfortable but in peril of being swished overboard. So much for sunbathing.

Cooking was even worse, and dinner preparations became fertile ground for some of my most psychotic fantasies ever. With the galley serving as the battleground, the cast of characters would read as follows: The enemy —Major Carbon Knife, Lieutenant Hot Pepper, infantry men (assorted forks, knives, tomatoes, apples, a can opener), special forces—fruit flies, heavy artillery—one hot tuna casserole. On the other side, the Allied Forces, it was just me.

Act 1, scene 1: Knives, spice bottle, and the rest of the galley troops are massing at the fiddles preparing to launch an attack on the Allied troops' vulnerable flank.

MAJOR CARBON KNIFE: Okay, boys. It's going to be a routine strafe bombing job. For convenience and the press we'll call it a "protective reinforcement reaction." We've already sent in the tomato.

LIEUTENANT HOT PEPPER: Yeah. It's amazing what a rotten tomato right in the chops can do.

MAJOR CARBON KNIFE: (musing) It's not what you'd call a weapon with a whole lot of character, but boy is she pissed!

LIEUTENANT HOT PEPPER: Yep. She's already starting the "you-should've-married-Mary Nutt" routine.

MAJOR CARBON KNIFE: (snappily) Let's break out the apples now. It'll drive her crazy. The forks can do an in-and-out on her ears.

Scene 2: A flying wedge of fruit flies has just been sent in, and Major Carbon Knife is observing the action.

MAJOR CARBON KNIFE: Wahoo! Look at those fellows go! (then turning to Hot Pepper) It's a nice touch, Lieutenant, those little green berets for the fruit flies. A very classy bit. Otherwise they'd look like any nickle-and-dime mercenaries.

LIEUTENANT HOT PEPPER: She's growing weaker, sir. Talking about next summer's vacation—a sedan chair through Turkey Run State Park.

MAJOR CARBON KNIFE: (calmly but with steely determination in his voice) All right, Lieutenant, dump the casserole right on her big toe. Report back to me immediately.

LIEUTENANT HOT PEPPER: (back with report) We've got her sur-rounded, sir. Stinkin' tuna all over.

MAJOR CARBON KNIFE: Okay. We can hold her now. You can tell the knives and forks to get back into the Tuppers. Hey, hey! What's that trigger-happy nut doing out there. What the hell! Oh, for Crissake, it's the can opener, and he's lowering his corkscrew. Oh, Lord! This goes against the Geneva Accords. Would somebody stop him. Uh-oh! She's got him. She just chucked him overboard. Damn those can openers! (then muttering to him-self) Yahoo dime store types—never learn. Okay. Everybody back to the Tuppers. (then with utter disbelief in his voice) What's that nincompoop husband of hers doing? Ah, for Crissake, he's taking her picture—tomato and all. Who does he think he is? David Douglas Duncan?

LIEUTENANT HOT PEPPER: (sighing) Well, sir, it's as bad as the cheese incident.

MAJOR CARBON KNIFE: Oh, yeah, what happened then, Lieutenant?

LIEUTENANT HOT PEPPER: Well sir, the husband fancies puns, and after she'd been knocked senseless by a ten-pound wheel of Gouda, her husband said, "How do you feel? Not so gouda?"

MAJOR CARBON KNIFE: Oh, God!

The End

CHAPTER 38

Under the almost continuous punishment of heavy winds and big seas, we began to worry about strain on the gear and not just the strain on ourselves. On December 10, after seventeen days at sea, George, our faithful helmsman, the self-steering vane, busted a gudgeon on the frame because of metal fatigue. Chris managed to fix this by using pieces of a spare gooseneck fitting. Five minutes after he had completed the repair on George, the Compass mount broke from electrolytic corrosion, so he proceeded to fix that. The next day Chris noticed that a pintle on George's frame had given way. Another piece of gooseneck was quickly called into service. But we were still very worried. The entire frame of the vane would jolt laterally back and forth as George tried to steer our six tons through this miserable weather. The remaining bronze fittings were now subject to more stress, and we sat

Leucothea *at sea*.

tensely trying to figure out where we could scrounge up bits and pieces for improvisation if they went. On top of this, we were belted by a really nasty squall just about dinnertime. We all stood with our noses pressed against the portholes as an awesome set of clouds raced above sending down sheets of rain that smoked the sea and sculpted waves into smooth dunelike shapes with crests whipped up like horses' manes.

If I had ever had any doubts about being one of the Chosen People, it was eradicated during the next three days when I continued in fine style a two-thousand-year tradition of persecution that was literally pounded into me. On December 12 I awoke for my morning watch, went topside into what was a beautiful morning with relatively organized seas, and was promptly doused by an offbeat wave that flung me to the cockpit floor, banging my nose. On December 13, under identical circumstances, I was knocked flat once more, this time hitting my shoulder on the coaming. On December 14 I was spared the indignities of the wave, but was treated to a close encounter of the third kind with a flying fish as it flew directly at my chest and for a split second resided in the top of my bathing suit before it managed to flip itself out.

Well, all things do come to an end. On December 14, at eight forty-five Chris picked up the Barbados radio beacon. We slid by the low-lying island with its glow of lights about two the next morning. We were in high spirits and just 157 miles from our destination—Grenada. That night I came on watch at ten o'clock. As soon as I was topside, I blinked in disbelief as I saw three vertical red lights blinking back at me. Impossible, I thought. We were

Under the lee of Grenada.

not supposed to see any signs of Grenada for at least four more hours. I called Chris. He came up and was equally bewildered. These lights matched the radio tower indicated on the chart at the northern end of Grenada. There was a current around here that swept in from the southwest and could have boosted our speed, but this seemed to be a somewhat implausible boost—four hours ahead of schedule. Chris was not willing to trust a manmade marker in the night, so he decided we should jibe to the south and steer clear of the coast.

As the tropical sky began to lighten and mythical green-clad islands rose from the sea, the distinctive profile of Kick'em Jenny, a small island north of Grenada, tipped us off that the three blinking red light in the night had not belonged to Grenada but were a new tower on Carriacou, not yet indicated on the charts. The one-and-three-quarter-knot current had indeed given us a boost and a sweep. We had been driven twenty miles north of our course to Grenada and were off the eastern shore of Carriacou. Chris's decision to lay off had been a wise one that saved our passage from coming to an inglorious and abrupt halt on the reefs three miles off Carriacou. We then sailed south along the coast of Grenada toward Saint George's harbor with the twin jibs flying and the gentle trades Chris had promised for the "piece of cake" crossing finally behind us.

At ten we broke out the champagne and sent up flags of the ten countries we had sailed to in the last three years. I thought the flags made us look more like a gas station than a sailing vessel, but I wasn't going to quibble. I lay back and watched: frigate birds carving lazy arcs in a cloudless sky, the twin jibs billowing at last with twelve-knot trade wind breezes, and the lushly sculpted islands floating like mirages on a sea of liquid sapphire.

PART IV

CHAPTER *39*

I had been rushing all day long. First, all the way out to Wilson Farm that morning for their excellent buttercrunch lettuce and fresh-picked strawberries, then back into Cambridge, where I hopped on my bike to go into Harvard Square to pick up some goat-milk cheese. It's senseless to take a car into the square as parking is virtually impossible. When I got back to the house, I remembered that I had some students' papers to deliver to Wheelock over in Brookline, which I had promised that day. As I was driving I suddenly remembered that ye gods! there's a Red Sox game, too late, and I shall be caught in horrible traffic. I was, but I managed to buy two bunches of flowers from a vendor walking through lines of cars in front of Fenway Park. I had forgotten all about flowers when I was at Wilson Farm that morning. Jackie Onassis probably doesn't have carnation bouquets on her dinner table, I think. I'm sure she has artfully artless spring bouquets of, say, lilies of the Valley in Steuben glass, or maybe Nicotiana and Peruvian lilies in ginger jars. I hoped that Chris remembered two red and two white and could fit the bottles in his backpack when he biked home from the studio that evening.

When I finally got home I asked if anyone had called. I always hope that there will be a call from my editor saying something to the effect that yes, we love the book so much we'll double the advance this time, and please take the shuttle to New York and we'll talk about the third chapter at Elaine's. That doesn't happen to me—the more money or Elaine's. My editor usually writes letters, and I do the calling. The only message for me is one from the plumber giving the name of a caulking compound good for toilet bases. Chris had tried Life Caulk, a marine one, and it left a stain on the linoleum. I immediately run out again to get beeswax. Toilet water leaking into the dining room from the powder room during a dinner party is really tackier than carnations.

Back again, it is time to arrange the carnations, which have been standing in a plastic pitcher full of water. In the pantry I discover that the ceramic vase I was planning to use has a lethal crack. Should I try the beeswax? It's five forty-five. There isn't time for it to set. I am desperate for a container. Eureka! I suddenly remember the Armagnac bottle. It has only a tablespoon of brandy left in it. Quickly I decant the brandy into an old Hellman's mayonnaise jar, rinse out the lovely brandy bottle, and pop in the carnations. They really look quite nice, better than carnations deserve to look. They probably feel better too. Enough of that treacly flower life. Bring on the VSOP, Very Special Odd Petals. There is a curmudgeonly group of intellects in Boston called the Odd Volumes. This could be their flower counterpart. I look at the arrangement again. Nice but not great. Any ikebana society worth its salt would most likely have apoplexy over such a concoction.

In an act of extraordinary organization (for me) I decide that it would be judicious to label the old Hellmann's jar as to its new contents. I can't find my stick-on labels, the ones that Chris bought me that were supposed to reorganize my life, order the hodgepodge that runs from my study to the kitchen. I do find a Band-Aid though. Oh! We sailors are so clever! I think —nothing to this little jury rig. I stick on the Band-Aid and write in small letters on it, brandy. I go to the refrigerator. The sole quenelles in pear-and-leek sauce are resting comfortably. What do I mean resting comfortably? They are wonderful. They are a culinary triumph. After many tries throughout the spring, I had finally done it. The first time they were like gefilte fish. The second time they were like fishy matzoh balls. But this time they worked. Chris said so. I had made them early that morning, and he had had one for breakfast. The first course would be pasta, "for starters" as they say; then, the quenelles with new potatoes, followed by a curly endive salad with balsamic vinegar dressing. For dessert, strawberries with a sabayon-type sauce and accompanied by Pirouettes. "The original" curled Pepperidge Farm cookie. Six years it is, no more, since I transported the forty-seven packages of Margaret Rudkin's finest across the three thousand miles of open water known as the Atlantic Ocean. Since then the cookies have become inextricably and forever associated with ocean sailing, even though I eat them on land now comfortably ensconced in a new old house in Cambridge.

The guests will be arriving in thirty minutes. I shower. Dress. The table looks great. The menu, which I've tossed around in my head, seems right for this night. It might seem a trifle studied, a little nouvelle, I reflect, but there will be none of this business of teensy-weensy entrées marooned on islands of sauce. I detest this pretension of putting sauce underneath the food. It's a culinary conceit that is ridiculous. In Italy they'd shoot off your kneecap for putting sauce underneath. I conjure up images of a few strands of pasta arranged in an arabesque design on top of a "simple ovoid" of Bolognese sauce on a white plate. How wretched! I suddenly think of my Uncle Jack. He asked a good question last week when I saw him in New York. What did we, here in this country, call pasta before we knew the word *pasta?* He had a few others: What word did we use before *ambiance* became so ubiquitous? And what did we say before that expression *into* came along, as *she's into stained glass,* or *he's into motorcycles.* He was making a list to send into "Metropolitan Diary" in the *New York Times.* This reminds me that I didn't check the *Times* today for evidences of Jack. Between "Metropolitan Diary" and the editorial pages my uncle gets more in the *Times* than a weekly columnist. In fact he has had to adopt a series of pseudonyms because the editorial page has a rule about the number of letters published yearly by one person. By February Jack had usually exceeded his limit. So he had thought up a slew of names—mostly anagrams of his own name, Jacob S. Hurwitz. There was Bijou Schwartz and Curtis J. Hazboro and Jay Essache. And then there was George Dreyfuss Hurwitz for his cat named George, who was also three-footed, hence the Dreyfuss. And there was Emma Faitch, an anagram of my Aunt Mildi's maiden name. The grandchildren were included too. Annie Sorkin appeared as Angel Sorkin, and Samuel became Essel Sorkin, all lending their names or letters of their names for Uncle Jack's pen, which wrote volumes on every subject under the sun from the bombing of Cambodia to the Nixon pardon to a scoreboard plan for boxing events to the importance of warning signals on ice cream trucks and not just school busses to the suggestion for an added tax to vehicle registration to be used for pothole repair.

On November 14, 1976, Uncle Jack was really counting a coup on the editorial page. He had two letters printed on the subject of Jimmy Carter's church denying admission to a black man. One was from Jacob Hurwitz and the other from Bijou Schwartz. I am thinking about all this as I am scrubbing the new potatoes. I can never eat new potatoes or fix them without thinking of the Dart River and the resignation of Richard Nixon. We had rowed up it from our anchorage to a tiny village on a creek off the Dart and bought a paper to read about the resignation, of which we had heard at two in the morning on our ship's radio. We scoured the paper in a pub called the Church House, and then on our walk back to the dinghy we had cut through a freshly harvested field and picked up the remnants of the new potato crop.

The guests have arrived. We've had drinks. We repair to the dining room. The table looks lovely. One woman comments on the "exuberant carnations." You would be too, I think, if you were in a brandy bottle. I make a mental note to warn Chris about the Hellmann's jar when we serve after-dinner drinks. There is the usual lively banter as we decide who sits where. We're definitely not place card types. Chris has just one rule, which is that we must sit boy-girl-boy-girl. We start to pull out the chairs. I notice that mine seems to resist. I pull again. It moves slightly, and so does the one to my left. Indeed all the chairs seem to move together . . . good Lord! I look down. Every chair is tied to the one next to it with a cord which has been deftly knotted into a near-facsimile of a bowline. Max! We are by this time all jiggling chairs. Chris and another guest are down on their hands and knees unknotting the handiwork of our four-year-old son, who has entered a stage that Gesell and Piaget didn't cover—knot tying. I was always finding evidences of his handiwork around the house. Two doors knotted together, kitchen drawers bound shut by elaborate knots. I should have realized that things had been ominously quiet when I was scrubbing the new potatoes and my mind was wandering down English country lanes and through villages with names like Dittysham and Stokes Gabriel.

"You always provide such interesting entertainment for your guests," said a woman as she got down on her knees to begin work on the chair she was hoping to eventually sit in.

CHAPTER 40

Max was a water baby from the start. I had realized this long before this evening when I found myself standing before our dining room table so gay with carnations and my mother's Italian pottery as I stared at these respectable knots, the very ones I had been trying to tie for years. It was very funny. Of course, this would have been an amusing quixotic entry in any

"The Charming Presence" bathes.

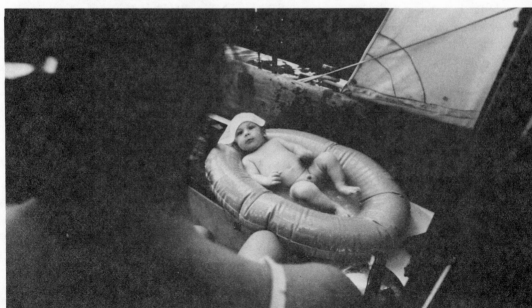

hostess's notebook, but for me it was more than just terribly funny. It was a moment loaded with irony and symbolic freight. This was indeed the "in-between" that Chris and I had sought, that I, in particular, had yearned for so desperately in Garrucha, and that Chris and I had pursued together and found when we settled in Cambridge to raise a family. It was certainly not a monochromatic suburb, and I had not joined the La Leche League and Chris was not coaching Little League. The house was not a suburban colonial, but a shingle-style Victorian built in 1891 by a nephew of Ralph Waldo Emerson with definite influences from H. H. Richardson. But we had not swallowed the anchor by any means, and Maxwell Balboni Knight, who had arrived almost a year to the day after our landfall in Grenada, possessed a buoyancy to match his dad's. By the time Max was six months old, he had been through the San Juan airport six times. We had left *Leucothea* in the Caribbean for three winters and would often fly down for cruises. At first I found the notion of sailing with an infant appalling. It is. But it is also fascinating.

For example, for years Chris had had this quirky thing about potato chips on board. He refused to allow anyone to eat them on our natural teak decks. "The oil, you know." He would say this in the same tone that you might use to say "Piranha, you know," in response to a question about what hazards you might encounter swimming the Amazon. Now I am not proposing that being able to munch potato chips during a gale in mid-Atlantic would have substantially balmed my spirits, but it embarrassed me to listen while he would explain the no-potato-chip rule to guests aboard for a day cruise who had unwittingly contributed potato chips to the lunch. He would then usher them below to munch in the torpid splendor of our main cabin. To be fair, Chris usually just explained the rule and that was enough to dampen anybody's longing for the chips. Life, however, has its compensations, and with them come some peculiar twists and exquisite paradoxes. Remedies for little hobgoblins and tiny tyrannies such as the no-potato-chip rule often come in strange packages. Ours came in the form of Max, who efficiently ended the no-potato-chip rule when just a baby, before he himself was even on solid foods. The elimination of this rule was merely a serendipitous fringe benefit of his mostly charming presence on our boat.

The first time Max was ever on *Leucothea* was in Fort-de-France, Martinique. He and I had flown in from New York to meet Chris, who had sailed up from Saint Vincent. Max was only months old, and this cruise was to be our first with him aboard. Chris was beside himself with excitement at finally being able to introduce his first child to *Leucothea*. Into Max's tiny three-month-old ear Chris would coo, "This is port, Max, and this is starboard. Say starboard. And this is George. George is nice. Be good to George. He's our self-steering vane, and while he sails the boat I can cuddle you. This is a winch, Max. Not a wench as Mommy used to call them before she knew better. Say winch, Max. Winch."

We had only been on the boat a short time before it became strongly apparent that Max's diaper would have to be changed. I was below organizing things in a cabin that was ajumble with sail bags, and there was not a square inch of clear surface area. Holding the reeking infant, Chris looked below through the companionway. "He needs a change, Kathy."

"Hmmmm," I said looking around for a place to change him. Then without a thought of potato chips, I answered, "Better do it up there. No room down here. Here's a diaper."

There might have been a fleeting shadow of doubt, a soupçon of hesitation in the voice as Chris said, "Well, Okay," but the next thing I saw it was bottoms up on the teak as Chris meticulously mopped up Max with generous portions of baby oil. This is what I call progress. There has never been another complaint about potato chips on deck.

Babies, especially on boats, make you sort out the significant from the insignificant, the serious from the frivolous, the real from the superficial; they also promote mental and moral growth, tolerance and sensitivity, and interesting forms of insanity. On our first cruise, which was two weeks in length, Max was three months old and still nursing. He was a robust little fellow and had never been sick. Still I was very nervous about taking him on a boat so far from home and kept hoping some sound medical opinion would say, "Don't do it," "Wait," "He should be older." Nothing of the sort was forthcoming. In fact, it was just the opposite. The morning after Max was born, my obstetrician, Dr. Ann Barnes, a veteran down-east sailor, came into my room at Boston Lying-In and presented me with a life harness for Max. "My kid's outgrown it," she said handing it to me. The orange straps, snap shackles, and rope looked incredibly out of place in the maternity ward.

"Dr. Barnes," I pressed, "Chris wants us all to go sailing in March down in the Caribbean. Now don't you think that's crazy?" I looked down at the six and a half pounds of adorable humanity that I cradled.

"What's crazy about it? I think it's great."

"What if he gets sick?"

"There are doctors, airplanes. Go now. This is the best time—before they can crawl."

Next I broached the subject with my pediatrician. His eyes lit up. "Ooooh! Who are you chartering from?"

"We have our own boat."

"You do? Wow!"

"Yes, but don't you think that . . ."

"What kind is she?"

"A Cheoy Lee ketch."

"Bermuda thirty?"

"Yes. Now don't you think Max is . . ."

"Bermuda thirty! Was she built before 'sixty-nine? You know, when they still used a lot of teak?"

"Yes."

"Oh, gee, I envy you. Where are you going? Virgin Islands?"

"No, Martinique and Antigua," I said trying to make it sound totally obscure and foreign.

"Fantastic! Oh God, my wife and I loved the food in Martinique."

"But what about Max?"

"What about him? He's a healthy kid."

"You mean you think this is reasonable."

"Oh, absolutely!" He pulled on the most serious medical-doctor look he could come up with. "Just keep him covered. The sun's your worst enemy, and don't get dehydrated, because you're still nursing."

So with everybody's blessing we began our cruise. He slept in a small plastic bassinet that folded up to the size of a pocketbook when not in use but when unfolded and in use fit perfectly on the main cabin sole between the two bunks. On our rough passage between Martinique and Dominica, Max was zipped into the Snugli, a front carrying pouch, which I wore. He slept blissfully. Chris and I had fun making mobiles for Max out of shells, old tangs, and snap shackles that hung in lively dangling arrangements above his bassinet. This first cruise was pretty near ideal.

Three months later, when Max was a supercurious and speedy six-month-old, we took another cruise. This time we sailed from Antigua to Tortola. Our first cruise seemed like a honeymoon next to this one. At three months Max had been extremely packable in every sense of the word. On several occasions we dined ashore in a lovely restaurant with our little bundle sleeping soundly in the portable bassinet. Such outings ceased when he was six months old. At three months there had always been somewhere on the boat I could wedge him if I needed both hands. At six months there was no place. Unable to crawl, he was nonetheless an extremely efficient creeper who could sneak away in a split second, usually to a precipitous edge. Mobile but far from stable was the name of his game. We took to putting cushions on all the floorboards in the cockpit or below. We could never put him in his bassinet and plan on him just staying there. This baby Houdini could slither over the edge and out. Hence, the bassinet was always on the floor in the main cabin.

By the time of our third cruise, Max was a full-fledged fourteen-month-old toddler. He had been toddling for over a month, and worse than toddling, he had been climbing anything within reach since he was nine and a half months. Just before his first birthday, I walked into the dining room one morning to find our nonwalker on top of the table. The next day I found him on a kitchen counter, and a few months later he was chasing Chris up a twenty-foot ladder. I had real nightmares prior to our third cruise. The mizzenmast would be small potatoes for our toddling Sir Edmund Hillary, not to mention climbing over the lifelines.

We had to do a Max overhaul of the boat, which entailed netting in everything aft of the doghouse and turning it into a giant playpen. We already had spray panels up along both sides of this section, but the stern area and the sections between the doghouse sides and where the panels ended had to be netted. We had to be careful to fix the net as close to the decks as possible as Max was a squincher and could squinch himself as flat as a planaria in a petri dish and slide under anything. By this time Max had outgrown his bassinet so we needed new sleeping space for him. Chris netted in an area in the forward V-bunk for Max. It was more like a cage than a crib as the netting extended from the bunk's edges almost to the ceiling, with a corner you could let down for a door. It sounds horrible, but Max loved it. And to this day when the seas get really rough and it's a little scary to be topside, Max's favorite place is the forward V-bunk, where he can sit for hours and peek out the porthole at the monster waves, and asking every third or fourth wave, "Was that one as big as the ones on the crossing, Mommy? I bet it was."

It was on the third cruise however, when Max was still a toddler and we were anchored off the Bitter End on the island of Tortola, that we had a memorable encounter. I had just finished feeding Max on deck and there was still a splattering of mango and mashed potato over everything when I noticed a white-haired gentleman and a woman rowing toward us in their dingy. As they rowed closer, I soon realized that the gentleman was none other than Dr. Benjamin Spock. After Dr. Spock and his wife, Mary Morgan, asked a couple of sailing questions and just as Chris was issuing an invitation for cocktails, Max presented his potato splattered face over the lifelines. "Ben!" cried Mary Morgan enthusiastically. "There's a baby on that boat!" Dr. Spock's smile froze. Chris held Max up to give the distinguished pediatrician a better look at what we considered a magnificent specimen.

"I can see from here," the doctor said, while starting to row madly in the other direction, "that you have an intelligent, calm, joyful baby!" He continued to exclaim while feverishly rowing toward the horizon, "Maybe drinks another time. Lovely child!" he yelled as he raced into the distance.

I tell this story with utmost respect for Doctor Spock. It shows the man has damn good sense. What could be more boring and less relaxing than drinks on board a small boat with a toddler and two eager parents who would much rather talk about their darling baby with a renowned pediatrician than talk about sailing.

There is no denying that sailing with a baby was difficult, and there were times when I was known to have said, after a two-week cruise with Max, that I needed a vacation. Anyone who says it's a breeze and never once longs for his and her child-free days is a liar. But there are some special things too, aside from slipping on mangoes mashed on teak. I can remember anchoring off Dog Island one night when Max was just six months old. Located off the western end of Anguilla, Dog Island is an isolated jump-off for the Anegada Passage. There are no people living on it. We had to scour the western side for an anchorage. A slot in the rocks offered good protection from the roll but no holding ground as the bottom was rocky. Finally we found good holding ground off a sand beach under the southwest point of the island. The roll was bad however, and we had to put out two anchors and angle our boat into the waves. It was a steep-to shore, so we were in tight with the beach just a short swim away, a beautiful beach with sand blown from the eastern side of the island drifting into high overhanging cornices. The water was startlingly clear, the clearest we had ever seen, and the reef fish were three times larger than any others we had seen in the Caribbean. Gulls and terns used the island for nesting. Dog Island, a singular place. A haven for all things wild and beautiful. A place where cruising boats rarely go. It seemed distinctly inhospitable to human beings. Dog Island remains lonely, untouched, but if the navy has its way, it will become a sublime bombing range for fighter jets.

Max and Mom afloat at the baths.
Virgin Gorda, B.W.I.

Max on lookout.

The air on board that night on Dog Island was hot and thick. Mosquitoes strafed us. I looked down at Max sleeping peacefully. His head was a lather of sweaty ringlets and mosquito bites. I thought of all the places we had been in our boat that were so much more welcoming to humans, so much more comfortable. I thought of those navy fellows who in some peculiar paranoia had decided that because this island was so isolated and inhospitable it should be used for target practice. Max would never remember this place, but this is the one of all of them that I have kept tucked away in my mind for him, and now, before he goes to sleep, for a bedtime story I sometimes tell him about the lonely island we sailed to when he was a baby, a place not made for humans but where the wind blew the sand into castles and the angelfish were as big as pancakes and the water so clear you could see a clown fish wink.

CHAPTER 41

I usually remember dinner parties in terms of the people and the food, but the one that I gave that spring night will always be inscribed in my memory as the one where Max tied together all the chairs—the knot-tying party. The woman who referred to our providing such interesting entertainment attended a party the previous year during which Chris had invited the guests to help him move the mainmast from the top of our car into the basement. He wanted it under cover to begin stripping it down for revarnishing in preparation for summer cruising. The boatyard had a rule that prohibited people from doing their own mast work on the premises. This mast-moving party occurred the same year as our tenth anniversary.

For this anniversary I had had dreams of Italy, a quick little trip, ten days or so in March. I was writing more children's books these days, and my idea of an appropriate celebration was a trip to Bologna to the International Children's Book Fair, the crowning event in the world of children's books. This coupled with the fact that Bologna was the ancestral home of Chris's mother's family, the Balbonis, seemed to make it the perfect place for the ten-year anniversary.

But starting in early February, there were ominous rumblings in the basement of our house. A mysterious box loaded with rusty unopened canned goods appeared one evening near the washing machine. I woke up in a cold sweat when I realized the origins of these rusty veterans—La Côte Bilge! These particular beauties were remnants of our second trans-Atlantic crossing of four years ago. Like a specter they had come back to haunt me.

The next morning Chris proudly announced that he was going to put all of those old cans out for the garbage collection. This made me even more nervous. Chris had never been known to part with a can of food no matter how rusty and battered. If the can had bulge in it, he would bid it a wistful adieu, but generally he clung to old cans like gold. Cans that I wouldn't touch with a ten-foot pole, Chris would gobble up before my eyes while I would sit alert to any sudden dilation of pupils, conflagration of rashes, construction of the throat, gagging, thrombosis, etc. As far as I was concerned, Chris played Russian roulette with canned food—botulism for bullets. So this was definitely a bad sign that these neonatal cans in Chris's chronology of preserved foods were being tossed out. Bad because it meant he was working up to something worse. I sensed that he was getting into bargaining position. Dreams of tagliatelle con fegatini, linguine Bolognese washed down with quantities of Gavi San Pietro were fading. There were murmurings about a ten-year refit, and I knew in my heart of hearts that Chris was talking about the boat and not the marriage.

We had not had *Leucothea* in the water for almost two years as the summer before was the one during which Chris had made the film on the *Observer* Single-handed Race, *American Challenge*. This had taken us back and forth across the Atlantic in airplanes, not boats, and had not left a weekend for sailing. Now, however, the trips to Manchester Marine were beginning to occur with startling regularity, and the smell of Teak Bright in Chris's clothes cut through my own pungent reveries of prosciutto di Parma.

Without becoming too elegiac, I can remember all too well when the last of my Bolognese dreams vanished. I was sitting on the couch with Max reading him a book. I turned the page and looked out the window, and what to my wondering eyes should appear coming up our street, not a miniature sleigh with eight tiny you know whats but our AMC Hornet with *Leucothea*'s mainmast, all thirty-two feet of it, resting on a framework that looked like a horizontal version of the Eiffel Tower. "Holy shit," I whispered. "Holy shit," squealed Max. And behind the wheel was that little old driver so lively and quick I knew in a moment it must be that singular nitwit—Chris.

My last Italian dream image was that of me sitting over a simple bowl of tortellini in the Café Diana discussing the new Czech version of *Alice through the Looking Glass* with some eminent editor. For dessert there would be a voluptuous bomba moca with a few tasteful inquiries concerning the speculations put forth by a well-known scholar that Beatrix Potter was gay.

That night we had our dinner party, the one with the interesting entertainment of moving the mast into the basement through the garage. It is a great icebreaker for guests who have never met. All our guests however were old and good friends. So we just sweated a lot before dinner—pasta primavera.

Chris had maneuvered not only the mast into the basement but himself into a full bargaining stance. Negotiations were about to open. For starters there was the one thousand dollars that Chris had saved by bringing the mast home instead of keeping it at the boatyard where the people there would have done the work. After three years in the blistering Caribbean sun, it needed work—at least seven coats of varnish, I was told. The number of coats and the number of dollars saved was impressive. It would cover a lot of airfare, but I knew that this was not why Chris was telling me this. Roughly the argument went as follows: With the amount of money we saved we could take a ten-day cruise in the Nantucket-Martha's Vineyard area, where we had never really sailed before, and we could do it without Max. We could hire a baby-sitter to move into our house and take care of Max, whom we had never left for more than forty-eight hours, and we could spend the balance of the thousand dollars on fresh food like beautiful beef tenderloin, fresh swordfish, striped bass (no canned goods allowed, he promised) and fine restaurants like Straight Wharf on Nantucket.

It was a compelling argument. I don't know what I had planned to do with Max in Bologna, but the idea of leaving him behind on another continent was unthinkable, while the notion of leaving him in Boston while we were in Martha's Vineyard or thereabouts was not only thinkable but appealing.

The tenth anniversary cruise begins.

"Just think," Chris reasoned. "Alone together for the first time in three and a half years. Ten days of eating beautiful dinners and finishing sentences. No *Star Wars* cassettes blasting in our ears."

Very compelling indeed. I thought about it. I thought about a quotation I had recently read in an Italian cookbook for some reason. "Tortellini is more essential than sun for a Saturday and love for a woman. But the origin of tortellini is lost in the mists of time."

It was a clear bright June morning when we slipped the mooring in East Boston. Finally we were off. The preparations involving child care, driving groups, etc. had seemed as Byzantine as those of seven years before when we had left the pier on the other side of Boston harbor for our first Atlantic crossing. Adrianne, the baby-sitter, and Max were on the pier waving madly to us. Max suddenly looked terribly small and vulnerable to me. Waving back, as we had rowed toward *Leucothea,* I shouted a constant stream of instructions to Adrianne concerning the care and feeding of our little boy. My last instructions were to Max himself. "Don't fall off the swan boats and mind the guardrails on top of the Hancock Building."

There was a ghost of a breeze. I conked out under the hot June sun. Jets from Logan roared overhead. Ten days with nothing to do! Lovely! This anniversary cruise was not only going to be relaxing but a very cornball, nostalgic affair. So our first stop would be Scituate, where Chris and I had taken refuge ten years earlier in a drenching rain when we were bringing *Leucothea* up from Falmouth on our way to Deer Isle for our wedding. We had discovered a wonderful seafood restaurant called the Satuit Lounge, right on the harbor, and had been salivating to return to it ever since. The wind soon died, and we were forced to motor the rest of the way to Scituate if we were going to make it in time for dinner.

Scituate seemed more built-up than I had remembered. The number of package liquor stores with ersatz colonial fronts had increased considerably. There was an intriguing antique shop on the pier with old hardware and interesting butter molds. The town, however, seemed just on the brink of going New England cutesy but luckily was not there yet. Part of its salvation was a genuine fish pier, thriving and with salty-looking trawlers tied up. We walked up the main street and found an excellent fish market where we bought fresh crabmeat for the next day's lunch. But tonight it was the Satuit Lounge.

It had been spruced up quite a bit. Perhaps *evolved* is more the word. The Satuit had gone from a simple clapboard structure with formica tables in jukeboxed booths to a brick wharf-style building. Inside there was still formica, but it had been woodified through some sort of photographic process. The result was a peculiar surface that appeared to be wood photographed to look like formica. The jukeboxes were gone. Wall-to-wall carpeting had been installed. I remembered somewhat wistfully how messy and steamy it had all seemed ten years ago when we had stood there dripping on the linoleum in our foul-weather gear. I had been standing near the counter then while we waited for a table, and the glass display case for pies had actually fogged in my presence. There were, needless to say, no more pie cases. Where before there had been only one room, now on our paper place mats the management encouraged us to visit "our new Ballyhoo Lounge," and God spare us, but we were also urged to inquire about their "function rooms." This particular piece of nomenclature for space offered for celebratory occasions I have always found especially unsettling. What could be more unfestive than a function room? Starker than a boiler room, more monotonous than an assembly line, the words *function room* simply do not lend themselves to celebratory thoughts. It is hard to imagine any party occurring in one except perhaps the Kapos annual Christmas fete at Auschwitz.

All these changes at the Satuit made us a bit nervous. However our fears were soon allayed. Where it really counted things remained unchanged, and we were soon diving into plate loads of the best fried clams and scallops that we have found anywhere on the Massachusetts coast. A veritable Merlin must have presided over the kitchen doing the batter, which was the lightest imaginable. The clams were the sweetest, the scallops most tender. Not so for our waitress. Initially she appeared quite surly, and I felt for sure she must be on a summer sabbatical from Durgin Park, which is notorious for its crusty waitresses. But she actually softened up quite a bit as she brought the food and, most important, was very generous with the tartar sauce. That is where it counts with waitresses in deep-fried seafood places. They can be mean as anything and totally incompetent, but as long as they are willing to raid the tartar sauce source and come up with something more than those paper thimbles of it, you know they are on your side.

At four-thirty the next morning we were happy to find our bow swinging to the northwest on the mooring. We slipped out of Scituate Harbor at five AM. It seemed odd now after three-and-a-half years of "child time" and clocking one's life to midnight feedings or nursery school schedules to be plotting a day according to wind and tides, but we had to reach the Cape Cod Canal with the following tide if we were to go through. We sailed out of the harbor with the trawler *Yankee Rose* and were flanked by her rust-streaked sister ship, *Orca*. The sun came up, gilding the water, and although I felt twinges of missing dear old Max, to be able to fumble around in blessed silence with only occasional words exchanged about mizzens and wind was nice.

I have never been a morning person. I have to slip into a day slowly, carefully—the way women used to put on silk stockings so they wouldn't run. I find the organization and efficiency needed to get a day going with children overwhelming. I am terrible at it. I lurch. I stumble. I stub my toes and bleat at my husband and child. I burn toast and spill milk. No one could call these silk-stocking mornings. It is more like a fat lady trying to stuff herself into a girdle. So this morning aboard *Leucothea* felt especially good as we skimmed down Mass Bay with the sun barely above the boom. It did not remain silent for long however, as Chris began fiddling with the blasted radio. In my dream morning it was supposed to be me, Chris, and the wind on this run; not me, Chris, the Boston marine operator, and a lot of cackling between the *Heidi Rose* and the *Lorraine Cecelia*.

The wind lightened and we motored some, but just before the canal we were wing and wing. A small boat loaded with jolly beer-drinking fellows came up beside us and wanted to know if *Leucothea* was the name of a fraternity house. This would have undoubtedly been enough to make the "runner on the white sea foam" turn puce. Pray that those fellows don't run afoul in their boat. Fat chance they would receive a scarf from the sea mew to gird their beer bellies.

We were in the canal a good hour before the tide changed and stopped at Onset to buy some fresh fish at Besse and Sons Fish Market, which had beautiful swordfish at a very good price. Onset itself is a mélange of Victorian houses and clam stands. It was an appealing town, its buildings abounding with cupolas and pergolas. There were saltbox houses with oodles of rickrack trim. There was a large green facing the bay with benches for older folks to sit and look at the sea. For some reason I cannot think anything but good of a town that provides benches for its older people to sit and think and watch the sea. Such benches with vistas are part of my criteria for rating towns. There was a nice curve of sand beach and a town pier in good repair. The town did not seem to be caught in the usual Cape Cod frenzy. As Cape villages go, it had a blessedly low cutesy-poo quotient. There were no gifte shoppes specializing in festive felt toilet paper-roll covers or sets of artichoke-shaped soup bowls. There was a slush stand, a couple of drugstores, a saltwater candy shop but no candle shop.

From Onset we had a lovely run down Buzzards Bay under twin jibs. The wind shifted to southerly just as we closed on Hadley's Harbor. We at first attempted to avoid the crowd of boats already at anchor behind Bull Island by going into the bight by Goat's Neck. It was, however, studded with rocks and shoals, so we beat a quick retreat and joined the crowd. It was easy to see why Hadley's was so popular. One of the most perfect harbors we had seen south of Cape Ann, it had many deep cuts, bays, and spreading fingers of water. In many ways it was reminiscent of our English river anchorages from years before. The English had called such long narrow bays bags, a term I loved and had always imagined was a leftover from Norman times and short for *baguettes,* those long loaves of French bread.

In any case, the islands were beautiful, all owned and preserved in a natural state by the Forbes family. I could not help but reflect upon how that good old China trade money could stretch a long way over time and distance —Whampoa to Naushon. The only flaw in the harbor scene was a loud lady on a lovely Concordia anchored next to us. However, it was soon dinner-time, and we went below for delicious swordfish pan-fried with lemons and capers accompanied by a bottle of Verdicchio. I read Chris a few paragraphs from T. H. White's *The Once and Future King.* Chris liked the description of the old pike—the despot of the moat "sad and full of grief in the eye."

That evening in Hadley's Harbor was all so civilized, so elegant in its own way. Yes, after three and a half years of parenthood, I was ready to admit that under certain circumstances sailing could be truly a civilized experience. We had come a long way from Garrucha. As Chris and I sat later on deck sipping our Grand Marnier and talking about Merlin or something, it was hard for me to imagine that anything could exceed this experience except perhaps dinner with André Malraux at the Ritz Carleton. But then

I would be so nervous. All was calm now. The loud-voiced lady was silent, presumably sleeping in the sea-kindly hull at anchor next to us. The open ocean was far away, ocean crossings a thing of the past, baby asleep in Cambridge.

CHAPTER 42

I was up at five-fifteen the next morning. I looked out the companion-way just to see the dawn, pink-and-orange, tinging the swath of sky between Bull and Naushon. I thought of how many Atlantic dawns I had seen. Then I went back to bed, something I could have never done on my previous dawn experiences as it was always my watch.

By nine AM we were under way again, this time heading for Woods Hole. At Eel Pond in Woods Hole we stopped in to visit Molly Bang, a distinguished children's book illustrator. I had never met Molly before, but a mutual friend in Cambridge urged me to visit her. Molly and her husband, Dick Campbell, who runs a boatyard, live in an erect little stone house overlooking the pond. From the tiny window on the top floor, Molly looks out on a small piece of the world, a round corner of the ocean trapped inland, and with this wedge of a view she paints and draws the most incredible scenes —phantasmagorical stories about fears and triumphs of the human spirit, everyday streets and houses and lives that suddenly become laced with goblins and bogeymen. From this tiny room Molly translates Japanese and Chinese folktales for young children. She has traveled far, to Japan, to India, to Africa, but it was within this tiny interior space that she has created and realized her lifework.

We drank tea, looked at her extraordinary books, and gazed out the window at some lovely boats. There was a classic little green schooner and a rugged channel cutter. She and Chris were talking boats. I was lost in Molly's award-winning book *The Grey Lady and the Strawberry Snatcher*. "Now there's an artist!" Molly said emphatically. I looked up wondering to whom she was referring. Her cool eyes were leveled on the Herreschoff 28 framed in the lower right-hand pane of the tiny window. The oddness of the moment struck me. Time bent. Past and present briefly intersected, and I was caught in the cross reflections of this salt pond as one artist perceived another through a tiny window on a piece of the world.

Our cruise so far had been high-style, an unalloyed joy. Not a tiff. Not a gear failure. No embarrassing docking scenes. We were ripe for something to happen. It did. We ran aground in Tashmoo Pond on Martha's Vineyard.

The cruising guide advised us to hug the can and steer clear of the nun. In fact we should have hugged the nun, trusted our eyes, and not placed blind faith in the cruising guide. The pond had obviously silted up since the last edition. We were left fairly high and dry on a nice sand bank. Luckily there was a rising tide, and Chris put out two anchors, one abeam to swing the stern toward deeper water and one astern to pull us out of the shoals. Much winching and flinching occurred. I swung out on the main boom in an effort to cajole our keel out of the mud. I am pleased to report that my weight could not budge our four thousand pounds of lead from the squishy bottom of Tashmoo pond. Finally, with the rising tide, some fast winching, and a dash of diesel, we got off.

We continued up the pond and anchored near the town pier. It was a lovely quiet anchorage. No town was within sight, only a few summer homes and fewer boats on moorings. Vineyard Haven was a pleasant mile's walk away. We spent an hour browsing in an excellent bookshop. Our selections were somewhat predictable. Chris purchased *The Privateer,* "a tale of sea-faring Yankee rebels, driven by Pride and Patriotism, Profit and Plunder. . . . Gentlemen and Scoundrels, Merchants and Mercenaries, Cunning and Courageous sailing turbulent seas." I bought the *Bluefish Cookbook* and found an intriguing variation on poached bluefish in which you wrap the fish in foil and pop it into the dishwasher (without soap) for one complete cycle. Alas the limitations of boat life. No dishwasher. I continued to read on in hopes of finding a recipe particularly suited for a gimballed alcohol stove.

That evening on Tashmoo Pond the sky clouded up soft and woolly as a sheep's back. Just before dinner as we were drinking a glass of sherry on deck, the air overhead was suddenly astir. A wonderful pattern of wing-beats could be heard. We caught our breath as we looked out and saw a swagged line of Canadian geese flying northwest. The leader pulled out ahead and set a course straight over the pond entrance where we had been aground earlier.

In an excess of nostalgia Chris and I recreated that night a dinner aboard *Leucothea* that we had enjoyed ten years before on our down-east honeymoon at anchor in Winter Harbor, Maine. My companion and I, this evening on Tashmoo, enjoyed tournedos chasseurs, cherry tomatoes sautéd in tarragon and shallots, instant hash browns that had held up admirably from our 'seventy-four crossing, and a Macon Château de Berze from our 'seventy-six meander through the French canals.

The next day we dropped in at Dick and Pat Newick's ship-in-the-woods house for showers. Dick, multihull designer of Phil Weld's *Moxie* and other illustrious sea birds, was on the phone in the wake of Phil Stegall's capsize in the Two-star race from Plymouth, England. Surprisingly, Stegall had overturned in his Newick trimaran in ten-foot seas with a triple reef in the main and small jib. Newick was trying to figure out what went wrong.

Dick works in an area no bigger than a large closet that is behind he and Pat's bed. A horizontal rectangular window over his drafting table frames not the sea but dense woods. Elegant drawings cover the table. The drawings appear sculptural as they combine the most subtle and natural forms one can imagine—the curve of a sea gull's wing, a shark's fin. That afternoon he took out the drawings for the prototype of Stegall's boat and those for his own boat that was under construction. He studied the shape of the outer hulls to see how they could be improved upon so the boat would not be tripped when pushed sideways by big seas. A focus of Newick's work in recent years is that of designing a self-righting trimaran. He told us a twenty-six-foot version of such a creature was then being built. "If it flips, the crew just goes for a swim for fifteen minutes and when they come back it's right side up."

There was a phone call, Damian McLaughlin, the Cape boatbuilder of Mike Birch's *Olympus Photo* and others. There was more talk about the Two-Star. A proa had lost its rig. Newick had done the original design, but the owner, contrary to Dick's advice, had radically changed the rigging. Dick had removed his name from the design, and now it appeared that a gale had removed the mast.

Listening to Newick can be infinitely entertaining and enlightening. On ballast: "It's a dirty word." On French racers: "They're just kids. Give 'em ten spinnakers, and they'll blow them all out. Phil Weld doesn't bash up equipment. He takes a spinnaker down before it blows out. He knows how much they cost and had to work for it."

We went down to the shed where Newick was building his own fifty-foot trimaran. It would include many of his new experimental ideas. Inside, the main hull, almost complete at that time, gave the appearance of a miniature cathedral. The laminated strips of exposed cedar joined in a Gothic confluence at the keel. Within the floating cathedral there was planned a small "apse" for Pat, a private place of her own where she could occasionally escape boat talk.

It becomes obvious rather quickly after studying Newick's designs that he is a form giver in the same way that Frank Lloyd Wright was a form giver. He has the courage to experiment, and he combines beauty and speed in an unparalleled way. Yet he is the first to speak up on what he calls the greed for speed and the high price that can be extracted from those who are too young, too impulsive when they foolishly tinker with wind and weather on these light seabirds.

We visited Edgartown, which I adored but Chris felt was a saltbox version of Palm Beach. In between the pâté-to-go shops and the Lilly

Pulitzer-type stores, there was a lot in the way of beautiful rose-thick lanes and lavish Victoriana that was delightful.

The summer matron who picked us up in her sputtering "island car" just outside Edgartown gave the best description ever of Oak Bluffs. "You must see Oak Bluffs," she said. "It's all gingerbready, Gothicky-wothicky. It was built as a place for high thinking and plain living." This bit of word work is hard to improve upon. Even quoting it verbatim cannot do it justice. Imagine the pithy trill of those words delivered with that unmistakable North Shore accent, which is not Harvard, nor what is sometimes thought to be Harvard, but actually Kennedy. In fact, this accent comes from somewhere between Pride's Crossing and Gloucester. In any case, it was the best piece of travel commentary we had ever heard, and we were not disappointed by Oak Bluffs.

One of the earliest planned communities in America, Oak Bluffs is composed of tiny "gingerbready" houses painted ice cream colors. These houses encircle what is referred to as the campground. In the middle of the campground is the tabernacle, a magnificent open-air structure. Ribbon-thin cast-iron trusses support the roof and presumably help the thoughts of the faithful fly heavenward. Bird song filled the tabernacle as gulls and swallows swooped in and out through the soaring loops and arcs. There was a sense of freedom to come and go to a meeting or whatever event might be held there. The combination of Aristotle with gingerbread was odd but satisfying.

At the campground office an elderly woman in a crisp summer dress explained to me the rules and procedures of ownership within the campground complex. The main rule was the requirement of church affiliation and a fervent belief in loving thy neighbor. This was essential in a community where houses were often no more than three feet apart. In her own words, "One rotten apple can spoil a summer." And the campground reserved the right to throw out the rotten apples. As far as I could understand, the houses were privately owned but the ground upon which they stood belonged to the campground association.

I was also given to understand that synagogues counted as "church affiliations" (We're not picky about that). I did not inquire about mosques and ashrams. As I was leaving the office, the lady walked me to the door. "Oh! It's going to be a clear day," she said with sudden delight, and proceeded to tell me in the same careful way she had explained the rules of the campground how indeed it would be a lovely day as "the fairies had spread their linen." Couldn't I see the dewy webs on the grass? This was a sign of clearing.

We left Tashmoo Pond on the flood in the early afternoon close: hauled and bound for Cuttyhunk. The wind was brisk from the southwest, and there was a knot and a half of current to boost us. We churned by Naushon, which from the weather side has the profile of a sleeping dragon. We dipped into Quick's Hole between Naushwena and Pasque, then aimed for Cuttyhunk.

In the harbor we were greeted by small flotillas of Canadian geese. Cuttyhunk has a different sense to it, an out-island feel. High contoured land with several sandy spits running into the sea, it appears very windswept. There are no tall trees, we soon discovered as we walked over the island that afternoon. The growth was low and sparse. Things seemed to cling to the island, plants and other living things in a kind of plucky defiance to Cutty-hunk's bold south exposure to open ocean. The island is not craggy with rugged rocks, but instead it has a smooth worn texture. Buffed like a piece of driftwood that has floated for a long, long time, the island seems to have the motion of wind and sea inscribed upon it.

We walked to Allen House, one of the two island guesthouses, to meet our friends, the Kootzes, who at that time were part owners of the establishment. Enna Kootz was busy deturquoising all the rooms. She and her husband, Leon, had never worked so hard since becoming proprietors. For many summers they had sailed their Swan 48 in Denmark, where they kept a home. Suddenly, that evening over a delicious dinner at Allen House with Leon and Enna, I realized why they had come to Cuttyhunk. The island has a decidedly Danish sense to its geography.

In the height of the summer, the harbor of Cuttyhunk is jammed with boats, but that mid-June evening when we rowed back in thick fog there were only a few dim masthead lights swaying in the night, and the fog-shrouded pilings from the fish pier stood like island druids, their shapes melting in and out of the milky sky. Several times during that night I got up to look out. The fog had grown thicker, but it felt quite cozy aboard *Leucothea* wrapped in her teak cocoon in that vaporous world between water and air.

By the next morning it had cleared some, and we left early. It was still quite hazy though. Pieces of island seemed to come and go as we sailed for Nantucket. Under Martha's Vineyard the fog thinned. There was little wind, but the incredible three-knot current in the Vineyard Sound pushed us to a four or five-knot speed over the ground. Twenty miles out of Nantucket the wind backed to westerly and cranked up to fifteen knots. We had a terrific sail.

Arriving in Nantucket about four that afternoon, we went directly to our good friend Meg De Give's food emporium, Provisions. Meg, also the pastry chef at Straight Wharf restaurant, had recently opened a kind of miniature version of the infamous Dean & Deluca's gourmet deli in New York's SoHo section. The store is chock-full of all sorts of goodies: chocolate truffles, goose liver pâté, terrific cheeses, exotic salads to go, and the most extraordinary array of sandwiches all made on homemade bread. Meg presides over all this with a kind of zany English charm and gadzooks enthusiasm. In the sandwich line, an unbeatable combination that she has concocted is the Brie and smoked salmon. "I woke up in the middle of the night," she recounted breathlessly, "and thought that sandwich up. It was all I could do to stay in bed and not run down to the shop and make it!"

Meg joined us later on board for drinks. She came bearing a hunk of perfect Stilton and some pâté. The talk on board *Leucothea* was relentlessly food—the little French couple tucked away someplace south of Boston who produce the exquisite pâtés for Provisions; the new shop girl, high on technique but low on style, who of all things "meringued" a lemon-curd tart. Meringuing the wrong thing in the world of haute cuisine is a kind of culinary shanghaing for true taste and under certain circumstances could be considered, good grief, tacky. "She'll learn. She'll learn," Meg bubbled on. "Under my splendid tutelage, she'll learn."

We were told that we had tasted nothing yet until we had tried the ginger cheesecake that the shop was making, but also very popular among the summer folk was a chocolate-chip cheesecake. Quiches, cheeses, and smoked fish were big sellers to sailors for quick elegant meals. We soon decided that we would have a sailing picnic the next day. But before the next day we bought three lobsters at the fish market and adjourned to Meg's tiny cottage for dinner.

It was a neat little Nantucket house with a prim row of petunias out front. We sat at a small polished mahogany table set with Meg's mother's elaborate Royal Derby Crown china directly on the wood. After the calculated ruggedness of the new country look that was so popular that year, the gilt and roses of the china was a welcome relief. A tiny Quaker-gray framed window by the table made it all perfect. We ate the lobster and talked into the night.

Actually we had two picnics provided by Provisions, for there was no way that we could consume all the food that Meg had packed in our basket at one sitting. For the first picnic we sailed to a windswept spit of land at the entrance to Nantucket Harbor where we flew kites and ate salmon-and-Brie sandwiches and madeleines and pâté and Granny Smith apples. The second picnic was a biking expedition to Sisco beach. We biked against a southwest wind through swirling fog to the beach, which was almost empty of people. We made our camp, just the two of us, in a dune pocket where I spread our grass mats and the food—mint-and-cucumber yogurt salad, smoked trout, fruit, chocolate caramel shortcake. As we ate, getting fat no doubt, the fog-spun world around us seemed reduced. It was as if Chris and

I were in a Zen watercolor. The horizon, not one hundred feet away, was a thin line where sand met water. There was no longer distance. We could not see the waves, only hear their rhythmic crush on the beach. In this reduced world one would notice with new wonder the way a clump of dune grass bent with the wind or the undulating line between sand and water.

The sun began to burn through. The fog rolled back. The beach revealed suddenly seemed public. We flew our octopus kite, which striped the sand with reflections from its colored tentacles. I found loads of big sea clam shells. The inside of these shells fascinated me; pearly and swirled, the inner surfaces seemed to hold views of tiny universes. Some were like moonscapes or earthscapes seen from a rocket's perspective. One could look into these shells and imagine swirling seas with continents massing in them or galaxies with exploding stars. I looked at each one and felt as though I were seeing still lives of the beginnings of things—views of a creation, of unimaginable evolutions—all right there on Sisco beach. Despite my philosophical musings I collected these shells with the incredibly mundane notion of serving hors d'oeuvres in them. How Bloomingdaleish! Marinated mushrooms in clam shells. Can hanging wicker baskets in the main cabin be far behind?

After the picnic we took a long bike ride over the island, in and out of the scent of salt ponds and roses, through patches of fog and sun, across the moors on sandy roads where one must keep the bike's speed up or risk gouging out where the sand thickens. Finally we were back to the cobblestone streets that jiggle the cellulite better than any reducing machine.

After almost fourteen miles of biking, we felt ready for dinner at Straight Wharf, a restaurant that from a previous nonsailing visit we considered the finest west of Paul Bocuse and others in the Michelin galaxy. This was to be the anniversary dinner. We had made our reservations weeks in advance.

Our table was situated right by the window framing a water view. The Nantucket lightship tied up to the wharf provided a huge vertical plank of red in the view making the picture as stunning as a Helen Frankenthaler canvas. Dinner began with smoked salmon for Chris and prosciutto and peach for me. Next came a fabulous fish soup, very Mediterranean, with tomatoes and saffron. Its fragrance absolutely transported me back to the Café New York in Marseilles and that wonderful bowl of bouillabaisse that I had so reluctantly given back to the sea the next day when the mistral blew up. People get het up about shredded spinnakers, but believe me, to blow one's bouillabaisse heading away from Marseilles is worse. It had taken me all these years to get back to something like it. For his main course Chris had the coulibiac, a mousse of sea bass layered with caviar and wrapped in brioche,

Kathy flies a kite with friends on Nantucket.

a truly grand and elaborate dish, which I think had its beginnings with the Romanoffs. I had the saddle of lamb in brioche with a delicate mustard sauce. Dessert was sensational—a chocolate apricot torte. The chocolate was of a density that real chocolate mavens find inspiring. We immediately decided that this would "sail well" and planned to buy a few slices in Meg's shop the next day.

Midway through our meal, both Chris's and my own eyebrows shot up in unison as we heard a lady at a nearby table intone to the wine steward that "the Puligney Montrachet complained over the coulibiac." I could not help but wonder if the dear old sea bass would have, if it could, complained over the fact that she smoked throughout her meal. We had noticed this family earlier, mostly because they looked as if they were directly out of *The Preppy Handbook.* There did not seem to be any father, but the mother presided over the table with lockjawed charm. There was a grandmother, two children of ten or eleven, and a stunning-looking girl of twenty with a golden helmet of perfectly clipped hair. The girl wore a boldly tailored white suit and possessed that sort of sporty white-duck crispness that one associates with Jordan Baker, the athletic beauty who cheated at tennis in *The Great Gatsby.* Obviously I was prepared to loathe somebody so young and golden, and she hadn't even said anything yet about Puligny Montrachet.

It was only a few minutes later that my eyebrows shot up again as the mother's voice, no longer intoning, scratched the air. "If you want to go play nouveau riche—just go on and do it, but not around me!" I swiveled my head to see who was the object of this venom. Was it the wine steward? That

Boston Harbor buoy.

indeed would be an overreaction to the wine. It was not the wine or the steward. It was her young son. For the next ten minutes, and it seemed like ten years, we saw this summer matron (old money, we must assume) flay her eleven-year-old son in one of the most bitter and tasteless displays of temper I had ever seen in public. It was hard to imagine what this youngster could have proposed that provoked this response on the part of his mother. Within minutes the child was reduced to tears, silently wiping his eyes with his napkin as the mother continued her tirade. Thank God the wine steward arrived with a bottle of champagne for dessert and she and he could continue their discussion. She was "on to some astounding California reds," etc.

I have a complaint about people who drink fine wines and yell at kids in public places reducing them to sobbing heaps or people who drink beer and yell at their kids in such a manner, but it is difficult to imagine that such people as this woman have taste in anything, let alone wine. And if she does, what is the point? May she crawl into a bottle of Beaujolais and rot or, more appropriately, turn it to vinegar.

There is one slightly redeeming feature to this story—the stunning blonde girl. She was no Jordan Baker, not to say that she was Mother Teresa either. But the girl I was ready to dislike moved over next to her crying brother and with tender gestures began to pat his shoulder and speak softly to him. She bent her shining head close to his and whispered funny things just to him. She crinkled her perfect little nose as she told him some story or other, and soon the boy was starting to smile.

I spent our last morning on Nantucket scurrying through fog-thick streets picking up presents for Max, whom I missed terribly now. It suddenly felt too long that we had been away. I could not wait to see his face as he unwrapped the cuddly triceratops. I wanted to talk dinosaurs and go on swan boat rides, and yes, I was even ready after a year's hiatus to take three-and-a-half-year-old Max on a *Leucothea* ride. We would go back to Deer Isle, where we had been married ten years earlier and where *Leucothea* had not been for nearly eight years since we had first begun our Atlantic circle. It was time to return, but first to the mainland to pick up Max.

CHAPTER *43*

April, 1983

Dear Holly,

Sorry I haven't written sooner. I'm finishing a book and raising kids, just two, but sometimes it seems like six. And I'm not any Super Mom either. Some days I'm a lousy Mom and some days I'm a lousy writer. But I have mentally, if not actually, made notes of all sorts of things I've wanted to write or call you about. First of all, we love the slide of the pottery you're making us for the Vermont house. It's perfect. I can just imagine a beautifully grilled trout on it with mushrooms and parsley. So I can't wait till you finish the set. The price is ridiculously low. I think you should charge more. I trust this is your "best friend" price. Second item, Yahoo, Chris and I are coming to California for the American Library Association meeting in the end of June. We're so excited. I've never seen Chris so keen about a nonsailing vacation. That's one of the main benefits of children; they help you appreciate things in a way that you might not have before. An example, this past Sunday morning (Easter) it was raining cats and dogs, really dismal. Max was very involved with his Easter basket. We did manage to get some cereal and bacon down him before he began consuming the herd? brace? flock? whatever of chocolate bunnies. Meribah had fallen asleep for a morning nap and Chris and I found ourselves miraculously and quietly alone in the kitchen. After our initial shyness with each other, and asking each other what our majors were and where we were from, we decided to have breakfast together. I am overstating it of course, but it had been eons since the two of us had sat down to breakfast or any meal alone without kids, Captain Kangaroo, or Jane Pauley. I was so excited naturally my thoughts ran toward enlarging upon our breakfast, which from all indications looked as if it were going to consist of shredded wheat with strawberries. I remembered some kiwis and Maroc tangerines lurking in the bilges of the refrigerator, and thus inspired (this is unbelievable but you of all people will understand)

I put on my foul-weather gear and got on my bike and peddled in this cold miserable April-is-the-cruellest-month driving rain into Harvard Square for croissants. I would have taken the car, but they are double-parked on Sunday mornings in front of the shop. Then like fury, because you buy them hot, I peddled home. I was going against a headwind too. On the computerized bike at the gym where I go it would have been registering 530 calories per hour. Well, I reached home in record time, and to quote Sendak in *Where the Wild Things Are*, "It was still hot." Not only that, but the baby was still asleep and Max, the king of all wild things, was still playing peacefully even though the chocolate rabbit population had been decimated. He had not gone into a sugar high or low or whatever condition they say those foods produce in children. Chris and I sat for one whole hour eating croissants and reading the *New York Times*. For one hour I was transported to that time, which now seems almost mythical to me, when we drifted through France on the still black water of the canals and the cabin was redolent with the smell of that bread, that incredible bread! But this was even better. We had the *New York Times* and two, for the moment, very decent children.

Another odd thing happened that Sunday, aside from Chris and I having breakfast together. Later on in the day, and I was not really prepared for it at all, Max asked us point-blank if there really was an Easter Bunny. I knew from the look in his eyes that he did not just doubt. He no longer believed. It was a very tense moment. He wanted me to tell the truth, but he wanted the truth to be different. Well, the truth was told. You've never seen a more crestfallen child than when he found out that I was indeed the big bunny. It was really rather sad and touching, but I felt we had no choice. He really wanted to know. I had even made the candy this year. There's this wacky cake-decorating shop on Mass Ave where you can buy the chocolate and the molds. I have all sorts—bunnies, hearts, carrots, seashells. You can buy every color chocolate from white to orange. It's very easy and fun to do. I might even take the course for intermediate-to-advanced chocolatiers. This is my little protest against nouvelle cuisine. Did you read the Garrison Keillor article on nouvelle cuisine in the Wednesday "Home" section of the *Times* back in February? It is absolutely wonderful, especially the part about the nouvelle Bulgarian restaurant in Breughel, North Dakota.

Swinging from Easter to Passover. I gave the seder this year. Twenty people! Max did not opt to ask the Four Questions. He preferred instead to read the list of plagues, which he did with a great deal of style. "Boils!" The word exploded from his mouth. But here's a weird little malaprop for you. When we got to death of the firstborn child, Max read it as "Born of the first death child." Sounds like a Joan Didion novel. After going through the intense holiday week, in spite of my own manic preparations (four pounds of haroseth and fifteen chocolate bunnies) I feel that it is not only worth it, but I've decided or realized that it is not language or toolmaking that distinguishes man from animal but, indeed, the capacity to celebrate that makes us human. This is my insight of the month. We're going to a fund-raising dinner at the Peabody Museum next week. Picture me discussing this with Stephen Jay Gould, the *Panda's Thumb* fellow. Look, they're teaching dolphins how to talk, but you and I know what they'll talk about, the weather, sharks, the Labrador current. The real question is will they celebrate once they're fluent? Will they plan a little dolphin seder if they're Jewish? Or will they be saying to some dolphin child, "Yes, Virginia, there is a Neptune"?

I read this awful book recently. The writing seemed so jagged (that is not to say uneven); the characters so crudely drawn. It was enough to send me straight back to Jane Austen. I just started *Sense and Sensibility*. I'm loving getting ready to detest Lucy Steele. I think you were reading *S & S* when you were with us in the Dutch Canals. I remember very clearly what I was reading. *The Alexandria Quartet*. By Belgium I had finished *Justine* and was a third of the way through *Balthazar* in the Ardennes; by Strasbourg I was starting *Clea*. It took an excruciating feat of willpower, something usually reserved for food, to resist starting *Mountolive* until we left Gibraltar.

I nearly forgot to tell you about the really good book I read recently. —*In the Flesh* by Hilma Wolitzer. Her language takes your breath away it is so beautiful. You would love this book.

If we were born again, an unfortunate phrase here as it always makes me think of such luminescent souls as Charles Colson and Billy Carter, but if we were, it sure would be fun to spend some time in one of those perfectly ordered little worlds of Jane Austen being pretty, a wonderful conversationalist, and preferably rich. Although, as she says in *Emma*, not having money was all right, but not having manners was unforgivable. It still holds. That reminds me of something Max said. He has had a substitute teacher in kindergarten this week who is absolutely a disaster. She has the most negative manner toward children imaginable. She's a caricature of the tight-ass, rigid teacher who thinks children exist to be controlled rather than taught. Need I say that she and Max are not hitting it off. I was trying to be sympathetic and I did say to him that she seemed "pretty bad." Whereupon he replied, "She's not bad. She's just got bad manners." Interesting!

I was just reading my favorite escapist literature, *Architectural Digest*, and here is my entry for the most pretentious phrasemaking of the month. A lady describing the rustic simplicity of her weekend retreat says that such a place should provide "a soothing and therapeutic preoccupation with the unstartling and the nonviolent."

How does that grab you? Is that not a perfect description of our "Zen pavillion" in the Vermont woods. I suppose our weekends are less violent than an Atlantic gale. But we have found that our darling little Meribah Grace can make such a racket during the middle of the night, not crying, mind you, just blabbering, that we are actually going to have to have a room with a door on it for her up there. The sleeping loft she shares with Max is wall-less. Hence, this month we begin to finish off the first floor, which will include a tiny bedroom that we hope will permit a more "soothing preoccupation" with sleep for the whole family.

Must go. Can't wait to see you.

Love,

Kathy

P.S. In case you're wondering why such a long detailed letter, it's because I think this is going to be the last chapter in my book on sailing; hence all the sailing allusions. I started out just to write you a simple letter. I had been working on the sailing book all afternoon and came across a recipe in the back of my sailing journal written in your handwriting for pasta with fresh vegetables. You see how ahead of the times you were in the culinary arts. This was before there was a primavera. It began to trigger all sorts of memories of your involvement, sailing and otherwise, with us. Do you remember, of course, how could you forget, gently shoving me out the door in East Boston so I wouldn't be late for our first Atlantic crossing. You're always there for the crises, and the good times. Are you

Boston Harbor light.

going to be there when Max (and probably Meribah too) says, "Mom, I want to sail across the ocean like you and Dad did"? I am totally alert to the fact that someday in the not too distant future the dream of crossing a large body of water will begin to germinate in his imagination, and that on another day Max and his dad will approach me with a modest proposal. What will I say? What will I do? Will I go with them or stay? And if I stay, will I know as a parent how to let go? I hope you'll be there to help me let go. I've crossed the damn ocean twice already. I've come full circle, but another voyage might begin. I imagine this one, this letting go, will be much tougher than anything that has preceded. Ye Gods, I hope I do it with a modicum of grace and manners.

Love again,

Kathy

P.S. I made sole quenelles in a pear-and-leek sauce that as the supreme Jewish accolade goes, "You could die from!"

Index